GREAT PREACHING ON
CHRIST

GREAT PREACHING ON
CHRIST

COMPILED BY
SHELTON L. SMITH

SWORD of the LORD
PUBLISHERS

P. O. Box 1099 • Murfreesboro, TN 37133
(800) 251-4100 (615) 893-6700 FAX (615) 848-6943
www.swordofthelord.com

Copyright 2002 by
SWORD OF THE LORD PUBLISHERS

ISBN 0-87398-342-4

Printed and Bound in the United States of America

Table of Contents

Preface 7
- I. R. A. TORREY
  Christ for Us; Christ in Us; Christ on Us; Christ With Us 9
- II. W. B. RILEY
  Christ—the Child of Prophecy 21
- III. BOB JONES, SR.
  Jesus, the Light of the World 37
- IV. T. DE WITT TALMAGE
  The Name of Jesus 59
- V. JOHN LINTON
  The Unavoidable Christ 69
- VI. CURTIS HUTSON
  Christ Is All 79
- VII. LEE ROBERSON
  The Poor Man's King 97
- VIII. H. A. IRONSIDE
  The Unchanging Christ 107
- IX. *My Substitute* 117
- X. D. L. MOODY
  "What Think Ye of Christ?" 125
- XI. W. E. BIEDERWOLF
  Why Christ Came 137

XII.	TOM MALONE	
	Why Jesus Became a Man	147
XIII.	R. G. LEE	
	Christ "Above All"	163
XIV.	B. R. LAKIN	
	The Lamb of God	181
XV.	ROBERT L. MOYER	
	Our Solitary Saviour	191
XVI.	JOHN R. RICE	
	Facing the Pierced Jesus	201
XVII.	JESSE M. HENDLEY	
	Wonderful Jesus!	223
XVIII.	SHELTON L. SMITH	
	"This Same Jesus"	239

Preface

The world's philosophers and historians may categorize Christianity as simply one of the great world religions, but even if they place it at the very top of their lists, they have seriously misjudged it. Christianity is first, foremost and finally about a Person, the Lord Jesus Christ. The history of Christianity is not about men finding their way to God, but about Jesus Christ presenting Himself as God and as the *only* way to God. In the first century, Christians were thus named because of their devotion to *Christ.* What preaching could be more central to the Faith or sweeter to the faithful than that which is concentrated and centered upon Him? He is the one message of the eighteen sermons in this book.

In this beautiful volume we have tried to present Christ so that the dual roles of His deity and His humanity are fully demonstrated. In the contemplation of His deity, His exalted character will inspire awe. The charm of His history will bring admiration as you view the perfection in His humanity. A review of His substitutionary and sacrificial works for us will remind us of both the blessed benefits we receive from them and the obligatory mandates laid upon us because of them. Best of all, as the liberals of our day try to diminish the greatness of Christ by searching for an elusive "historical Jesus," the last message in this book assures us that the Jesus presented in these messages and in the Bible is the same Jesus who is calling us today! The Apostle Paul testified that "this Jesus, whom I preach unto you, is Christ" (Acts 17:3). Critics who assailed the early Christians accused them of "saying that there is another king, one Jesus" (Acts 17:7).

Christ is presented from His eternal glory to His work in creation, to His Messianic presentation in Old Testament prophecy, to His supernatural birth in Bethlehem, to His perfect life, to His substitutionary death on Calvary, to His triumphant resurrection, to His miraculous ascension, to His glorious second coming, and to His eternal millennial reign. These powerful biographical pictures of Christ are delivered by some of the great preachers of the church age—men who have proven their devotion to Christ by a lifetime of faithful service, through which they have gained intimate knowledge of the Saviour they loved. This knowledge is passed on to us through *Great Preaching on Christ*.

Our prayer is that your love for Him will grow and that this will translate into a life of devoted and faithful service to Him, our wonderful Saviour, who is indeed worthy of our love and our labors.

REUBEN ARCHER TORREY
1856–1928

ABOUT THE MAN:

Torrey grew up in a wealthy home, attended Yale University and Divinity School, and studied abroad. During his early student days at Yale, young Torrey became an agnostic and a heavy drinker. But even during the days of his "wild life," he was strangely aware of a conviction that someday he was to preach the Gospel. At the end of his senior year in college, he was saved.

While at Yale Divinity School, he came under the influence of D. L. Moody. Little did Moody know the mighty forces he was setting in motion in stirring young R. A. Torrey to service!

After Moody died, Torrey took on the worldwide revival campaigns in Australia, New Zealand, England and America.

Like many another giant for God, Torrey shone best, furthest and brightest as a personal soul winner. This one man led 100,000 to Christ in a revival that circled the globe!

Dr. Torrey's education was obtained in the best schools and universities of higher learning. Fearless, quick, imaginative and scholarly, he was a tough opponent to meet in debate. He was recognized as a great scholar, yet his ministry was marked by simplicity.

It was because of his outstanding scholastic ability and evangelistic fervor that Moody handpicked Torrey to become superintendent of his infant Moody Bible Institute. In 1912, Torrey became dean of BIOLA, where he served until 1924, pastoring the Church of the Open Door in Los Angeles from 1915 to 1924.

Torrey's books have probably reached more people indirectly and helped more people to understand the Bible and to have power to win souls, than the writings of any other man since the Apostle Paul, with the possible exceptions of Spurgeon and Rice. Torrey was a great Bible teacher, but most of all he was filled with the Holy Spirit.

He greatly influenced the life of Dr. John R. Rice.

I.

Christ for Us; Christ in Us; Christ on Us; Christ With Us

R. A. TORREY

"For in him dwelleth all the fulness of the Godhead bodily."—Col. 2:9.

The Gospel of Jesus Christ is ever larger than our thought. When we first come to know Christ and His Gospel at all, Christ is so wonderful as we see Him that we think there can be nothing beyond what we now see. But as we go on studying and pondering the Word of God and getting better acquainted with Jesus Christ Himself, we soon find that what we know of Christ at first—glorious as it is—is a very small part of all that there is to know.

We are constantly getting new views of Christ and seeing Him in new relations to our own lives. We never get to the end of our new discoveries if we study Him.

Some of you may see some things in Christ's relations to us that you never saw before, yet I would not for a moment dare to say that this will be a full presentation of Christ and of His relations to us.

When shall we ever cease to make new discoveries about Him in whom "dwelleth all the fulness of the Godhead bodily"? I never expect to be able to preach an absolutely full Gospel until He comes and I see Him fully as He is, see Him in all the fullness of His infinite beauty and glory.

I. CHRIST FOR US

The first view of Christ and His relationship to us is found in Galatians 3:13:

"Christ hath redeemed us from the curse of the law, being made a curse for us: for it is written, Cursed is every one that hangeth on a tree."

Here we see Christ *for* us, taking our place, bearing our sin, suffering our penalty that we might go free, taking our place in order that we might take His place.

This view of Christ is the fundamental one, that upon which every other view must rest. We cannot hope to see Christ in any other relation of blessing to us until we have first seen Him clearly in our place, suffering for us, bearing our own sin in His own body on the tree.

Here is where many go astray. They try to understand Christ *in* us and talk about Christ in us before they are clear about Christ *for* us.

The Bible is full of this thought of Christ for us. We find it in the Old Testament and we find it in the New Testament.

For example, we find in the Old Testament one of the clearest and most definite statements about it in Isaiah 53:6:

"All we like sheep have gone astray; we have turned every one to his own way; and the Lord hath laid on him the iniquity of us all."

We find another and an amazing statement about it in II Corinthians 5:21:

"For he hath made him to be sin for us, who knew no sin; that we might be made the righteousness of God in him."

Peter also gives us a very clear and definite statement of this great truth in I Peter 2:24:

"Who his own self bare our sins in his own body on the tree."

And our Lord Himself, when here on earth, even before His atoning death was accomplished, set forth the same great truth in Matthew 20:28:

"The Son of man came not to be ministered unto, but to minister, and to give his life a ransom for many."

Christ for us was the meaning also of all the bloody sacrifices of the Old Testament system.

This is a most blessed view of Christ. Oh, to how many a guilty conscience this view has brought perfect peace! How many a man and woman, crushed with the sense of the awfulness of their sins and the impassableness of the gulf that yawned between them and an infinitely holy God, have found rest when they came to see Christ for us—Christ bearing their sin in His own body on the cross, their sin put away forever, God's wrath at their sin fully and forever satisfied, and absolutely nothing between them, sinful as they were, and God, holy as He is.

Have all of us gotten clearly and fully this first view of Christ—Christ *for us* on the cross? Do we realize that all of our sins were laid upon Him and settled forever? Do we realize that "we have redemption through his blood, the forgiveness of sins"? Do we realize that "there is therefore now no condemnation [absolutely none] to them which are in Christ Jesus"? Do we realize that, no matter how vile we may have been, God now has absolutely nothing against us? Do we realize the full meaning of what we sing:

> **Jesus paid it all,**
> **All to Him I owe;**
> **Sin had left a crimson stain,**
> **He washed it white as snow.**

Oh, the joy of seeing that through Christ for us on the cross there has been an absolute interchange of positions between Christ and us, that He took our place when He hung upon the cross for us, and that the moment we accept Him, we step into His place of perfect acceptance before God, that He 'became sin for us' in order 'that we might become the righteousness of God in Him.'

Do we really believe that couplet we so often quote:

> **Near, so very near to God,**
> **Nearer I cannot be;**
> **For in the person of His Son**
> **I am as near as He.**
>
> **Dear, so very dear to God,**
> **Dearer I cannot be;**
> **For in the person of His Son**
> **I am as dear as He.**

Have you got this first blessed view of Christ—Christ for you? If you have not, this is the first view to get.

II. CHRIST IN US

But there is a larger view of Christ than the one of Christ for us on the cross. Yet it is built upon this first view, is inseparable from it, and is impossible without it. If you try to get it without first getting a view of Christ *for* you, you will fail and your view of Christ will be untrue.

You will find this second view of Christ in Galatians 2:20:

"I am crucified with Christ: nevertheless I live; yet not I, but Christ liveth in me: and the life which I now live in the flesh I live by the faith of the Son of God, who loved me, and gave himself for me."

The view of Christ which we have here is Christ *in* us.

This is a larger view of Christ than the one of Christ *for* us. It is good to see Christ *for* you on the cross; it is even better yet to have Christ *in* you. But you will never have Christ *in* you until you have first accepted Christ *for* you. That is, you will never have Christ as an indwelling Presence until you have first accepted Christ as an atoning Saviour.

Never forget that. This is the mistake many are making today: they are trying to get Christ *in* them while ignoring Christ *for* them. They are trying to live the Christ-life while ignoring or even sneering at the atonement of Christ.

The so-called Church of Christ, Scientist, the Unitarian Church and many professing Christians in Methodist, Congregational, Baptist and various other churches are trying to build the superstructure before they have laid the foundation. It cannot be done.

But when you have accepted Christ *for* you, then you can go on to get Christ *in* you. You cannot build the superstructure until you have laid the foundation.

But when you have laid the foundation, you do not need to stop with it. For it is not only our privilege to have Christ for us on the cross, but it is also our privilege to have Christ in us.

This is a most blessed view of Christ. Just to think of it: the second Person of the Trinity, who came down and dwelt in and as Jesus of Nazareth, is ready to come down and dwell in us, ready to take up His abode in us.

Listen to Christ's own promise made the night before His crucifixion: "If a man love me, he will keep my words: and my Father will love him, and we will come unto him, and make our abode with him" (John 14:23).

In point of fact, Christ does dwell in every believer. Paul clearly teaches that in II Corinthians 13:5: "Know ye not your own selves, how that Jesus Christ is in you?"

Yes, Jesus Christ is in every child of God, hidden away, it may be, so that we are not distinctly conscious of His presence; for there is a part of our being deeper than consciousness.

Cranch, the Transcendental poet, wrote:

> **Thought is deeper than all speech,**
> **Feeling than all thought;**
> **Soul to soul can never teach**
> **What to itself was taught.**

But he might have gone further and said that *being* was deeper than all *feeling*.

So Christ dwells in many of us, hidden away in our spirit, deeper than our conscious thought or feeling and, alas, so hidden that He is not very manifest in our daily lives. Yet, nevertheless, He is there.

I say to every regenerate person here: Jesus Christ does actually dwell in you, whether you know it or not. But it is our privilege to have His conscious indwelling. It is our privilege to have Him not merely hidden away in the spirit, deeper than our conscious thought and feeling, but to have Him take complete possession. It is possible for us to surrender our whole being to Him and say, "O Lord Christ, Thou who dwellest in the inward sanctuary of my being—spirit, soul and body—live out Thy life in me." And He will. And then He will flood your soul with joy unknown before.

This is the joy of which Peter speaks, "joy unspeakable and full of glory" (I Pet. 1:8). With this conscious indwelling of Christ, we can obey God's commandment given through the Apostle Paul, "Rejoice in the Lord alway," and also know the peace of which he speaks a few verses farther down, "The peace of God, which passeth all understanding." And it is then that we can say with the psalmist, "My cup runneth over."

This, beloved brethren, is the secret of true living: Let Christ live in you. Give up trying to be anything or do anything in your own strength. "Have no confidence in the flesh"; it is worthy of none.

Recognize that all that is of self is bad, wholly bad. See self on the cross where Christ put it when He died as our Substitute and our Representative, and leave self there. That is the proper place for self, and just surrender absolutely to the indwelling Christ to live His life in you. Do not try to crucify yourself; the crucifixion of yourself has already been done. Paul wrote, "I am crucified with Christ."

To what time does he refer when he speaks of himself as having been "crucified with Christ"? The rest of the verse tells us that he was crucified with Christ when Christ "gave himself [up] for" him.

When Jesus Christ was nailed to the cross and actually crucified, every one of us who is in Christ was crucified with Him. Our part is to realize that our crucifixion was accomplished more than nineteen centuries ago, and look at self where Christ has put us by His atoning death—on the cross.

III. CHRIST ON US

Now we come naturally and easily to the third view of Christ. You will find it in Romans 13:14: "Put ye on the Lord Jesus Christ." Here we have Christ *on* us, Christ's clothing us with His own likeness, Christ Himself as the very clothing we wear. So we are outwardly like unto Himself.

Is not this in some respects even a larger view of Christ than the second? It is possible for one to have Christ *in* Him but so hidden away and hindered that one sees very little of Christ *on* him. But here we see that it is possible to have Christ *on* us, so that men see Christ when they see us.

We have all known men and women who so lived that they made us think of Christ. Christ was on them; He clothed them; He was the clothes they wore.

They say that "clothes make the man." Well, the spiritual clothes we wear do make the man, and Christ Himself is the clothes we ought to wear. That is the exact force of the figure Paul used in Romans 13:14, "Put ye on the Lord Jesus Christ." It is possible to live outwardly as well as know inwardly a Christlike life.

But let it be said again that just as we shall never have Christ *in* us until we have Christ *for* us, so we shall never have Christ *on* us until we first have Christ *in* us. Christ *on* us will be the outworking of Christ *in* us.

There are those who are trying to get Christ *on* them without first getting Christ *in* them. In other words, they are trying to imitate Christ and become like Christ in their own strength. It cannot be done.

You will never live like Christ until you surrender self and self efforts utterly and let Christ come in fully and live His own life out in you and through you. As Paul puts it in the verse already referred to (Gal. 2:20), 'It is no longer I that live, but Christ liveth in me.'

But the great need of today is men and women who have Christ on them, men and women who live like Christ in all the various relations of life: husbands and wives, fathers and mothers, and children too, in the home; men and women in business; men and women in social life; men and women in their church relations.

It is good to be able to say, "I believe in Christ for me. I believe Christ bore all my sins in His own body on the tree, and through so believing I have found peace."

It is good, very good, to be able to say that; but it is better still to be able to say, "Christ Himself dwelleth in me."

But something even better yet is what this old world needs—to see Christ on you.

Let me give you a hint of how people can see more of Christ on you. As already said, Christ must be allowed to live in you in fullness if men are to see Christ on you; but that is not all.

Turn to II Corinthians 3:18: "But we all, with open face beholding as in a glass the glory of the Lord, are changed into the same image from glory to glory."

The thought is this: Christ is the Sun; we are the mirrors. We catch His rays and reflect them out upon the world.

If you wish men to see more of Christ on you, from glory to glory, keep looking up into His glorious face and thus keep reflecting the glory you see there. Spend much time alone with Jesus. Ah, there is the danger in our crowded lives of letting our work for Christ crowd out our communion with Christ. If you do, you will soon not have much of Christ on you.

IV. CHRIST WITH US

There is still a fourth view of Christ better than any we have had yet. "What?" someone will say. "Something better than Christ for us on the cross?" Yes. "Something better than Christ in us as an indwelling Presence and Person?" Yes, something better yet.

We have not gotten to the bottom of this wonderful Gospel even yet. We have not scaled the loftiest heights of the Gospel of Christ even yet.

You will find this something better, this best of all, in Acts 1:11:

"This same Jesus, which is taken up from you into heaven, shall so come in like manner as ye have seen him go into heaven."

You will find it again in John 14:1–3:

"Let not your heart be troubled: ye believe in God, believe also in me.

"In my Father's house are many mansions: if it were not so, I would have told you. I go to prepare a place for you.

"And if I go and prepare a place for you, I will come again, and receive you unto myself; that where I am, there ye may be also."

You will find it also in Philippians 3:20, 21:

"For our conversation [citizenship] *is in heaven; from whence also we look for the Saviour, the Lord Jesus Christ:*

"Who shall change our vile body, that it may be fashioned like unto his glorious body, according to the working whereby he is able even to subdue all things unto himself."

Here we have the living, personal, visible Christ actually and fully with us. It is good to have Christ *for* us; it is better to have Christ *in* us; it is better still to have Christ *on* us; but it is immeasurably best of all to have Jesus Himself *with* us.

The great cry of every heart that truly knows and intelligently loves Jesus is found in the last prayer of the Bible, "Even so, come, Lord Jesus."

An aged, honored and faithful minister of the Gospel once wrote these strange words: "We are not to expect a personal return of our Lord, but be satisfied with Him as coming more and more clearly in all the wonders and glories of this century." How could anyone who really loved His Lord thus write?

Suppose a bridegroom had left his bride for a time. In the meantime, he had given her much and was constantly sending her larger gifts; but she, like a true bride, was looking for his own return.

One day a friend comes in and says, "You must not expect a personal return of him you love, but be satisfied with him as 'coming more and more clearly' in all these gifts of his love." What would any true bride say? With breaking heart, she would cry, "I do not want his gifts; I want himself!"

And so cries the true bride of Christ: 'Come, Lord Jesus, come quickly.'

Dr. James H. Brookes used to tell about a beautiful young woman in his church whom he married to an officer in the United States Army. Not long after the marriage, the officer was ordered to a new post, where it was impossible to take his bride with him.

As they separated, he said to comfort her, "This appointment may not be for long, and I may soon be sent somewhere else, where I can take you with me."

During the days of his absence he was constantly sending her beautiful gifts of one kind and another. But that loving heart was not satisfied with the gifts: it wanted him far more than any gift.

One day in the back parlor as she was going through a box just received, looking at one beautiful gift after another that spoke of him whom she loved, suddenly she heard a familiar step at the door. With fast-beating heart, hoping that it might be he, she looked up and saw him entering the door. She sprang up and, in the haste of her love, knocked the box over, scattering the gifts. But she paid no attention to them in rushing to him. What mattered gifts? She had him!

I think I have never longed for the coming of my Lord as I have this past month; and He will come: "...this same Jesus, which is taken up...into heaven, shall so come in like manner as ye [the apostles] have seen him go into heaven" (Acts 1:11).

"For the Lord himself shall descend from heaven with a shout, with the voice of the archangel, and with the trump of God: and the dead in Christ shall rise first:

"Then we which are alive and remain shall be caught up together with them in the clouds, to meet the Lord in the air: and so shall we ever be with the Lord."—I Thess. 4:16,17.

In that hour, and not until then, Christ *on* us will be perfectly realized. The best of saints has Christ on him only imperfectly today, but "when he shall appear, we shall be like him; for we shall see him as he is" (I John 3:2).

In that day the weakest and most imperfect child of God will be transformed into His own perfect likeness. "We shall be like him; for we shall see him as he is."

I look at some of you and I look at myself and cry, "How unlike Christ we are!" But when that glad day comes and He comes, we shall be transformed into His own perfect image.

I have often thought that when Christ comes again and we look into His glorious face just as it is, such will be the transforming power of that look that the most imperfect of us will be so like Christ that you can scarcely tell us apart.

But that great day will not be a glad and glorious day for all. If we are to "have confidence, and not be ashamed before him at his coming" (I John 2:28), we must have first accepted Christ for us—that is, we must have put our trust in His atoning work—must also have "Christ in you [us] the hope of glory" (Col. 1:27), and we must have Christ on us.

This, then, is the Gospel as I see it, the marvelously glad tidings: Christ *for* us on the cross; Christ *in* us as an indwelling and all-governing Presence; Christ *on* us as the vesture of our daily life; Christ ever *with* us as a living, visible Presence transforming us into His own perfect likeness.

W. B. RILEY
1861–1947

ABOUT THE MAN:

Dr. W. B. Riley was for forty-five years pastor of First Baptist Church, Minneapolis, and pastor emeritus three years. His ministry there built this church to the largest membership in the Northern Baptist Convention.

But all over America Dr. Riley moved and swayed audiences. Thousands were won to Christ in great campaigns.

Riley's ministry was one of preaching the Gospel as well as fighting foes of the Gospel. He sometimes prefaced what he wrote with: "As one who has given his life to the defense and propagation of fundamentalism."

William Jennings Bryan once called him "the greatest Christian statesman in the American pulpit."

The teaching of evolution was a hot issue in his day, so his debates became another phase of his ministry. Bryan had died in 1925, so the mantle for fighting evolution passed to Riley.

One can well compare Dr. Riley with Charles Spurgeon in the largeness of his work: 1. Like that prince of preachers in London, the Minneapolis pastor-evangelist-crusader carried on for several decades an effective ministry; his church grew about as large as Spurgeon's. 2. Like Spurgeon, he turned out many books, including a 40-volume sermon-commentary. 3. Even as Spurgeon, he was a prophet to a whole nation of moral decline and infidelity in the church. 4. As Spurgeon withdrew from the Baptist Union, so Riley withdrew from the Northern Baptist Convention. 5. Like Spurgeon, he founded a growing training college and seminary. 6. Like Spurgeon, he was an editor, editing *The Christian Fundamentalist* and *The Northwestern Pilot*.

Truly, in the days of his strength, Dr. Riley was one of America's greatest preachers.

II.

Christ—the Child of Prophecy

W. B. RILEY

As one reads chapter 2 of Matthew, he is profoundly impressed with two oft-recurring phrases: "for thus is it written [or spoken] by the prophet" and "that it might be fulfilled."

Dr. W. J. Dawson, speaking of the latter, said, "It chimes upon the ear like the sound of a persistent bell."

Verses 16 through 23 narrate things which in themselves seem tragic and disastrous and to which men give the word "accident"; but the divine explanation is, "that it might be fulfilled." Whether there be an accident is debatable.

If one reads the Bible believingly, he is impressed that God's hand is upon everything; that even the incidents of life are appointed of Him or else on their occurrence are immediately taken possession of and employed in the execution of His purposes.

Many of these must be overruled and turned from evil to good before God can use them; but this also is easily within His power, as the whole of chapter 2 of Matthew and many another passage of Sacred Writ suggest.

I invite your attention to "Christ—the Child of Prophecy."

1. The Place of His Birth

"Now when Jesus was born in Bethlehem of Judæa in the days of Herod the king, behold, there came wise men from the east to Jerusalem,

"Saying, Where is he that is born King of the Jews? for we have seen his star in the east, and are come to worship him.

"When Herod the king had heard these things, he was troubled, and all Jerusalem with him.

"And when he had gathered all the chief priests and scribes of the people together, he demanded of them where Christ should be born.

"And they said unto him, In Bethlehem of Judæa: for thus it is written by the prophet,

"And thou Bethlehem, in the land of Juda, art not the least among the princes of Juda: for out of thee shall come a Governor, that shall rule my people Israel."—Matt. 2:1-6.

The place of His birth was definitely named. It appeared in prophecy before it appeared in history. In Micah 5:2 we read:

"But thou, Beth-lehem Ephratah, though thou be little among the thousands of Judah, yet out of thee shall he come forth unto me that is to be ruler in Israel; whose goings forth have been from of old, from everlasting."

Matthew is but recording the fulfilling of that Word. John, who is supposed to be a philosophical writer and not to deal in questions literal and historical, declines to pass over this important event and records that some who had looked upon Jesus, said: 'Hath not the Scriptures said, That Christ cometh of the seed of David, and out of the town of Bethlehem, where David was?'

Gordon spake truly when he said, "Prophecy is the mould of history." The latter answers to the former point by point. In other words, God's revelation does reveal.

From the first He has marked for men a plain path.

When He spake to Adam in Eden, it was in no uncertain words, and He was not misunderstood.

When He addressed Himself to Noah concerning the Flood, His language was clear, and not a word of all He uttered failed.

When He called Abraham to quit Ur of the Chaldees and go away to Canaan, Abraham had no difficulty in understanding.

If one is as childish as was Samuel in the temple, and as slow to interpret the meaning of the divine voice, God simply repeats Himself until His purpose is understood.

Let no man speak of the Bible as "enigmatical"; let no man call the book of the Revelation a "cryptogram." Clouds sometimes obscure the face of the heavens, but beyond them the sun shines undimmed. Though men may be clouded in intellect and Satan may seek to befog the path, the "Light, which lighteth every man that cometh into the world" never goes out. In spiritual things there is an everlasting day for the children of light.

This place of His birth was fully described. It has always been a custom to repeat the names of towns. There is an Albany, New York and an Albany, Oregon; there is a Rochester in New York and a Rochester in Minnesota. When we write letters or send Christmas gifts, we are careful to set down, not the city alone, but so to locate the city that mail clerks can do their work without mistake. God was not less careful concerning His love gift. He said, "Bethlehem of Judea is the one I mean."

Even in matters of lesser moment, God's revelation is equally clear. When He commissioned Jonah, it was not to foreign missions but to Nineveh. When he converted Saul, He described the very street and house and master of the house whither He would have him led, that he might be instructed.

The reason men miss the way so easily is that they do not study the Word; they leave the Guide Book in neglect, then complain when they find themselves on strange, rough and robber roads.

James likens the man who is a hearer of the Word and not a doer, to one who "beholding his natural face in a glass...and goeth his way, and straightway forgetteth what manner of man he was" (1:22–24).

James also tells us, "Whoso looketh into the perfect law of liberty, and continueth therein, he being not a forgetful hearer, but a doer of the work, this man shall be blessed in his deed" (vs. 25).

There are two things to be seen in Sacred Scripture. The first is a reflection of our own face, the likeness of our own character.

It is said that Sir Peter Lely demanded of the artist that he paint him as he was, not leaving out a pimple or a mole, but making the likeness accurate to life. The Bible does that! To look into it, therefore, is to meet rebuke; to look into it is to understand all spiritual defects.

The Bible also presents our possible likeness—Christ—and sets up for us lofty ideals and marks a plain path to their attainment. If we fall short, the fault will not be in God's revelation.

So absolutely do I believe with the great Lorimer that—considered from the standpoint of the individual life as husband, father, child, citizen, neighbor, friend, Christian—the Bible marks the path to the ideal, that when I fall short, I will blame myself; when I mar life, I will accept the moral responsibility of my own conduct and never charge it to an incomplete revelation! It speaks, rather, of a neglected one!

Oh, ye "wise men" from the East; ye "wise men" from the West; ye "wise men" from so many quarters of the globe—hear God while He marks the plain way to Jesus: "In Bethlehem of Judæa: for thus it is written by the prophet."

Thus was the place of His birth divinely honored.

"Thou Bethlehem, in the land of Juda, art not the least among the princes of Juda: for out of thee shall come a Governor, that shall rule my people Israel."—Vs. 6.

It is a far cry from Genesis to Matthew. One has not only to travel through many books in coming, he is compelled to pass through many centuries also if he travel from one to the other. Yet in this passage God has not lost His way, nor have His plans failed, for in Genesis 49:10 we read:

"The sceptre shall not depart from Judah, nor a lawgiver from between his feet, until Shiloh come; and unto him shall the gathering of the people be."

Judah would not have been greatly honored had Jesus been merely a mortal child, begotten by a mortal man, though that mortal one had been destined to rule Israel as David did.

Who thinks much about the place of David's birth? It was not so important as the birth of Moses; it was not so important as the birth of Saul of Tarsus. The towns in which these first saw the light were not immortalized in that circumstance for the simple reason that many towns have had the honor of giving birth to babes destined to mortal greatness.

But only one town in all the world marked the birth of God in mortal flesh. That lifted Bethlehem from littleness to largeness, from obscurity to never-dying fame; for there the Son of God first saw the light.

"Son of God!" did I say? Yes, and I say it without hesitation, without apology! Oh, I know how the modern man who assumes to represent all scholarship smiles at my obsolete notion. I can hear him now summoning to his aid his latest scientific phrase. I can see him with knit brow, attempting to state his position so as to patronize Jesus, yet at the same time tell the public that He is something short of the Son of God.

Unitarianism is expert in compliments to the "man of Nazareth" and equally accomplished in denying essential deity! Such a procedure is vain praise! To call Christ "a great man"; to call Him "the most moral of men"; to speak of Him as if He had "unusual prevision"; to line Him up with the world's moralists and say He "outmatched" them; to insist that He was the "sociologist and psychologist of all ages," of all sons the "pattern one"; to say that His example was "never equaled"; that one might with better face be privileged to follow these remarks with the denial of His virgin birth, the discrediting of the shed blood, an ethereal explanation of His physical resurrection, the lowering of His deity to the level of the socalled divinity of other men—all this is a gospel unknown to the four writers, Matthew, Mark, Luke and John, and is a fresh crucifixion of the Nazarene.

No!

"But thou, Beth-lehem Ephratah, though thou be little among the thousands of Judah, yet out of thee shall he come forth unto me that is to be ruler in Israel; whose goings forth have been from of old, from everlasting."—Mic. 5:2.

2. The Peril of His Infancy

"Then Herod, when he had privily called the wise men, enquired of them diligently what time the star appeared.

"And he sent them to Bethlehem, and said, Go and search diligently for the young child; and when ye have found him, bring me word again, that I may come and worship him also.

"When they had heard the king, they departed; and, lo, the star, which they saw in the east, went before them, till it came and stood over where the young child was.

"When they saw the star, they rejoiced with exceeding great joy.

"And when they were come into the house, they saw the

young child with Mary his mother, and fell down, and worshipped him: and when they had opened their treasures, they presented unto him gifts; gold, and frankincense, and myrrh.

"And being warned of God in a dream that they should not return to Herod, they departed into their own country another way.

"And when they were departed, behold, the angel of the Lord appeared to Joseph in a dream, saying, Arise, and take the young child and his mother, and flee into Egypt, and be thou there until I bring thee word: for Herod will seek the young child to destroy him.

"When he arose, he took the young child and his mother by night, and departed into Egypt:

"And was there until the death of Herod: that it might be fulfilled which was spoken of the Lord by the prophet, saying, Out of Egypt have I called my son."—Matt. 2:7-15.

That peril was precipitated by a plain prophecy. The chief priests and scribes of the city had one important accomplishment—they knew the Scriptures—hence, when they wanted to find out about the first coming of Christ, they looked into them, and lo, it was written that He should come from "Bethlehem in the land of Juda." And those scribes and Pharisees were literalists. They supposed God had said what He meant and that God had meant what He said. They had had no wise men to say to them, "The letter killeth." They knew no better than to believe the Book! Literalists they were, but it is commonly conceded that they were right!

That raises the question as to whether literalists concerning the second coming may not also be correct.

Dr. B. H. Carroll, the great Southern preacher, counted himself a postmillennialist; yet as a great and honest student of the Bible, he said:

> No other event of history is so well accredited and so universally believed and so widely honored as the first coming of the Lord Jesus Christ. The fact of His coming and all the circumstances attending His life here upon the earth were so clearly and vividly foreshown in prophecy that a profound expectation of that coming took possession of the whole earth.

When He came, His birth, His life, His doctrine, His death, His burial, His resurrection and His ascension into Heaven are facts more accredited by evidence than any other historical event.

And as He came the first time personally, literally, visibly, audibly, tangibly, so He will come the next time personally, literally, visibly, audibly and tangibly.

Thank God for the fact that Simeon and Anna have successors in the twentieth century! They believed that "a virgin shall conceive and bear a son." And when they saw Jesus, they rejoiced in God's perfect fulfillment of His promise.

The church of Jesus Christ has in it a large company today who believe that Christ shall cleave the sky, 'that every eye shall look upon Him,' that 'His feet shall stand upon Mount Zion'!

Think you that they are destined to disappointment? No! God's prophecies are plain. So plain was this one that it put the Child in peril. They knew right where to find Him.

Dr. A. W. Archibald is justified in likening the stream of Messianic prophecy running through the ages preceding the birth of Jesus to the great Gulf Stream, which seems to rise yonder at the southern point of Florida, but takes its way in definite and ever-increasing flow to all parts of the Old World and laves almost every continent. He reminds us that the prophecies of the Messiah had been so clear that even people outside of Israel, like Suetonius, who wrote *The Lives of the Caesars*, and Tacitus, joined their voices in declaring that a Ruler should come and that He should rise out of Judah. Virgil also caught the vision. In his fourth *Eclogue* he wrote:

> **Come, claim thine honors, for the time draws nigh,**
> **Babe of immortal race, the wondrous seed of Jove!**
> **Lo, at thy coming how the starry spheres**
> **Are moved to trembling, and the earth below,**
> **And widespread seas, and the blue vault of heaven!**
> **How all things joy to greet the rising age!**

When men, therefore, talk about the "Judaizing influence" that led Peter, James and John to deify Jesus, they forget that God had so moved upon the world—Gentile as well as Jewish—as to create an expectation answering to His plain prophecy and that that very expectation imperiled the infancy of Christ.

Mark, however, that **that peril was thwarted by a clear providence.**

"And when they were come into the house, they saw the young child with Mary his mother, and fell down, and worshipped him: and when they had opened their treasures, they presented unto him gifts; gold, and frankincense, and myrrh.

"And being warned of God in a dream that they should not return to Herod, they departed into their own country another way."—Matt. 2:11,12.

We have those among us who laugh at dreams, and no wonder. The dreams of the great majority of us are simply disturbances produced by physical gormandizing. God is not in them! That is no proof that God is not in any dream.

Many of the gifts of the Spirit are already gone. Open the First Epistle to the Corinthians, and in chapter 12 is a catalogue of those gifts: "wisdom," "knowledge," "faith," "healing," "working of miracles," "prophecy," "discerning of spirits," "divers kinds of tongues." Where are they?

Oh, poverty-stricken church! God's angels seldom visit thee! Thine ear has been so full of the sound of frivolous revelry, the rumbling machinery of merchandise, that an angel's whisper is heard no more.

No wonder we miss the way. No wonder men deny the supernatural. No wonder men smile at the suggestion of an overruling providence. No wonder men reduce the whole world to a mechanism completed, wound up and set going, with the machinery of which God never interferes.

To me, the great lesson here is that a God, General Manager of the Universe, can set aside what He will, and though all the thunders of Herod bear down upon a defenseless Babe, God knows how, by the whisper of an angel, to thwart the inhuman purpose and preserve His own.

Mark you further, **this peril was averted by human obedience.** God could work apart from man. As a rule, He does not. God joins Joseph to Himself, and these two outwit the enemy of Christ:

"When he [Joseph] arose, he took the young child and his mother by night, and departed into Egypt:

"And was there until the death of Herod: that it might be fulfilled which was spoken of the Lord by the prophet, saying, Out of Egypt have I called my son."—Matt. 2:14, 15.

How easy it is for God to raise up His man and make him the medium of the divine preservation.

I was reading a few days since of the time when the leader of the Mohammedan forces, having crushed Christianity again and again, came at last to the Atlantic and, spurring his chafing steed into the sea, exclaimed:

> Great God! If my course were not stopped by this sea, I would go on to the unknown kingdoms of the West, preaching the unity of Thy holy name, and putting to the sword the rebellious nations who worship any other god but Thee.

And how later they turned northward, conquering Spain, and poured over the Pyrenees into France and moved on for the conquest of Europe and the obliteration of Christianity.

Suddenly, in A.D. 732, God raised up Charles Martel who not only overthrew the oncoming hordes but hammered away until three hundred thousand of his enemies lay dead on the field, and turned the tide of paganism and kept Christianity from perishing out of Europe.

What cannot God work? Yet let us never forget that His will is to be done by men and through men, and that the obedient one brings preservation not only to the Infant Christ but to His body, "the church."

3. The Pathos of His Escape

"Then Herod, when he saw that he was mocked of the wise men, was exceeding wroth, and sent forth, and slew all the children that were in Bethlehem, and in all the coasts thereof, from two years old and under, according to the time which he had diligently enquired of the wise men.

"Then was fulfilled that which was spoken by Jeremy the prophet, saying,

"In Rama was there a voice heard, lamentation, and weeping, and great mourning, Rachel weeping for her children, and would not be comforted, because they are not.

"But when Herod was dead, behold, an angel of the Lord appeareth in a dream to Joseph in Egypt,

"Saying, Arise, and take the young child and his mother, and go into the land of Israel: for they are dead which sought the young child's life.

"And he arose, and took the young child and his mother, and came into the land of Israel.

"But when he heard that Archelaus did reign in Judæa in the room of his father Herod, he was afraid to go thither: notwithstanding, being warned of God in a dream, he turned aside into the parts of Galilee:

"And he came and dwelt in a city called Nazareth: that it might be fulfilled which was spoken by the prophets, He shall be called a Nazarene."—Matt. 2:16–23.

The horror of life is in man's inhumanity to man. Selfishness has always been the chief sin. Satan made his first appeal to Eve and Adam at that point, "Ye shall be as gods," and he succeeded.

Herod would have none greater than himself; and in order to end a possible rival, he put scores of innocent infants to the sword. We look back at that bloody past and remember that his conduct was not so uncommon. The wholesale destruction of infants was advocated by the philosophers who preceded Jesus. Plato and Aristotle endorsed the inhuman custom. Cato insisted that the duty of the state was to keep great wealth together; therefore, not to get too many children. It was declared of the Roman Senate that nearly every member of that body had exposed to death one or more of his own children.

Under Augustus, in whose reign Christ was born, ten thousand men were put into the arena to die for the entertainment of their fellows. In Trojan's games, eleven thousand animals and ten thousand gladiators fought; while Claudius had nineteen thousand mariners engaged in a sea fight for his amusement. The empress sat at his side to enjoy with him and others the bloody and ghastly scene.

We think sometimes that our own age is not so brutal a one; but man's inhumanity to man has not come to an end. There are those who plot and plan to rob their fellows. Even in ordinary business, honesty is not too common. In social relations, lust lives and thrives.

Men wreck their own sisters and, like some fiends of the pit, make their work a joke.

If the time has passed when every village and district and province and empire have wailed for their dead, and every house has been a house of mourning, the time is still on when battles rage, rapine and brutality blaze, and when moral death and mourning in consequence of brutality in business, debauch by drink, lust in the name of love, still beggar the land.

Human rage is impotent against God. Herod could slay some children and set Rachel weeping, comfortless in spirit, but Herod himself can be called to judgment, and is, for the next verse reads: "But when Herod was dead...." Oh, with what ease God lays a man aside! With how slight a touch He lays low the man who brutally struck others.

Two of our missionaries in Turkey found a decree sent forth from the Sultan, that the Gospel should not be preached anymore in that land, and Christians should be driven from it. When one of them reported this to his brother, the great missionary answered: "The Sultan of the universe can change the order."

Next morning, the Turkish ruler lay dead.

One of the best-known pages of history recites the story of how the Spanish Armada, when it was just ready to crush the cause of Christ, was struck by a rushing wind that not only drove it back, but wrecked its every vessel and left its fleet strewing the shores with its dead.

Macaulay tells about the landing of William of Orange in England in 1688, that man who really brought religious liberty to the land. The great historian even dares to say:

> The wind blew straight from the east, while the Prince wished to sail down the channel, and turned to the south, when he wished to enter Forboy; sank to a calm during disembarkation, and as soon as disembarkation was completed, rose into a furious storm and struck the pursuers in the face.

It may be true that Satan is the "prince of the power of the air," but it is also true that the "four winds of heaven" are at the command of God and that satanic powers are also impotent against Him.

Some of us have seen in the city of Chester what they call "God's Providence House." It was built over 280 years ago. In the seventeenth century the plague visited the city, and in all Water Street this was the only home that did not suffer. Then the owner had this inscription carved on the main beam under the gable:

GOD'S PROVIDENCE IS MINE INHERITANCE

We have a goodly heritage if we dwell in "God's Providence House."

In truth, we may take a step further in this chapter.

Inhumanity may be compelled to aid the divine plan. Herod's own position enters into the fulfillment of prophecy. It had been written, "Out of Egypt have I called my son." That it might be literally fulfilled, Herod drove Joseph forth with the holy Child.

There is no conflict between the utmost freedom of human agencies and a perfect conformity to the divine plan. Herod was wrong and he knew he was wrong. His ways were wicked and he knew they were wicked. But God through him illustrated a truth:

"All things work together for good to them that love God."—Rom. 8:28.

"Shall we continue in sin, that grace may abound? God forbid."—Rom. 6:1,2.

There is usually a larger meaning in every event than at first appears, and we have to get to that larger meaning if we are to find God.

Dr. Joseph Parker once engaged in a debate with Mr. Holyoake, an excellent speaker and a skeptic. In the course of it, when arguing against a divine providence he put to Dr. Parker the question:

"What did providence do for the martyr Stephen when he was being stoned to death?"

The audience felt its force. For a brief moment it was supposed that Parker could make no reply. But he, after a second of prayer for help, answered:

> What did providence do for Stephen when he was stoned to death? God does not always reveal what He does. He did not visibly appear to the martyr; He did not save him from death.

But I tell you in that moment He did more for Stephen than save his life. God enabled Stephen to say, "Lord, lay not this sin to their charge." To have worked this miracle in the spirit of Stephen, God did more for Stephen than to have saved his life.

It is said that the answer had an overwhelming effect. But to me, it was not as full as it might have been. God did more for Stephen: He made a revelation of Himself to him that made death easy. And in the shedding of Stephen's blood, He laid another stone in the foundation of the blood-bought church. He so far overruled that wickedness that Stephen's death was worth more to the world than his life could have been.

Our God knows how to take care of His own.

Truly, as Cowper wrote:

**God moves in a mysterious way
His wonders to perform.**

But God arrives!

He may let His children turn back from Kadesh-barnea and let the last one of a generation perish in the wilderness, but in the process, He will cure Israel of idolatry and bring their children into Canaan—a conquering host.

He may let Joseph go to prison and languish there for two years in utter forgetfulness, but in the prison He will equip him to be premier and in His own time bring him forth and put him in the place of power.

He may let a slattern nurse drop Walter Scott and lame him for life, but He will take the child intended for military service and make of him the greatest literary genius of the age.

He may let disease and poverty and deputies' warrants sorrow the youth of William Shakespeare, and yet by his sadness so instruct him that he will write like a seraph.

He may let a Paul be put into prison in Rome and be led forth at the behest of evil men and beheaded, but in Paul's martyrdom He will present to the world the conception of a Christian character, and for full twenty centuries stir the souls of men to increasing courage and to sacrificial service.

Our text truly is an illustration of James Russell Lowell's words:

> **Truth forever on the scaffold,**
> **Wrong forever on the throne;**
> **Yet that scaffold sways the future,**
> **And behind the dim unknown**
> **Standeth God within the shadow**
> **Keeping watch above His own.**

ROBERT REYNOLDS JONES, SR.
1883–1968

ABOUT THE MAN:

Called the greatest evangelist of all time by Billy Sunday, Robert Reynolds Jones, better known as Dr. Bob Jones, Sr., was born October 30, 1883, in Shipperville, Alabama, the eleventh of twelve children. He was converted at age eleven, a Sunday school superintendent at twelve and ordained at fifteen by a Methodist church.

"Dr. Bob" was a Christ-exalting, sin-condemning preacher who preached in the cotton fields, in country churches and in brush arbors. Later he held huge campaigns in American cities large and small, and preached around the world.

Billy Sunday once said of him: "He has the wit of Sam Jones, the homely philosophy of George Stuart, the eloquence of Sam Small, and the spiritual fervency of Dwight L. Moody."

He saw crowds up to 10,000 in his meetings, with many thousands finding Christ in one single campaign.

But Dr. Bob was more than an evangelist. He was also an educator—a pioneer in the field of Christian education, founding Bob Jones University in 1927.

Behind every man's ministry is a philosophy. Dr. Bob's was spelled out in the sentence sermons to his "preacher boys" in BJU chapels. Who has not heard or read some of these: "Duties never conflict!" "It is a sin to do less than your best." "The greatest ability is dependability." "The test of your character is what it takes to stop you." "It is never right to do wrong in order to get a chance to do right."

"DO RIGHT!" That was the philosophy that motivated his ministry, saturated his sermons, and spearheaded his school.

His voice was silenced by death January 16, 1968, but his influence will forever live on, and Christians will be challenged to "DO RIGHT IF THE STARS FALL!"

III.

Jesus, the Light of the World

BOB JONES, SR.

(Preached in Chicago Arena Citywide Campaign, May 1946)

"Then spake Jesus again unto them, saying, I am the light of the world: he that followeth me shall not walk in darkness, but shall have the light of life."—John 8:12.

"Ye are the light of the world. A city that is set on an hill cannot be hid.

"Neither do men light a candle, and put it under a bushel, but on a candlestick; and it giveth light unto all that are in the house.

"Let your light so shine before men, that they may see your good works, and glorify your Father which is in heaven."—Matt. 5:14–16.

Jesus made both of these statements: "I am the light of the world" and "Ye are the light of the world." There is no contradiction here.

I look about me on a lovely day and say, "The sun is the light of the world." Then in the evening the sun goes down behind the western horizon, and the moon comes out in her glory, and I say, "The moon is the light of the world." There is no contradiction in those statements. The sun is the light of the world, but the moon becomes the light of the world because the sun shines upon the moon.

1. A Christian, the Light of the World

Jesus Christ is the light of the world, but a Christian becomes the light of the world when Christ shines into his heart.

I should like to stop in passing long enough to say that I have seen the moon in eclipse. I have watched her shine in her beauty and glory until a shadow came over her face. And they told me that a part of the world had come between the sun and the moon.

I have seen eclipses in Christian lives too. I have known men to shine in wonderful beauty for God until they permitted the world to come between them and their Sun.

It may be that some soul here tonight has experienced an eclipse. Over your sky the world has cast its shadow. You are no longer what the Lord meant you to be when He said, "Ye are the light of the world."

Henry Drummond said, "The greatest proof of the Christian religion is a Christian." A Christian is the unanswerable argument to the reality of the Christian religion.

If you want me to judge a civilization, show me the type of men and women that civilization produces. You judged the civilization of Germany by the type of German soldier in World War II. You judged Japan by the type of Japanese soldiers who fought in that war. You judge a civilization by the sort of people the civilization produces. You judge a school or college by the type of character the school or college turns out. You judge a god by the sort of life that god can produce.

Now the world, to some extent at least, judges Jesus Christ by the kind of lives we Christians live. Someone has said that every Christian is writing a gospel, a chapter day by day. What is the gospel according to you? What kind of chapter did you write in your bible this past week? What sort of chapter are you going to write tomorrow? Remember, "Ye are the light of the world."

"Let your light so shine before men, that they may see your good works, and glorify your Father which is in heaven."

A story was told of a blind man who went one night down a back alley with a lantern in his hand. Someone asked, "Why do you carry that light? It doesn't do you any good."

He said, "Oh yes, it does; it keeps other men from stumbling over me."

If you Christians do not carry your lanterns down the alley of life, men are going to stumble over you into everlasting night and ruin.

"Ye are the light of the world....Let your light so shine before men, that they may see your good works, and glorify your Father which is in heaven."

Your Lord, whom you claim to love and trust, has commanded that of you, and not to obey is to disobey God.

Did you ever stop to think of the fact that everything God ever created obeys His voice, except man?

When this universe was wrapped in chaos and darkness, God said, "Let there be light." In obedience to His matchless voice, the sun unveiled its face and the world was lighted.

When Christ was on earth, He looked for fruit on a fig tree and found none. He cursed it, and in obedience to His matchless voice, it withered and died.

When out on tempest-tossed Galilee His disciples awoke Him and said, 'Master, we are in the midst of a storm,' in the dignity of His glory and power He said, 'Wind, cease blowing; water, be still.' They said, "What manner of man is this, that even the winds and the sea obey him!" (Matt. 8:27).

The wind obeys Him. The sea obeys Him. The highest archangel and the tiniest insect on mother earth obey Him. But you do not obey Him. He said, 'Let your light shine,' but you have not been letting it shine. He said, 'Ye are the light of the world; let that light shine before men,' but you have disobeyed God. Oh, may God move upon our hearts and give us a sense of our responsibility and obligation. O God, help us to obey Your voice!

Think about it: God created you for the purpose of letting your light shine before men. You are to take His light and give it out into the darkness of this world.

When I was a boy in the country, I heard an old-time, ultra-Calvinistic preacher say something that startled me very much. As he looked out over the crowd, he said, "God made some of you people to go to Hell, so you will just have to go. There is no way out for you."

This little country boy said to himself, *If God made me to go to Hell, I want to go to Hell. My ambition is to be what God made me to be.*

Listen! If God made me to go to Hell, such a thing as Hell would be an absurdity. Anything that does what God made it to do is happy. God made the fish for the sea, the birds for the air. The fish play in the water and the birds sing in the air. But put the fish in the air and the birds in the water, and they die.

God did not make fish for the air, and God did not make birds for the water. Anything in its place is happy. And if God had made men for Hell, the idea of a Hell would be an absurdity. God would change the flames of Hell into flames of matchless glory.

Say, God made you to walk in the light as He is in the light that you might have fellowship with Him and He might have fellowship with you. God made you for Heaven. Hell was made for the Devil and his angels. And if you go to Hell, you will be an intruder.

Say, God made Heaven for you. God made streets of gold for you! God made cloudless skies for you! God made the Holy City beyond the stars for you! And if you go to Hell, you will be an intruder. That is what makes Hell. All the agony and sorrow that you have on this earth come to you because you are out of your sphere; you are not where God wants you; you are not in fellowship with God.

Oh, I am so glad I can tell every soul that God wants to save him. I am so glad I can look into the face of every human being under the stars of heaven and tell him that God loves him and Jesus died for him.

I can go to the home of the rich man and listen in vain for my footfalls on carpeted floors; I can look at his beautiful pictures on magnificent walls; I can go to his table laden with the luxuries of life; I can sit beneath his gorgeous chandeliers of trembling crystal, blazing from the walls like bouquets of diamonds.

Then I can go out on a street corner and see a poor beggar who lifts his trembling hand and asks for a penny.

If it were left to me I might say, "Come, ye rich man," or, "Come, ye poor man." But I leave that to Jesus. He looks down on the rich man's prosperity and the poor man's poverty and says, "Come, anybody. I'll take you. I want you. I would like to have you."

I may see in this city a manly, sober, moral, upright young man who works hard all day and goes home at night to his little cottage where he is greeted by his loving wife and little children. Out yonder in the ditch is his drunken brother, a poor besotted wretch who staggers down a back alley with bloated face and bloodshot eyes to a cabin door to curse a ragged wife and hungry child. If it were left to me, I might say, "Come, ye moral man." But I leave it to Jesus. He looks down on the moral man's manhood and the drunkard's debauchery and says, "Come, anybody. I'll take you. I want you. I would like to have you."

You may see in this city a girl, pure, decent and refined. She has in her eyes the luster of purity. The roses of modesty bloom in her cheeks. The most beautiful thing in the world is that kind of girl. But out yonder in an earthly hell is her fallen sister, a soiled dove of the underworld. She walks down the street with faded face and sad eyes. If it were left to you, you might say, "Come, ye girls of purity and respectability." But you leave it to Jesus. He puts His arms around this old world, locks His nail-pierced hands on the other side, hugs it to His bosom, warms it with His love and says, "Come, anybody. I'll take you. I want you. I would like to have you."

Anybody in this country whom nobody else wants can be sure that Jesus wants him. Go hunt up the poor man and tell him that Jesus would like to have him.

"Ye are the light of the world." Let your light shine! Be an invitation to everybody who sees you to come to Christ.

"I am the light of the world" is a marvelous statement. We read all that Jesus said and take everything for granted. But think of Somebody living nearly two thousand years ago, walking the dusty roads of earth, standing in the darkness of the world, and saying, "I am the light of the world."

Jesus, the Light of the Intellectual World

Jesus never wrote a book. As far as we know, He wrote but one time, and nobody knows what He wrote then. But in spite of the fact that He never wrote a book, He is the light of the intellectual world.

Woe be to those who leave Jesus Christ out of their scholarship! For my philosophy of life, I would rather sit at the feet of a woman who lives in a cabin and who can scarcely write her name but who knows Jesus, than to sit at the feet of the greatest scholar the world ever saw, if that scholar is not a Christian.

"The world by wisdom knew not God" (I Cor. 1:21). You cannot think accurately unless you come to know Jesus.

I was saved when I was eleven years old. We did not have good schools. We did not have the advantages you have in the great schools now available. This little country boy found Jesus in a little country church. The next morning when I went back to school, I had a real intellectual stimulation. I could understand things and see things that I had never understood nor seen before.

Jesus not only comes into your heart when you are saved, but He also stimulates your faculties. He helps you to see. He lights up your intellectual sky.

These men without God—don't let them disturb you! Young people, don't let the worldly-wise scholars who know not God disturb you. Poor, blind, weak, stumbling, ignorant men—how little they know!

Years ago I heard this story:

In Louisville, Kentucky a woman taught her parrot to say "Good night" when she put him in the cage at night and "Good morning" when she took him out of the cage in the morning.

One day the bird got in a fight with a cat. She rescued the bird. That night she put the bird in the cage and said, "Good night, Polly."

The bird said, "Good night."

The next morning was a lovely spring morning. The lady went out to the cage and said, "Good morning, Polly."

The bird said, "Good night."

She said again, "Good morning, Polly."

The bird said, "Good night."

"Oh," she said. "Polly, what's wrong with you? Good morning!"

The bird again said, "Good night."

"Well," she said, "Polly, don't you know when it is daylight? Good morning, Polly!"

The bird said, "Good night."

The woman got up near the cage and found that the bird's eyes had been scratched out by the cat the day before. There were no more "Good mornings" for that poor, blind bird.

O man without God, you cannot see! O Christless woman, you have no eyes! Jesus Christ is the light of the intellectual world.

Jesus Christ, the Light of the Social World

Conditions are terrible in this world, but have you ever wondered what they would be had Jesus never come?

Suppose there had never been a manger in Bethlehem. Suppose there had never been a cross at Calvary. Suppose there had never been an open sepulcher. Suppose there had never been a Sermon on the Mount. What a world it would have been! Everything worth having came from Jesus.

Jesus Christ made womanhood what it is in this country. In countries where His name is unknown, women have always been slaves and burden-bearers. It was Jesus Christ who took the chains of slavery from the hands of women.

It was Jesus Christ who put woman on the throne and crowned her queen. Oh, tell me why all women and girls do not fall in love with Him! He is the best Friend you ever had. One of the saddest things is, so many women and girls are turning the freedom that He bought for them into license to do wrong.

Jesus Christ made childhood all it is in the world. No pagan writer ever said anything about childhood's golden days. Childhood had no golden days for a pagan. It was Jesus who touched babyhood into beauty. It was He who was the first Teacher to open His arms and say, "Suffer the little children to come unto me, and forbid them not: for of such is the kingdom of God" (Mark 10:14). Little babies fell into His arms.

Somebody else recalls that Jesus is the God of little things. He puts wings on archangels and feathers on sparrows. He puts all the resources of nature back of the frailest flower that blooms.

Some time ago while in Oregon, I went up on a mountain with some friends. I saw a little flower—I know not what kind—coming up through the ice and snow. That little flower was trying to shake the ice out of its hair to get up to the sun.

This friend said, "They come up in the spring before the ice and snow melt. They can't wait to get to the sun."

I thought, *How much wiser those flowers are than some people! They walk away from the light, but those flowers climb up through the ice and snow to get to the light.*

One morning down in Georgia when I went for a walk, I saw a beautiful wildflower blooming in a cluster of bushes. The little flower was lifting its perfumed lips for the kiss of the morning. As I stood there, I talked to it a little while. "Little flower, did you get lonely last night?"

"No, I never get lonely at night. God keeps the stars awake to watch over me while I sleep."

"Little flower, wouldn't you like to have some breakfast?"

"I have had my breakfast, thank you. I draw my sustenance from soil and air."

"But, little flower, you haven't dried your face."

"I wait every morning for God's sun to dry my face."

"Little flower, what do you do when you get thirsty?"

"Oh, I just tell God about it, and He tells the sun to draw me a drink of water."

"Little flower, what do you do when the sun gets hot?"

"Oh, I just tell God I'm too hot, and He sends the winds through the forest to cool my cheek."

"Little flower, I suppose I'm the only person who ever saw you; but you haven't bloomed in vain. Out here in this little spot where you are, you have talked to me about God, my Father."

Young people, never mind; shine where God puts you. I tell our students at Bob Jones University that the most important light in the home is not the chandelier in the parlor; it is used only when company comes—a company light. The most important light in your home is that little back hall light. It is not so bright; it doesn't light so much space, but it is kept burning all the time; and it keeps people from falling down and getting hurt when they must get up during the night.

Listen! Maybe you are a little back hall light. Maybe you haven't much ability or talent. Maybe God has hidden you away in a little secluded spot. Then shine for God where you are! That song, "Brighten the Corner Where You Are," is a wonderful song in its thought.

"Ye are the light of the world." Jesus is also "the light of the world"—the light of the intellectual world, the light of the social world.

Christ, the Light of the Religious World

Religion is one thing and Christianity is another. Everybody has some kind of religion.

What is religion? Religion is reliance—the thing on which you rely for salvation. And your religion is no stronger than your reliance. A Christian is one who, knowing that he cannot save himself, relies upon Jesus Christ and His atoning blood for salvation.

The Christian religion is one of song. Atheists cannot write music. Pagans cannot sing sweetly. It is Jesus who puts a song in the heart. It is He who makes us sing.

It is the sorrow of my life that I cannot sing. I cannot stay on pitch, for I haven't a sense of pitch. But I have a song in my heart, and I wish I could sing it. It is a song that Jesus wrote. He put it in my heart that night He saved me at age eleven. Someday I will be able to sing it. You have heard lovely music tonight, but wait until you hear me sing! When I get to Heaven, that land of cloudless sky, I will dip my tongue in the melody of the sky, ask the heavenly orchestra to set the pitch for me, and I will sing that song that Jesus put in my heart!

Who else but a Christian can sing his way through the sorrows of life?

Who else but a Christian could sing, as Paul and Silas did, in a dismal dungeon when backs were lacerated and feet were in stocks?

Who else but a Christian can go down into the valley of the shadow of death and say, "Glory to God!" "O death, where is thy sting? O grave, where is thy victory?"

Who else but a Christian can see the coffin go down and say, "The LORD gave, and the LORD hath taken away; blessed be the name of the LORD"?

Oh, it is wonderful to have a religion of light and song!

Christ May Become the Light of the Individual World

Everybody in this house lives in a little world of your own—a world of your own individuality, a world of your own peculiarity, a world of your own personality, a world where you hope, dream, yearn and long—a little world all your own.

You have things in your heart you can't tell anybody else. All music, all art, all the architecture, all human achievement is just a feeble effort of man to draw from his depths and get something out of his soul that he can't tell.

When Bob III, my grandson, was small, he was in my office one day, and I said, "Bobby, someday Pop [his name for me] will move out, if the Lord tarries, and your daddy will move in here. And you might move in his office, Bobby, and I want to be sure you are a Christian. Do you know Jesus, Bobby? Have you trusted Him?"

"Yes, Pop; I've trusted Him."

"Bobby, tell me how you know it."

"Pop, it is so hard to tell—I can't get it out. It is down there, but I just can't exactly tell it."

There is always something you can't tell. There are unexplored depths. You can find the word, but it doesn't say all you feel.

There are men in this house with storms in your hearts that would sink all the ships at sea. I am talking to men who have come to where the road parts. You look down this way and say, "I don't believe I can afford to go that way; that might lead me to disgrace. And this other road might lead me to defeat. I don't know what to do."

I will tell you what to do: look up to Jesus! He will show you which way to go. Down yonder where it looked like disgrace, you will find honor. Where you thought it would be defeat, you will find victory.

I am talking to some woman here tonight who years ago locked up in your heart a secret sorrow, and you threw away the key. One day you thought you would tell somebody, but you were ashamed to do it, so you vowed never to tell it; to suffer alone. Your dreams have faded, your hopes have been dashed, and you have gone through weary, lonely, sad hours alone. Many times when everybody else has been asleep, you have stayed awake to weep. You poured out burning tears on your pillow. The next morning maybe you heard the prattle of little feet coming to the bed. You turned the pillow over to hide your tears and began to smile. You do not know what to do.

I can tell you what to do: Trust Jesus Christ; yield your life to Him. He will turn those tears into pearls, string them for you, put them in a crown of joy, and place the crown on your head. He will chase away the midnight darkness.

Oh, what a Saviour! There was never a cloud He could not drive out of the sky.

He can also drive the darkness out of the valley of the shadow of death. "Though I walk through the valley of the shadow of death, I will fear no evil."

Listen! Death is never a valley when a Christian gets there. It looks like a valley on my journey there, but when I get there, death is never a valley.

You never knew a Christian who at the last moment dreaded to die. He may dread it until the time comes; he may instinctively draw back; but wait until he peeps through the gate and sees what is on the other side!

Years ago there was a frail invalid woman who had a fine husband. They prayed that God would send them a baby—and they kept praying and kept praying. One day God did send a little baby into their home. The little thing was on the mother's arm as the doctor leaned over the bed. The husband and the nurse were there.

The new mother spoke: "Doctor, am I dying?"

The doctor said, "I am awfully sorry, but I must be honest with you. Yes, you are dying."

"O Doctor, I so wanted this little baby. Doctor, I wouldn't mind dying if I could take my little baby along. Can I, Doctor?"

The doctor answered, "I'm awfully sorry. That little gate of death is so narrow that you will have to go alone. There is no room in that gate for even the wee little baby."

Doctor, do not tell her that! Do not say that to her, Doctor! She cannot take the baby; you are right about that. And her husband at the gate of death will have to say good-bye. That is all true. But there is Somebody who can go through the gate of death with her. "Yea, though I walk through the valley of the shadow of death, I will fear no evil: for thou art with me."

Oh, there is no dark valley for the Christian!

Years ago down South an old man was dying. His son, who had been to a university that had shattered his faith, stood at his bedside. As he watched his father, he asked, "Father, how does the valley look?"

"The valley?"

"Yes, how does the valley look?"

"What do you mean by the valley?"

"The doctor says you are in the valley of the shadow of death. And you have always talked about your faith and your Saviour and your religion. Now how does the valley look?"

The old man replied, "The valley? The doctor says I am in the valley? You tell that doctor he doesn't know what he's talking about. Tell him I'm on the sunlit summit. Tell him it is the brightest day of my life!"

I say it again: Death for a Christian may look like a valley as he journeys that way, but when he gets there, the light of the heavenly city floods the valley!

Christ, the Light of This Dark World

When I was a young man, I was holding a campaign in a certain city. We had had only rain, mud and slush. I had not seen the sun in eight days. I had been under some strain. I was sitting on the front porch of a little frame hotel one Sunday morning. The vines had grown clear up beyond the second floor.

I looked down at the mud and up at the clouds and said to myself, *It looks as if that great big sun could clear up the sky. Sun, can't you get rid of those clouds? You are able to do it.*

While sitting there thinking, I saw a great big cloud rent in twain, and back of it a misty veil. I watched that misty veil shot through with holes of light. As the great big sun stepped out from behind the cloud and waved at me, I threw it a kiss.

I was carried back in my thoughts to the time two thousand years ago when midnight's blackest darkness hovered above this earth and wise men groped their way through the darkness, looking for light.

One day a star appeared. That star led them across plains, mountains, rivers and over hills. And, like all true light, it led them to Jesus, and it began to shine over His cradle.

That star did not go out at that cradle. It was shining in the temple when He was twelve years of age and talked to the doctors. It was shining at Jordan when He was baptized. In His temptation in the wilderness, on the mountaintop, on the pinnacle of the temple, it was shining. It was shining in His miracles when He made the blind to see, the deaf to hear, the dumb to speak; when He cured the palsied, cleansed the leper, raised the dead.

One day the world said, "Let's put it out." (The world does not want light; its deeds are evil.)

I called on a neighbor in my town just at twilight. The lady said, "Come in. Tom will be here in just a minute."

I walked into the parlor and wondered why she didn't turn the light on. It was getting dark.

Then when her little boy came in and started to turn on the light, she said, "Don't turn it on, Son; Mother's hair isn't combed."

When Jesus came into a room, He pressed the button. Those Pharisees said, "Cut it off! We don't look right in the light."

So the world said, "Let's get rid of His light," and Jesus was put on a cross, the heavens put on mourning and bowed to the earth to weep, the earth staggered under its load, and darkness settled down. It looked as if the light was gone.

But wait! Maybe it isn't. A moment later the light flashed into the heart of the dying thief. It got rid of the darkness of his soul and got it ready to go Home to God.

Then they took Jesus down off the cross and put Him in a tomb. For three days there was darkness. Some of the disciples said, 'Let's go back to work.' Peter said, 'I'll go back to fishing. The light is gone.'

But three days later the star poured its light into the sepulcher. Some angels were flying around, and the sepulcher looked so much like Heaven, so they thought they had gotten home and flew in!

Men and women, that star arose never to set. After awhile the old world will catch fire and burn; and the moon, colored as red as blood, will hang its crimson livery upon the wing of the night; and the sun will drag up to the door of Heaven and refuse to shine; and breath from the nostrils of God will blot out the stars; and universal midnight will come.

But there will be no midnight for a Christian. Heaven is a city of light!

Jesus, the Light of Eternal Heaven

John on the isle of Patmos, when the darkness of loneliness and the war of sorrow had settled upon him, got out his old prophetic telescope, and I imagine he said, "I want to see what I can find up yonder where I am going to stay forever."

He turned that telescope to the sky, looked through it, then said, "What a beautiful gate—it is a solid pearl. And that wall is of jasper. I want to see everything before night comes. If I am going there, I want to look it over."

Then he said, "There must be a lot of gold up there; they use it for pavement. And I never saw any water as clear as crystal! And the tree—what a tree! And it is for the health of the nations.

"I must not miss anything, for it will be night after awhile. Before the sun goes down, I want to see everything in it that I can.

"What a city! Nobody is wearing mourning up there."

And John did not see any wrinkled faces. The fingers of Time had not pinched wrinkles around anybody's eyes. And no shoulders were drooping under the weight of their years.

John did not see any babies crying in pain. I want to live in a city where babies do not cry.

John said, "I wonder where the graveyard is. Oh, there is no death there!"

Then he took hold of his telescope again and said, "It is way past nighttime—the days must be longer up there." He kept looking and looking on through the hours and hours, and it was just as bright after hours passed as it was when he first looked. Then John cried out in matchless ecstasy, "There is no night there! The sun never sets!"

Think of living forever in a city where there are no graveyards, where nobody dies, where no babies cry in pain, where nobody wears mourning! Think of it!

Think of a city where there is no sin, where nobody dips his tongue in the slime of slander to try to ruin somebody's reputation. Think of it!

Oh, that city is my home! There shadows never come. There evening twilight nor morning twilight ever comes—it is always noonday splendor. Oh, the glory of that city! And there are no tears there.

Dr. Len G. Broughton, the great Southern preacher, gave up medicine to become a preacher. He was pastor of a church in Virginia, was having a very wonderful ministry, and he was very happy. But in his church was an old bachelor, a refined, cultured

JESUS, THE LIGHT OF THE WORLD

gentleman. One day this bachelor said to Dr. Broughton, "I am a timid person and of so little use to God. I don't feel that I'm any good. But I have been praying that God would show me something I could do. I believe I have found it. Will you let me usher? I can do that for Jesus."

Dr. Broughton spoke to the chairman of the committee, and the chairman said he would like to have him do it. Everybody knew how self-conscious and timid he was.

Dr. Broughton said:

> The next Sunday morning this refined, cultured gentleman came in his cutaway coat, his gray trousers, his patent leather shoes and his nice gloves. He ushered people down the aisle with such dignity. Everybody looked at each other and smiled. I never saw anybody so radiantly happy. He was back that night. He was at prayer meeting. He did not miss a service. Weeks went by and he kept coming to every service. He was so happy—he felt that he had found something he could do for God.
>
> One day he got sick, and the doctor said his condition was rather serious. I used to go to see him every day. One day I was on the way over there, and I met the physician who said, "Dr. Broughton, Tom cannot possibly live through the day."
>
> I said, "Well, I knew he couldn't live."
>
> As I went up the front steps, his mother came down to meet me and said, "Dr. Broughton, I want you to ask my boy if he is ready to die."
>
> I said, "I know he is ready."
>
> She said, "Well, I know it too; but you know, I am his mother, and I just want him to say he is ready."
>
> I said, "Well, I'll ask him."
>
> I went in and sat down by his bed and said, "Tom, I want to read you a chapter out of the Bible. Tell me what to read."
>
> He said, "Dr. Broughton, there is one chapter in Revelation I have read every day since I've been sick, the chapter that says He shall wipe away all tears. I hate to be a baby, but I had been so happy since I began ushering. I felt I was doing something for God. Since I cannot be there, I cry. Then I read that chapter."
>
> I said, "I will read it to you, Tom." I read it and got down

on my knees and had prayer. After I got up, both of us went to crying, not because we were sad, but because our hearts were melted.

A great stream of tears would flow down Tom's cheeks and across the consumptive flush. I had a big silk handkerchief in my pocket that had been given to me which I hadn't even unfolded. I took it and began to wipe away his tears. I kept trying to dry them. They came as fast as I could dry.

He smiled at me through his tears and said, "Dr. Broughton, the next time they are dried, Jesus will do it."

I told him good-bye and left. In about an hour they called me to say he was dead.

Oh, the tears, the burning tears on the cheeks of God's people; someday Jesus will take His nail-pierced hands and wipe them all away. My mother was pretty good doing that, but nobody can dry them like Jesus!

In that city we will never get tired. Everybody gets tired. This is a weary world. Life is such a strain.

The memory of my mother is the memory of a tired face. The only time I ever saw her look rested was when they put her in her coffin and stretched her hands across her breast. As she slept the sleep of death, she looked so rested.

I do not know what people mean when they say they are rested. All my life I have been under a strain. The only time I can remember when I felt completely rested was a few years ago out in the middle of the Atlantic Ocean, coming back from Palestine. On a certain day out at sea, it suddenly occurred to me that I was not tired.

Oh, weary, tired bodies, tired minds and tired hearts—when you get to Heaven you can work all you want to and never get weary. Nobody gets tired there. Think of a Heaven like that! What a place it will be!

I have seen the vista of rolling hills and verdant valleys, of winding streams and forests with their changing colors. I have seen the sky on wintry nights bejeweled with countless stars. I have seen the hand of God sweep the eastern sky with the glory of a dawning day. I have seen Him put His canvas on the western horizon, dip His brush in fire, and paint the exquisite tints of golden sunsets.

I have caught the odor that floats through park and tropical islands on summer evenings. I have heard the music of the organ, the piano, the violin as they have responded to the master's touch. I have heard the matchless music of the human voice. But all I have ever heard and dreamed and yearned for and hoped for cannot compare with the first rapture that will thrill my heart when I look within that city gate!

> **I want to go there.**
> **I mean to go there.**
> **I intend to go there.**
> **I do.**
>
> **I want to go there**
> **I mean to go there.**
> **I intend to go there.**
> **Don't you?**

Christian, Let Your Light Shine

When Jesus calls us Home, I am going to ask Him to let me sit in a window up in Heaven and pull up the shade a little and let a little light come down, for there is so much darkness in the world.

Down South after the Civil War, a widow's husband had fallen in battle. Her fortune had been swept away. She was cultured and refined but had never known what it meant to work. When starvation was staring her in the face, she went to the field to supervise her own farms. While she worked, her little boy played in the hedge.

The little fellow grew up to be about twelve years of age. He said, "Mother, I'll take over the farms for you." So she stayed at home, and the boy took over the fields.

He would go to the fields early in the morning, and every evening just at twilight he would come home. There was one little place where he could look through the branches of the trees and see the light in the cottage window—a signal that everything was all right at home. As the days and months and years passed, he got in the habit of stopping there and looking for the light.

One evening when he reached that spot and looked through the grove, the light was not there. He went on quickly to the house, struck a match and lighted the lamp on the table. There in the bed was his mother, cold and lifeless.

He went over, put his arms around her, reached down and kissed her lips of clay. Near her head he saw an envelope. He opened it and read:

> My dear son:
> I have a feeling that someday you may come home from the field and the light may not be in the window. I have a feeling that someday I may have to move that lamp and place it in Heaven's window. So if you do come home and the light is not in the window, remember where it will be. Walk in that light and meet your mother someday.

Fathers and mothers and young people, go home and put lights in your windows, and keep those lights burning. And if Jesus tarries and you have to move, you will let them shine back. Death does not dim them. The lights are made brighter if they are carried through the valley of the shadow of death.

When I was a boy, we had no good schools out there in the country, so my parents sent me thirteen miles to high school. Always a great mother's boy, I didn't see how I could leave her. I would stay at home and sit on the back steps, hold her hand and kiss her sweet face over and over.

When I got ready to leave for school and to be gone two weeks, it seemed such a long time. When my mother came out to tell me good-bye, she had some food packed in a box.

"Now, Son, eat this in your room. You will be timid for the first two or three days, so don't go hungry." She kissed me and said, "Be a good boy."

I went away. Then when I came home, my mother met me at the gate and asked, "Have you been a good boy?" And every time I left—were it just one day or several hours—she would say, "Now, Son, you are going away; be a good boy." And when I returned, she would always ask me the same question, in the same tone of voice: "Have you been a good boy?"

One day when she came out to tell me good-bye and to kiss me, her lips were a little warm, and she had a strange flush in her cheeks which I had never seen before, and the strange expression in her eyes concerned me. She said, "You are going away, Son; be a good boy." I told her good-bye and went off.

At the end of ten days I had an opportunity to go home again. My father heard me drive up, so he came out to meet me. He said, "Son, I'm glad you have come; your mother is very sick. I was going to send for you tomorrow."

That memorable night is before my mind tonight. Those fevered arms—I can feel them now as she put them around me, pulled me down to her, kissed me and said, "Have you been a good boy?"

When I left home the next time, there was no mother to go with me to the gate, no mother to kiss me good-bye, no mother to tell me to be a good boy. But I had a kiss I had never had before—Mother throwing me one from Heaven. And I saw a light that day brighter than I had ever seen—Mother's lamp shining from the window in the sky. I heard a voice—Mother's voice and Mother's sigh, mingled with music that angels make on harps of gold—saying, "You are going away, Son; be a good boy."

Christians, listen! Let's trim our lights and let them shine. Some of us haven't much longer in this world. But let those lights shine to lighten the pathway of men to God.

I am talking to somebody tonight whose mother prayed for you before she died. She is up in Heaven tonight. I am talking to somebody whose father is up there. There is some man here whose wife has gone on or maybe somebody whose child has gone on. The lights are shining back. Best of all, Jesus Christ is up there. They are with Him tonight in fellowship.

You can come into the light too. Somebody is here who has never known what the light means. You are living in darkness. You can come into the light tonight. God help you!

"Ye are the light of the world....Let your light so shine before men, that they may see your good works, and glorify your Father which is in heaven."

T. DE WITT TALMAGE
1832–1902

ABOUT THE MAN:

If Charles Spurgeon was the "Prince of Preachers," then T. DeWitt Talmage must be considered as one of the princes of the American pulpit. In fact, Spurgeon stated of Talmage's ministry: "His sermons take hold of my inmost soul. The Lord is with the mighty man. I am astonished when God blesses me but not surprised when He blesses him." He was probably the most spectacular pulpit orator of his time—and one of the most widely read.

Like Spurgeon, Talmage's ministry was multiplied not only from the pulpit to immense congregations, but in the printed pages of newspapers and in the making of many books. His sermons appeared in 3,000 newspapers and magazines a week, and he is said to have had 25 million readers.

And for 25 years, Talmage—a Presbyterian—filled the 4,000- to 5,000-seat auditorium of his Brooklyn church, as well as auditoriums across America and the British Isles. He counted converts to Christ in the thousands annually.

He was the founding editor of *Christian Herald*, and continued as editor of this widely circulated Protestant religious journal from 1877 until his death in 1902.

He had the face of a frontiersman and the voice of a golden bell. Sonorous, dramatic, fluent, he was, first of all, an orator for God. Few other evangelists had his speech. He poured forth torrents, deluges of words, flinging glory and singing phrases like a spendthrift; there was glow and warmth and color in every syllable. He played upon the heartstrings like an artist. One writer described him as the cultured Billy Sunday of his time. Many of his critics found fault with his methods; but they could not deny his mastery, nor could they successfully cloud his dynamic loyalty to his Saviour and Lord, Jesus Christ.

IV.

The Name of Jesus

T. DE WITT TALMAGE

(Delivered at Queenstown, Ireland, in 1890)

"A name which is above every name."—Phil. 2:9.

I. THE NAME OF JESUS

On my way from the Holy Land, and while I wait for the steamer to resume her voyage to America, I preach to you from this text, which was one of Paul's rapturous and enthusiastic descriptions of the name of Jesus.

1. A Good Name

By common proverb, we have come to believe that there is nothing in a name; so parents sometimes name their children not thinking that that particular title will be either a hindrance or a help.

Strange mistake. You have no right to give to your child a name that is lacking either in euphony or in moral meaning. It is a sin for you to call your child Jehoiakim or Tiglath-Pileser. Because you yourself may have an exasperating name is no reason why you should give it to those who come after you.

But how often we have seen some name, filled with jargon, rattling down from generation to generation, simply because someone a long while ago happened to be afflicted with it.

Institutions and enterprises have sometimes, without sufficient deliberation, taken their nomenclature. Mighty destinies have been decided by the significance of a name. There are men who, all their lives, toil and tussle to get over the influence of some unfortunate name.

While we may, through right behavior and Christian demeanor, outlive the fact that we were named with the name of a despot or an infidel or a cheat, how much better it would have been if we all could have started life without any such incumbrance.

When I find the apostle, in my text and in other parts of his writing, breaking out in descriptions of admiration in regard to the name of Jesus, I want to inquire what are some of the characteristics of that appellation. And, oh, that the Saviour Himself, while I speak, might fill me with His own presence, for we never can tell to others that which we have not ourselves felt.

2. An Easy Name

This name of Jesus is an easy name. Sometimes we are introduced to people whose name is so long and unpronounceable that we have to listen sharply, and we must hear the name given to us two or three times before we venture to speak it. But within the first two years, the little child clasps its hands, looks up and says "Jesus."

Can it be, amid all the families represented here today, there is one household where the little ones speak of "father" and "mother" and "brother" and "sister" and not of the "name which is above every name"?

Sometimes we forget the titles of our best friends, and we have to pause and think before we can recall the name. But can you imagine any freak of intellect in which you could forget the Saviour's designation? That word "Jesus" seems to fit the tongue in every dialect. When the voice in old age gets feeble and tremulous and indistinct, still this regal word has potent utterance.

> **Jesus, I love Thy charming name,**
> **'Tis music to my ear;**
> **Fain would I sound it out so loud**
> **That Heaven and earth might hear.**

3. A Beautiful Name

Further, I remark it is a beautiful name. You have noticed that it is impossible to disassociate a name from the person who has the name. So there are names that are to me repulsive—I do not want to hear them at all—while those very names are attractive to you. Why the difference? It is because I happen to know people by those names who are cross and sour and snappish and strange, while the persons you used to know by those names were pleasant and attractive.

As we cannot dissociate a name from the person who holds

the name, that consideration makes Christ's name so unspeakably beautiful.

No sooner is it pronounced in your presence than you think of Bethlehem and Gethsemane and Golgotha, and you see the loving face, hear the tender voice and feel the gentle touch.

You see Jesus, the One who, though banqueting with heavenly hierarchies, came down to breakfast on the fish that rough men had just hauled out of Genessaret; Jesus, the One who, though the clouds are the dust of His feet, walked footsore on the road to Emmaus.

Just as soon as that name is pronounced in your presence, you think of how the Shining One gave back the centurion's daughter; how He helped the blind man to the sunlight; how He made the cripple's crutches useless; how He looked down into the babe's laughing eyes and, as the little one struggled to go to Him, flung out His arms around him and impressed a loving kiss on his brow and said: "Of such is the kingdom of heaven."

Beautiful name—Jesus! It stands for love, for patience, for kindness, for forbearance, for self-sacrifice, for magnanimity. It is aromatic with all odors and accordant with all harmonies.

Sometimes when I see that name, the letters seem to be made out of tears. And then again, they look like gleaming crowns.

Sometimes they seem to be as though twisted out of the straw on which He lay; then as though built out of the thrones on which His people shall reign.

Sometimes I sound that word "Jesus," and I hear coming through the two syllables the sigh of Gethsemane and the groan of Calvary. And again I sound it, and it is all a-ripple with gladness and a-ring with hosanna.

Take all the glories of book bindery and put them around the page where that name is printed. On Christmas morning wreathe it on the wall. Let it drip from the harp's strings and thunder out in organ's diapason. Sound it often, sound it well, until every star shall seem to shine it, and every flower shall seem to breathe it, and mountain and sea, and day and night, and earth and Heaven acclaim in full chant: "Blessed be His glorious name forever; the name that is above every name."

**Jesus, the name high over all,
In Heaven and earth and sky.**

To the repenting soul, to the exhausted invalid, to the Sunday school girl, to the snowy-white octogenarian, it is beautiful.

The old man comes in from a long walk and tremblingly opens the door, hangs his hat on the old nail, sets his cane in the usual corner, lies down on a couch, and says to his children and grandchildren: "My dears, I am going to leave you."

They say, "Why, where are you going, Grandfather?"

"I am going to Jesus." And so the old man faints away into Heaven.

The little child comes in from play and throws herself on your lap and says, "Mamma, I am so sick! I am so sick!" You put her to bed. The fever gets worse and worse. Come midnight she looks up into your face and says, "Mamma, kiss me good-bye; I am going away from you."

You say, "My dear, where are you going?"

She answers, "I am going to Jesus." The red cheeks which you thought were the mark of the fever only turn out to be the carnation bloom of Heaven.

Oh, yes, it is a sweet name spoken by the lips of childhood; spoken by the old man.

4. A Mighty Name

Still further, it is a mighty name. Rothchild is a potent name in the commercial world; Cuvier, in the scientific world; Irving, a powerful name in the literary world; Washington, an influential name in the political world; Wellington, a mighty name in the military world. But tell me any name in all the earth so potent to awe and lift and thrill and rouse and agitate and bless as this name of Jesus.

That one word unhorsed Saul, and flung Newton on his face on ship's deck, and today holds four hundred million of the race with omnipotent spell.

That name in England means more than Victoria; in Germany, more than Emperor William; in France, more than Carnot; in Italy, more than Hubert of the present, or Garibaldi of the past.

I have seen a man bound hand and foot in sin, Satan his hard taskmaster, in a bondage from which no human power could deliver him; yet at the pronunciation of that one word he dashed down his chains and marched out forever free.

I have seen a man overwhelmed with disaster, the last hope fled, the last light gone out; yet at that name pronounced in his hearing, the sea dropped, the clouds scattered, and a sunburst of eternal gladness poured into his soul.

I have seen a man hardened in infidelity, defiant of God, full of scoff and jeer, jocose of the judgment, reckless of an unending eternity; yet at the mere pronunciation of that name, blanch and cower and quake and pray and sob and moan and believe and rejoice.

Oh, it is a mighty name!

5. An Enduring Name

Still further, it is an enduring name. You clamber over the fence of the graveyard, pull aside the weeds and see the faded inscription on the tombstone. That was the name of a man who once ruled all that town.

The mightiest names of the world have either perished or are perishing. Gregory VI, Sancho of Spain, Conrad I of Germany, Richard I of England, Louis XVI of France, Catherine of Russia—mighty names once that made the world tremble; but now, none so poor as to do them reverence. And to the great mass of people they mean absolutely nothing; they never heard of them. But the name of Christ is to endure forever.

It will be perpetuated in art, for there will be other Bellinis to depict the Madonna; there will be other Ghirlandaios to represent Christ's baptism; there will be other Bronzinos to show us Christ visiting the spirits in prison; other Giottos to appall our sight with the crucifixion.

The name will be preserved in song, for there will be other Handels to write *The Messiah;* other Dr. Youngs to portray His triumph; other Cowpers to sing His love.

It will be preserved in costly and magnificent architecture, for Protestantism as well as Catholicism is yet to have its St. Marks and its St. Peters.

That name will be preserved in the literature of the world, for already it is embalmed in the best books. And there will be other Dr. Paleys to write the *Evidences of Christianity*, and other Richard Baxters to describe the Saviour's coming to judgment.

But above all, and more than all, that name will be embalmed in the memory of all the good of earth and all the great ones of Heaven. Will the delivered bondman of earth ever forget who freed him? Will the blind man of earth forget who gave him sight? Will the outcast of earth forget who brought him home? No! No!

To destroy the memory of that name of Jesus Christ, you would have to burn up all the Bibles and all the churches on earth; then in a spirit of universal arson, go through the gate of Heaven and put a torch to the temples and the towers and the palaces; and after all that city was wrapped in awful conflagration and the citizens came out and gazed on the ruin—even then, they would hear that name in the thunder of falling tower and the crash of crumbling wall, and see it wrought in the flying banners of flame; and the redeemed of the Lord on high would be happy yet and cry out: "Let the palaces and temples burn; we have Jesus left!"

Blessed be His glorious name forever and ever—the name that is above every name.

II. WHAT NAME WILL YOU CALL CHRIST?

Have you ever made up your mind by what name you will call Christ when you meet Him in Heaven? You know He has many names. Will you call Him Jesus, or the Anointed One, or the Messiah, or will you take some of the symbolical names which on earth you learned from your Bible?

Wandering someday in the garden of God on high, the place abloom with eternal springtide, infinite, luxuriance of rose and lily and amaranth, you may look up into His face and say, "My Lord, Thou art the rose of Sharon and the lily of the valley."

Someday as a soul comes up from earth to take its place in the firmament and shine as a star forever and ever and the luster of a useful life shall beam forth tremulous and beautiful, you may look up into the face of Christ and say, "My Lord, Thou art a brighter star— the morning star—a star forever."

Wandering someday amid the fountains of life that toss in the sunlight and fall in crash of peal and amethyst in golden and crystalline urn, and you wander up the round banked river to where it first tingles its silver on the rock, and out of the chalices of love you drink to honor and everlasting joy, you may look up into the face of Christ and say, "My Lord, Thou art the fountain of living water."

Someday, wandering amid the lambs and sheep in the heavenly pastures, feeding by the rock, rejoicing in the presence of Him who brought you out of the wolfish wilderness to the sheepfold above, you may look up into His loving and watchful eye and say, "My Lord, Thou art the shepherd of the everlasting hills."

But there is another name you may select. I will imagine that Heaven is done. Every throne has its king. Every harp has it harper. Heaven has gathered up everything that is worth having. The treasures of the whole universe have poured into it.

The song full. The ranks full. The mansions full. Heaven full. The sun shall set afire with splendor the domes of the temples and burnish the golden streets into a blaze and be reflected back from the solid pearl of the twelve gates; and it shall be noon in Heaven, noon on the river, noon on the hills, noon in all the valleys—high noon. Then the soul may look up, gradually accustoming itself to the vision, shading the eyes as from the almost insufferable splendor of the noonday light until the vision can endure it, then crying out: "Thou art the sun that never sets!"

At this point I am staggered with the thought that notwithstanding all the charm in the name of Jesus and the fact that it is so easy a name and so beautiful a name and so potent a name and so enduring a name, there are people who find no charm in those two syllables.

Oh, Come This Day to Christ

Oh, come this day and see whether there is anything in Jesus. I challenge those of you who are farther from God to come at the close of this service and test with me whether God is good and Christ is gracious and the Holy Spirit is omnipotent. I challenge you to come and kneel down with me at the altar of mercy. I will kneel on one side of the altar, and you kneel on the other side of it; and neither of us will rise until our sins are forgiven and we ascribe, in the words of the text, all honor to the name of Jesus—you pronouncing it, I pronouncing it—the name that is above every name.

**His worth if all the nations knew,
Sure the whole earth would love Him too.**

Oh, that God today, by the power of His Holy Spirit, would roll over you a vision of that blessed Christ and you would begin to weep and pray and believe and rejoice.

You have heard of the warrior who went out to fight against Christ. He knew he was in the wrong. While waging the war against the kingdom of Christ, an arrow struck him and he fell. It pierced him in the heart; and lying there, his face to the sun, his lifeblood running away, he caught a handful of the blood that was rushing out in his right hand, held it up before the sun and cried out, "O Jesus, Thou hast conquered!"

And if today, the arrow of God's Spirit piercing your soul, you felt the truth of what I have been trying to proclaim, you would surrender now and forever to the Lord who bought you.

Glorious name! I know not whether you will accept it or not; but I will tell you one thing here and now, in the presence of angels and men: I take Him to be my Lord, my God, my pardon, my peace, my life, my joy, my salvation, my Heaven.

Blessed be His glorious name forever—the name which is above every name.

Hallelujah unto Him that sitteth upon the throne and unto the Lamb forever and ever! Amen and amen and amen!

JOHN LINTON
1888–1965

ABOUT THE MAN:

The story of John Linton is another of those sagas that shine with the wonder-working grace of God.

One of twelve children, this immigrant boy from Scotland gravitated to the life of a wastrel, a wanderer. This wicked youth seemed to be destined to a life of cheating, lying and stealing.

But God moved in when John was thirteen. He had left home, had lied to suspecting police, had hid in barns; then finally he was taken in by a Christian woman and mothered. Here John learned the sweet lesson of the Heavenly Father's patience, tenderness and forgiveness to an erring child. So he confessed Christ and claimed His forgiveness. This was the turning point in his life.

Shortly he emigrated to Canada. And at James Street Baptist Church, Hamilton, Ontario, John Linton heard God's call to preach the Gospel.

He attended Gordon Bible College in Boston. Under the consecrated teaching there, Linton "grew like a hothouse plant." His pastor persuaded him to go to a Baptist college in Woodstock, where he could finish high school work as well.

College life became a geographical game of musical chairs—Boston, Woodstock, Toronto, Manitoba. All the while he was preparing to be a "good preacher" he was busy "practicing preaching."

He graduated with a master's degree, married a childhood sweetheart and became a pastor. It was during his pastorate at High Park Baptist Church, Toronto, that he became vitally interested in revival and evangelism. Linton entered that field of ministry—and God blessed—across Canada, across America, until his decease in 1965.

John Linton is not normally listed among the elite of the evangelists in this century: Moody, Sunday, Bob Jones, Sr., Appelman, John Rice. But he was not some lesser light—God mightily moved through his ministry. He left a trail of converts to Christ as well as revived, restored, rejoicing churches.

His gospel soundness, his compelling delivery, his Scotch brogue and his devotion to our Lord made him widely acceptable. You cannot hear the inimitable Scotch brogue in his sermon, but you can enjoy its sweet and powerful message.

He died at age 77 in the pulpit while conducting evangelistic services.

V.

The Unavoidable Christ

JOHN LINTON

"The same day at evening...when the doors were shut...came Jesus and stood in the midst."—John 20:19.

It is an upstairs room in a house in the city of Jerusalem. It is the third day after the death of Jesus of Nazareth. His disciples, trembling with fear of the Jews who had killed their Master and might do the same with them, disturbed in mind over news of the empty grave, are secretly met in this room. They are talking in whispers lest any should discover their hiding place. The doors are safely locked and securely barred.

Suddenly they are conscious of a presence. There was no footstep on the stair, no hand was heard trying the lock; yet something, somebody is there. Then before the wondering eyes of the disciples, the Lord Himself appears standing in the midst! The doors are still shut, the bars still intact and untouched; but locked doors cannot keep out the risen Son of God. Jesus passed through those doors as if they had never been, for "when the doors were shut...Jesus...stood in the midst."

My message in a nutshell is this: Jesus Christ, the crucified and risen Son of God, still lives. Men may try to shut and lock the door of mind and conscience against Him; nevertheless, they cannot, for Jesus will come into their consciousness, will demand attention to His claims, and will compel every man to decide either for or against Him. Though the doors are shut, Jesus will stand in the midst.

There are three propositions I will ask you to consider: First, Jesus Christ is a fact. Second, Jesus Christ is a unique fact. Third, Jesus Christ is an unavoidable fact.

1. Jesus Christ Is a Fact

Jesus of Nazareth is a historic personality. Profane history tells us this, apart from the Bible. The existence of *Christus* in Roman history is a fact as well verified as the existence of Julius Caesar, Nero or Constantine.

The date on the coin in your pocket or on the nickel you put in the plate tells you Christ is a historic fact. Do you think the world's calendar is based on the birthday of a Man who never lived? Who would say so? So far as I know, no enemy of Jesus Christ today would deny His existence. Jesus of Nazareth was born. He lived. He died. He was a historic personality. Jesus Christ is a fact.

2. Jesus Christ Is a Unique Fact

Christ is unique because of His claims. He claimed to be the Son of God. He claimed to be coequal with God. He claimed to be God. The Unitarians who deny this do not have a foot of ground to stand on. Jesus said, "I and my Father are one." For any man to say He merely meant that He was one with His Father in aim and purpose is mere trifling. The Jews put Him to death "because that thou, being a man, makest thyself God" (John 10:33).

But mark the unique element in this claim. He not only claimed to be God, but He proved His claim! He sustained His claim to deity by miracles wrought sometimes before thousands of people. He told His enemies they ought to believe for the very works' sake.

Now suppose someone stood up in Chicago or Washington or London and claimed to be God; who would believe it? But if that person could recover the sick and heal the blind and raise the dead, yes, and even rise from the dead himself, the world would be ready to consider his claim. This Jesus did. He claimed to be God, and by His wonderworks He proved it. This is unique.

And His claims had authority behind them. He spake as never man spake. That does not mean He was the most eloquent man ever heard. It means that when Jesus Christ spoke, He had the authority of the Godhead behind Him. His was the most authoritative voice ever heard on this earth. His friends and enemies alike knew this. And we know it today.

Here is a marvelous thing: although nineteen hundred years have passed since He spoke, His words have not lost one iota of their authority; and when He speaks today from the Word of God, the human heart recognizes this unique authority.

How different from other teachers and moralizers! When you read the teachings of Plato or Socrates or Seneca or any other teacher of morals and ideals, you do not feel you have to decide for or against them. You do not feel you have made a great moral decision, eternal in its consequences for weal or for woe, when you decide either to accept or reject their teachings. You do not feel that Heaven or Hell depends on what you do with them. Of course not. They were mere men, known as good men, wise men, but men and men only. Yet no honest man can hear or read the words of Jesus Christ and intelligently comprehend His claims without being gripped by the compelling authority of them.

Moreover, if a man decides to reject the claims of Christ, it takes an effort to do so. That is why some men lock and bar the door of their consciousness to keep Christ out. It makes them uncomfortable and uneasy when Christ stands within the chamber of their thoughts.

But why? Other teachers do not trouble them in this way. Why Christ? Because He is not only a fact, He is a unique fact, unique both in His claims and in the divine authority of attending those claims.

3. Jesus Christ Is an Unavoidable Fact

There are some men, I repeat, who have barred and locked the door of their minds against Jesus Christ. They do not want to think of Him. They are not willing to acknowledge His claims and to yield Him the control of their lives. And because they feel convicted in His presence, they decide to shut out all thought of Him. So they fill their minds and their time with other things—business, pleasure and a barricade of a thousand and one worldly interests so that Christ cannot get at them.

But one day when they think they are secure behind their barred doors, suddenly through some experience Christ stands before them—for "when the doors were shut...came Jesus and stood in the midst."

The other night in a church where I was preaching there was such a man. The Spirit of God wrought mightily in conviction, but he was unwilling to face Jesus Christ. He rose up in the middle of the sermon and walked out. What was he doing? Trying to shut Christ out.

A ministerial friend of mine went to Toronto General Hospital to visit a dying man. He said cheerfully and kindly to him, "I just came in to have a little chat with you."

The dying man answered, "All right, Mr. Brown, if you don't talk religion." What was he doing? Using his dying strength to shut Christ out.

But, my friends, write in your book and let no man nor devil erase it: It can't be done. You may think you have shut Jesus out, you may have every door and entrance barred against Him; but Jesus is the inescapable, the inevitable, the unavoidable Christ—for "when the doors were shut...came Jesus and stood in the midst."

Adam and Eve hid themselves from the presence of the Lord amongst the trees of the Garden, but God followed them to their hiding place, and they stood ashamed in His presence.

Jonah rose up to flee unto Tarshish from the presence of the Lord, but the ship was never built that could smuggle a man out of God's presence, and Jonah found himself face-to-face with God.

The psalmist had learned the lesson of my text when he said:

"Whither shall I go from thy spirit? or whither shall I flee from thy presence?

"If I ascend up into heaven, thou art there: if I make my bed in hell, behold, thou art there.

"If I take the wings of the morning, and dwell in the uttermost parts of the sea;

"Even there shall thy hand lead me, and thy right hand shall hold me."—Ps. 139:7-10.

The poet had this thought when he wrote these words:

> **Within Thy circling power I stand;**
> **On every side I find Thy hand.**
> **Awake, asleep, at home, abroad,**
> **I am surrounded still with God.**

Sometimes Christ stands in the midst through adversity.

Here is a man whose way God has prospered. He had made much money, but he had forgotten God. In love, God pulls down everything about his head. I say "in love," for it is better to be poor and go to Heaven than to be prosperous and go to Hell. Standing amid the ruins of his former prosperity, he sees how fleeting are earthly joys, and he is forced to think of God and eternity. Through adversity, Christ has appeared and is standing in the midst.

Sometimes Christ enters through sickness.

I knew a commercial traveler some years ago who was shutting Christ out. One day sickness laid him low. As he came to the gates of death, lo, Christ appeared and stood beside him. The man later said to me, "I have forgotten God. If God spares me, I shall serve Him." And God did. I baptized him. He became a faithful teacher in the Sunday school and an officer in the church.

Sometimes Christ enters through the death of a loved one.

A young married man in a former pastorate was a stubborn unbeliever. His entire family, all saved, prayed for him continually; but he had sternly forbidden them to speak to him about Christ.

He had one only child, a sweet little girl of three. One day God put His hand on that little life and took her to His heavenly Home.

Now where our treasure is, there will our heart be also. Because this young father believed his child had gone to Heaven, he began to hope he might see her there again. So he opened his heart to God and became an earnest Christian.

I seldom conduct a funeral without thinking of this text. I see men standing in the presence of death who for years have been shutting Christ out. They have banished from their minds the thought of death, of Christ and of eternity.

Then some friend, some loved one, dies, and decency compels them to attend the funeral. How often I have seen unsaved men tremble in the chamber of death listening to a funeral sermon, because standing before them was the unavoidable Christ compelling them to think.

My unsaved friend, you cannot shut Jesus out of your thoughts. The door of your bedchamber cannot keep Him out. He will stand before you in moments of silence when no one else is near.

You may stop your ears to the voice of the preacher, but you cannot drown the still small voice of the unavoidable Christ who speaks to your inmost soul.

You may dismiss the preacher's invitation, but Jesus will walk with you down the street. He will follow you into your home. He will stand beside your bed. He will visit you in your dreams. On the morrow He will travel with you to your business. He will stand beside your bench or desk. He will show you His hands and feet, and He will call on you to decide for or against Him.

Facing Christ, every man is forced to make a choice. He may not wish to make it, but the choice is inevitable, inescapable. Pilate, you remember, tried to escape that choice, just as someone reading this has tried to escape it. He delivered Jesus and then washed his hands! He decided against Him but tried to deceive himself and others into thinking he had not done so.

My friends, one of the greatest delusions abroad today is for a man to think it is possible to be neutral in the presence of Jesus Christ.

I go to a man and I ask, "Friend, will you go to Heaven when you die?"

He answers, "I hardly think so."

I ask, "Will you go to Hell if you die?"

He answers, "I don't think so."

He had never wholeheartedly joined himself to Christ and God's people, so he doesn't think he is fit to go to Heaven. But he has never outwardly opposed God or God's people, so he doesn't think he is bad enough to go to Hell.

Oh, listen! You are bound either for one place or the other. "No man," said Christ, "can serve two masters." He said, "He that is not with me is against me." He said also, "To whom ye yield yourselves servants to obey, his servants ye are."

Every man who reads this message is either serving the world, the flesh and the Devil, or he is serving the Lord Jesus Christ. Which is it? Neutrality in the presence of Christ is impossible. A man is one thing or the other, and to think differently is a delusion.

If you are for Christ, you will accept Him as your Saviour. And if you do not accept Him, you reject Him.

Dr. Mahood has pointed out that every man must do one of three things with Christ: compliment Him, crucify Him or accept Him.

Some compliment Him. Many infidels have complimented Jesus

Christ as the best man who ever lived. But you might as well crucify Him as compliment Him. He said, "Why call ye me, Lord, Lord, and do not the things which I say?"

Some crucify Him. That's what the multitude is doing today. Those who neglect Him are crucifying Him.

Others accept Him. Which will you do today? God help you to do now what you will wish you had done when you stand before Him.

And that brings me to another fact. Someone says, "I do not think your text applies to some people who have so long and so often shut Christ out that He has ceased to plead and strive with them. They do not come to church; they will not listen to preachers; they will not hear saved people speak a word to them. God is not in all their thoughts, and He seems to have little chance of ever getting into their thoughts. What of them?"

I answer, "When the doors were shut…came Jesus and stood in the midst." Every one of them shall find himself face-to-face with the unavoidable Christ at the judgment throne of God.

Oh, He is the inescapable, inevitable, unavoidable Christ. Men will find that closing their eyes in death does not get them out of God's hands.

Unsaved men will not come to church. They will not go near evangelistic meetings; but there is a meeting where every unbeliever will attend, where every infidel will be present. "Every one of us shall give account of himself to God." Every man who has tried to avoid Christ, Christians, radio or TV preaching and church services, will stand lone before the great white throne of God. He will not escape that meeting. He will have to stay until his case is all settled. He will have to listen to God then. He will have to face Christ then. The eyes of the assembled universe will be centered upon him, the light from the throne will be turned full upon him, and when the sentence is pronounced, he will have to hear it.

And then what? Then God will do for such men what they have long wanted—leave them alone. They have shut the door of mind and heart against Him. Very well. God will leave them shut up in their eternal prison house. What that means no tongue can tell.

A man may reject Christ here, but he is not cut off from the blessings and mercies of God. Yonder, however, in the eternal world, the sinner unsaved shall be separated, not only from God, but from God's people, from all light and mercy and truth.

Oh, what will it be with no Great Physician to heal, no blood to cleanse, no God to hear a penitent sinner's cry—shut out from the Saviour who waited to save, and shut in with the Devil whom they served instead?

> **What if thine eye refuse to see,**
> **Thine ear of Heaven's free mercy fail,**
> **And thou a willing captive be,**
> **Thyself thine own dark jail?**
>
> **O doom beyond the saddest guess,**
> **As the long years of God unroll;**
> **To make thy sordid sinfulness**
> **The prison of thy soul.**
>
> **We shape ourselves the joy or fear**
> **Of which the future life is made**
> **And fill our future atmosphere**
> **With sunshine or with shade.**
>
> **The tissue of the life to be**
> **We weave with colors all our own.**
> **And in the field of destiny**
> **We reap as we have sown.**

You unsaved men and women who may read this message, God be merciful to you who will not have mercy on yourselves. Do you not see that life's greatest folly is to shut Christ out of your heart? Do you not see that the sin you love will eventually destroy you? Do you not know that to serve the Devil now is to share the Devil's destiny?

Jesus Christ has not yet left you. You know that. You would not be reading this if He had. He is merciful and compassionate and stands ready to save you.

Why not receive Him? Why not take Him now? Far better to meet Christ now as your Saviour than to meet Him hereafter as your Judge.

CURTIS W. HUTSON
1934–1995

ABOUT THE MAN:

In 1961 a mail carrier and pastor of a very small church attended a Sword of the Lord Conference, got on fire, gave up his route and set out to build a great soul-winning work for God. Forrest Hills Baptist Church of Decatur, Georgia grew from 40 people into a membership of 7,900. The last four years of Curtis Hutson's pastorate there, the Sunday school was recognized as the largest in Georgia.

After pastoring for 21 years, Dr. Hutson—the great soul winner that he was—became so burdened for the whole nation that he entered full-time evangelism, holding great citywide-areawide-cooperative revivals in some of America's greatest churches. As many as 625 precious souls trusted Christ in a single service. In one eight-day meeting, 1,502 salvation decisions were recorded.

As an evangelist, he was in great demand.

At the request of Dr. John R. Rice, Dr. Hutson became associate editor of THE SWORD OF THE LORD in 1978, serving in that capacity until the death of Dr. Rice before becoming editor, president of Sword of the Lord Foundation, and director of Sword of the Lord Conferences. He continued in these ministries until his death on March 5, 1995, literally changing the lives of thousands of preachers and laymen alike, as well as winning many more thousands to Christ.

Dr. Hutson was the author of many fine books and booklets.

VI.

Christ Is All

CURTIS HUTSON

(Preached at Sword Family Conference, Bill Rice Ranch, 1974)

"*Christ is all, and in all.*"—Col. 3:11.

Dr. Bob Jones, Sr., told the story of being in a meeting where people were giving testimonies. He kept noticing an old man on one side holding the back of a pew. Every now and then he would try to pull himself up by holding the back of that pew. Finally, after several attempts, he succeeded.

As he got to the floor, shaking and in tears, he said, "Dr. Bob, I'm an old man. My wife has gone to be with the Lord. My children are all grown and married. My health is about gone. I don't have much money. Come to think of it, Dr. Bob, about all I have left is Jesus." And he sat down.

Dr. Jones said after some other testimonies, the old man began to pull himself up out of the pew again. As he made his way up to the floor the second time, he said, "Dr. Bob, come to think of it, that is just about all I need."

A missionary was teaching a young fellow the 23rd Psalm. He began, "The Lord is my shepherd; I shall not want." The little fellow repeated: "The Lord is my shepherd; that's all I want."

Christ is all we need and all we want.

1. Christ Is All in Revelation

First, Christ is all in revelation. I mean, Christ is all in this Book I hold in my hand. I believe the Bible to be not PART but ALL of God's revelation to man. Jude said:

"Beloved, when I gave all diligence to write unto you of the common salvation, it was needful for me [the marginal rendering in the Scofield Bible is "constraint was upon me, i.e., of the Spirit"] *to write unto you, and exhort you that ye should earnestly*

contend for the faith which was once delivered unto the saints."—Vs. 3.

According to *Strong's Concordance,* *"once"* in Jude, verse 3, doesn't mean "once upon a time," but "once for all."

I have heard people say, "God gave me a new revelation yesterday." I know what they mean by their expression; however, they didn't receive a new revelation, but an illumination upon the already given revelation.

I have discovered some truth in the Bible which seemed to jump out at me. I said, "Boy, the Lord just gave me a revelation!" No, He gave that revelation to the Bible writer when it was penned. What I received was illumination. God shined a light so I could see the truth.

Christ is all in revelation; that is, Christ is everything in this Bible. I don't need many proof texts for this.

In John 5:39 Jesus said, "Search the scriptures; for in them ye think ye have eternal life: and they [the Bible] are they which testify of me." From Genesis to Revelation, verse after verse talks about Jesus Christ.

A young preacher once asked an older preacher how he should study the Bible and what he should look for in the Bible. The old preacher answered, "Young fellow, you never really discover the true meaning of any passage in the Bible until you find Jesus Christ in that Scripture."

I am told that in Washington, D.C., there is a copy of the Constitution of the United States of America. If you look at it from a certain angle, you see the picture or impression of George Washington, our first president. Just so, I have learned in these years of studying the Word of God that you can look at the Bible from any angle and see Jesus Christ.

After Jesus' resurrection, He walked down the road with His Emmaus disciples. They didn't know who was walking with them. "Beginning at Moses and all the prophets, he [Jesus] expounded unto them in all the scriptures the things concerning himself" (Luke 24:27).

Now the three divisions of the Old Testament are: the books of Moses, "the Pentateuch," the first five books of the Old Testament; the Prophets, the prophetical books; and the Psalms, the songbook.

Jesus preached through the entire Old Testament and pointed out Himself in verse after verse after verse.

Say, wouldn't you like to have heard that sermon! I would like to have heard Jesus as He started in Genesis and "expounded unto them in all the scriptures the things concerning himself."

Here is God slaying a little innocent animal, taking the skin, clothing Adam and Eve, and saying to them, "That animal is a picture of Me, a picture of My death on the cross. Through My death you will wear a robe of righteousness, and your sins will be covered and done away with." I would like to have heard that, wouldn't you?

Christ is all in this Book. In Genesis He is the Promised Seed; in Exodus He is the Passover Lamb; and all the way to the book of Revelation where He is the Coming King.

2. Christ Is All in Creation

Not only is Christ all in revelation, but He is all in creation. I'm not an evolutionist. I believe God created man out of the dust of the earth. And I am amazed at preachers who do not know the importance of believing in the Genesis account of creation.

Our public schools teach evolution. I don't mind so much their teaching evolution as a theory, but when they teach evolution as a fact, that upsets me.

If man evolved like the evolutionists teach, where are you going to put the Fall of man? If man was not created like the Bible says, and placed in the Garden like the Bible says, and given a prohibition like the Bible says, and if we didn't disobey God like the Bible says, then we are not sinners.

Romans 5:12 says, "Wherefore, as by one man sin entered into the world, and death by sin; and so death passed upon all men, for that all have sinned."

Romans 5:19 tells us, "For as by one man's disobedience many were made sinners." We are sinners by virtue of our birth as well as by our choice. We inherited the sin nature when we were born. Jesus didn't have that. I think that is what He meant when He, talking of Satan, said, "The prince of this world cometh, and hath nothing in me" (John 14:30). He literally was saying, "He has nothing in Me to get hold of; I don't have a sin nature."

I think that is the meaning of Hebrews 4:15: "For we have not an high priest which cannot be touched with the feeling of our infirmities; but was in all points tempted like as we are, yet without sin," or apart from the sin nature. He was not a sinner but the spotless, sinless, virgin-born Son of God who died on the cross in our place, bearing all our sins and satisfying the just demands of a holy God.

I am saying, Christ is all in creation.

"In the beginning was the Word, and the Word was with God, and the Word was God.

"The same was in the beginning with God.

"All things were made by him; and without him was not any thing made that was made."—John 1:1–3.

He is all in creation.

Dr. B. R. Lakin said, "I have no confidence in biological baboon boosters who pray, 'Our father who art in the coconut tree.'" You know, the ones who say:

> **Once I was a tadpole, long and thin;**
> **Then I was a bullfrog with my tail tucked in.**
> **Then I was a monkey hanging from a tree;**
> **Now I'm a professor with a Ph.D.**

3. Christ Is All in Salvation

Jesus is not only all in revelation and all in creation, but He is all in salvation. It is not Jesus plus something; it is Jesus, period.

He said in John 14:6, "I am the way, the truth, and the life: no man cometh unto the Father, but by me." And Acts 4:12 reads, "Neither is there salvation in any other: for there is none other name under heaven given among men, whereby we must be saved."

First John 5:12 states, "He that hath the Son hath life; and he that hath not the Son of God hath not life."

I'm glad to be a Baptist, but I'm not saved because I'm a Baptist. I'm saved because Christ loved me and died on the cross, paid my sin debt, suffered my Hell, and because I have accepted Him as my Saviour.

A missionary was visiting a little fellow who was religious. She told him how Jesus Christ became his Substitute, died on the cross and paid his sin debt at Calvary. He had never heard the story exactly like that.

The missionary left. A few days later she came back, and he was smiling. It was evident something had happened to him. There was a different look on his face. It was showing on his countenance.

The missionary asked, "Billy, what has happened to you?"

He answered, "Miss Missionary, I always knew Jesus Christ is necessary, but I didn't know until three or four days ago that He is enough."

Dr. George Truett told about a man who died in a cheap hotel room in Texas after having spent his fortune seeking peace and not finding it. Dr. Truett said, "I think he found the peace he was looking for." When they found his body, they found on a table nearby a sheet of paper with this poem penned:

> **I've searched in vain a thousand ways,**
> **My fears to quell, my hopes to raise;**
> **And all I need, the Bible says,**
> **Is Jesus.**

Jesus is the "open sesame" to Heaven.

A fellow went to his pastor and asked, "What can I do to get saved?"

The preacher replied, "You have to have 100 points to go to Heaven."

"I don't know if I have any points or not."

"Tell me what you have done, and I'll tell you if you have any points."

"I keep the Ten Commandments."

The pastor said, "That's five points."

"I've joined the church and been baptized."

"That's five more points."

"I have been faithful to my wife and been a good father."

"That's five more points. That totals fifteen points."

"I give a tithe of my income."

"That's five more—twenty points."

"I pray every day and read my Bible."

"That's five more points."

When the fellow ran out of good things he had done, he had only thirty-five points.

The pastor asked, "Is there anything else you have done for which you can get more points?"

The man answered, "I can't think of another thing—yes, I did do one other thing. One night in a country church I heard a preacher tell how Jesus Christ loves sinners and how He bore all our sin in His own body on the cross. He preached that night that Jesus Christ died and suffered Hell and paid my debt at Calvary. When they gave the invitation, I went forward and trusted Jesus Christ as my Saviour."

The pastor said, "That's 100 points!"

Jesus Christ is all in salvation.

A little fellow went to his pastor and said, "Pastor, I want to get saved. What can I do to get saved?"

The pastor said, "I'm sorry. It's too late."

"You mean I'm too late to be saved?"

"No, not too late to be saved, but too late to do anything to be saved. You see, son, Jesus did it all two thousand years ago."

> Why was He there as the bearer of sin
> If on Jesus my guilt was not laid?
> Why did He shed His life-giving blood
> If His dying my debt has not paid?

Jesus paid it all. God showed His acceptance of the price Jesus paid when He raised His Son from the dead and let the prisoner go free.

Christ is all in salvation. It is not Jesus plus baptism. It is not Jesus plus joining the church. All these are good, but the point I am trying to make is, Jesus Christ is all in the matter of salvation.

Christ is all in revelation: He is everything in this Book. Christ is all in creation. Christ is all in salvation.

4. Christ Is All in the Church

I am talking about the local assembly, the local church. What is the church? What happens in the church?

In the church we have the ordinances: the Lord's Supper, baptism, and we have preaching. Let us take these one at a time.

First, look at the Lord's Supper. What do you think about when you come to break the bread and pour the fruit of the vine in the cup? Paul said in I Corinthians 11:26, "For as often as ye eat this bread, and drink this cup, ye do shew the Lord's death till he come." Paul says every time we observe the Lord's table, we look backward to His dying on the cross and forward to His coming to be crowned King of Kings and Lord of Lords. Take Jesus out of the Lord's Supper, and you have nothing but some unleavened bread and juice. Take Jesus out of it and you have no ordinance.

Second, look at baptism. I baptized thousands of converts at Forrest Hills Baptist Church; but if we take Jesus out of baptism, we don't have anything.

When I baptized children, I said to them, "I want you to understand what baptism is. When I put you under the water, that means Jesus Christ died and was buried. When I bring you up out of the water, that means Jesus Christ arose the third day, according to the Scriptures. Baptism is a picture of the death, burial and resurrection of Christ."

I'm a Baptist, and I believe in baptizing converts, but I don't preach baptismal regeneration.

One fellow preached on baptism every time he went into the pulpit. He was called to a church. He went and on Sunday morning preached on baptism. He went back Sunday night and preached on baptism. Wednesday night he preached on baptism. The next Sunday morning—baptism; the next Sunday night—baptism; the next Wednesday night—baptism.

The deacons became concerned. They met together and then called the preacher aside and said to him, "Listen, we are Baptists and we believe in baptism, but don't you know anything but baptism, baptism, baptism?"

He said, "Yes, I know a lot of other things."

"Well, why don't you preach on something besides baptism?"

He said, "Suppose you give me a text, and I will preach on it."

One of the deacons picked out a good text: "And now also the axe is laid unto the root of the trees: therefore every tree which bringeth not forth good fruit is hewn down, and cast into the fire" (Matt. 3:10). He said, "Suppose you preach on that text next Sunday." (He didn't see where he could get baptism out of that.)

The next Sunday morning the preacher got up and said, "My text this morning is, 'The axe is laid unto the root of the trees: therefore every tree which bringeth not forth good fruit is hewn down, and cast into the fire.'" He added some preliminary remarks, then said, "And, bless God, why do you think they were cutting those trees down? Why, they were clearing a path to get to the creek to have an old-fashioned baptizing."

I believe in baptism, but take Christ out of baptism, and you have nothing. Take Christ out of the Lord's Supper, and you have nothing. And what did Paul say? "For we preach not ourselves, but Christ Jesus the Lord" (II Cor. 4:5). Take Jesus Christ out of preaching, and you have nothing.

In his sermon "The Preeminence of Christ" Dr. Jack Hyles said:

> If preachers would just preach about Jesus on Sunday morning, preach about Him on Sunday night, preach about Him on Wednesday night, then look for Jesus in this book and that book and preach Jesus, Jesus, Jesus, and have the choir sing about Jesus, we could have revival.

There is something about that name, Jesus! Jesus Christ is all in revelation, all in creation, all in salvation and all in the church.

5. Christ Is All in the Christian Graces

I won't begin to cover them all, but I think I can cover the chief three quickly: faith, hope and charity (love).

Christ is all in faith. It dawned on me one day that faith is not important at all; it is the object of faith that is important.

For instance, if you put your faith in your good works to get you to Heaven, it will send you to Hell. If a man's faith is in anything other than the death of Jesus on the cross, his faith is going to send him to Hell. It is the object of faith that makes faith important. It is not believe and be saved, but "Believe on the Lord Jesus Christ, and thou shalt be saved." It is not believe and have everlasting life, but "He that believeth on the Son hath everlasting life." It is not believe and be not condemned, but "He that believeth on him [the Son] is not condemned."

Take Jesus out of faith, and your faith is nothing. You can go to Hell on your faith. Romans 10:17 says, "So then faith cometh by hearing, and hearing by the word of God."

John 1:1 says, "In the beginning was the Word, and the Word was with God, and the Word was God." Verse 14 says, "And the Word was made flesh, and dwelt among us, (and we beheld his glory, the glory as of the only begotten of the Father,) full of grace and truth."

Faith comes by hearing, hearing by the Word of God, and Jesus is the Word of God.

Jesus is all in faith. He is our Hope. Paul said:

"For the grace of God that bringeth salvation hath appeared to all men,

"Teaching us that, denying ungodliness and worldly lusts, we should live soberly, righteously, and godly, in this present world;

"Looking for that blessed hope, and the glorious appearing of the great God and our Saviour Jesus Christ."—Titus 2:11-13.

Christ is all in love. You may stand and say, "I love Jesus." You may sometime be tempted to boast that you love Jesus; but did you ever think about I John 4:19: "We love him, because he first loved us"? If I love Him, I can't take credit. I only love Him because He first loved me.

He is all in faith. He is all in hope. He is all in charity. I am saying, Jesus Christ is all in revelation, all in creation, all in salvation, all in the church, and all in the Christian graces.

6. Christ Is All in Our Expectation

If Jesus doesn't come, I expect to die. Of course, I believe I may be alive when Jesus comes. The Apostle Paul thought he would be alive when He came, for Paul said:

"For the Lord himself shall descend from heaven with a shout, with the voice of the archangel, and with the trump of God: and the dead in Christ shall rise first:

"Then we [including himself and those he is addressing] *which are alive and remain shall be caught up together with them in the clouds, to meet the Lord in the air: and so shall we ever be with the Lord."*—I Thess. 4:16,17.

If Jesus doesn't come and I live out my life-span, then the next thing before Heaven is death. And Christ is all in death.

I am thinking of Psalm 23 where David said, "Yea, though I walk through the valley of the shadow of death, I will fear no evil: for *thou art with me;* thy rod and thy staff they comfort me."

I am thinking too of the death of my mother-in-law. I led her to Christ on a Father's Day, gave her a new Bible and baptized her. She left on vacation several years later to go to Chattanooga. I left to go to Florida to speak in a Bible conference.

While on that vacation in Chattanooga, my wife's mother became sick. My wife called me and asked me to pray for her. Later she called back and said her mother was much sicker than they thought, and might die. Later she called and told me her mother had died.

My wife told me about her mother's death:

> Curtis, before Mother died she would lie under the oxygen tent, and every once in a while she would open her eyes wide and look around and say, "Is Momma here?" Then she would smile and say, "Yes, Momma, I see you."
>
> Then she would open her eyes wide and say, "Is Bunk here?" [Bunk was her cousin William.] "Yes, Bunk, I see you."
>
> Then she would open her eyes and say, "Is Uncle Riley here?" [her uncle who had died a couple weeks before]. Then she would smile and say, "Yes, Uncle Riley, I see you."
>
> Then she said something to her sister, Alma [who was still alive]. "Alma, get behind me and push." She was that close to Heaven. "Alma, get behind me! Alma, push. Alma, push, PUSH, PUSH."

You say she was just a crazy old lady. No, she saw Alma; she saw Riley; she saw Bunk; she saw Momma when she died.

I read biographies of great men and have written down the dying words of many great saints.

Among the last words of John Wesley were, "Best of all, Christ is with us."

Among A. J. Gordon's dying words were, "Victory! Victory!"

Among Billy Bray's dying words were, "Glory! Glory! I'll soon be with the Lord! Glory be to God!" And off he went to Heaven.

D. L. Moody's dying words were, "This is my coronation day! It is the day I have been looking forward to for years!"

I have stood by the side of dying saints and watched them as they seemed to see the other world. The old man who founded Forrest Hills Baptist Church was Mr. John Chastain. He built a little white frame building and put six pews on either side that would seat fifty or sixty people comfortably.

I used to go see Uncle John and play the accordion and sing for him. He was a very poor man. He lived in an old run-down house. The last time I went to see Uncle John, I played and sang "The Great Homecoming Week." I laid the old accordion down, and John began to smile. He said, "Do you see 'em?"

I got cold chills and said, "No, I don't see them."

He said, "They are all around here. The room is full of 'em. They are out there in the yard."

Those old walls had not been painted in years, and the paint was peeling off. He looked over at the walls and said, "Aren't those beautiful walls!"

I said, "If you say so, John."

He said, "They are the most beautiful things I ever saw." And he said, "Look at all those beautiful flowers!" (There wasn't a flower in the room.) Uncle John was that close to Heaven.

Jesus Christ is all in death. And after death, the resurrection, because Jesus is coming and the dead are going to be raised.

I was raised in a church that didn't believe in the resurrection of the dead. In fact, my pastor said to me one day just before a funeral service, "Now, Curt, when I die, don't you tell them that anything is coming out of the grave. 'Dust thou art, and unto dust shalt thou return.'" And he added a little bit to it—"and dust thou shalt remain."

I was taught there was no bodily resurrection. I thought when you died, you were buried and that was the end. I don't know how I overlooked verses like John 5:28, 29:

"Marvel not at this: for the hour is coming, in the which all that are in the graves shall hear his voice,

"And shall come forth; they that have done good, unto the resurrection of life; and they that have done evil, unto the resurrection of damnation."

I don't know how I overlooked Acts 24:15: "There shall be a resurrection of the dead, both of the just and the unjust."

I don't know how I overlooked Job 19:25, 26:

"For I know that my redeemer liveth, and that he shall stand at the latter day upon the earth:

"And though after my skin worms destroy this body, yet in my flesh shall I see God."

I don't know how I overlooked I Corinthians 15:22, 23:

"For as in Adam all die, even so in Christ shall all be made alive.

"But every man in his own order: Christ the firstfruits; afterward they that are Christ's at his coming."

I conducted my mother's funeral. When we buried her in the country churchyard, some of those old country preachers came by and tried to comfort me. They would put an arm around my shoulder and pat me on the back and say, "Now, Curt, she's gone. You will remember her footsteps around the house; you will remember those times when you had a fevered brow and Mother helped you. But she is gone now. You will never see her again."

I wanted to say, "Hush! Get away!" I'm glad I knew that when the trumpet sounds, the dead in Christ will rise.

An old country preacher friend was taught as I was until he began studying and found there is to be a resurrection. So one Sunday morning he preached on "When the Clods Begin to Fly."

People sometimes ask funny questions, such as, "Do you believe that when we are resurrected, we will come through the ground without making any opening; or do you think we will actually make holes in the ground when we come out?"

Really, I don't know, but when Jesus was resurrected, they found the stone rolled back. And before Jesus resurrected Lazarus, He said, "Take ye away the stone."

I would like for the graveyard to start opening up and dirt start flying like popcorn so these modernistic preachers who don't believe in the resurrection can be thoroughly convinced!

Christ is all in resurrection. Every resurrection passage has connected with it the coming of Christ. What was it Job said?

"For I know that my redeemer liveth, and that he shall stand at the latter day upon the earth:

"And though after my skin worms destroy this body, yet in my flesh shall I see God."—Job 19:25, 26.

Of what is this speaking? The Redeemer's coming and standing with His feet upon the earth.

What does I Thessalonians 4:16, 17 say?

"For the Lord himself shall descend from heaven with a shout, with the voice of the archangel, and with the trump of God: and the dead in Christ shall rise first:

"Then we which are alive and remain shall be caught up together with them in the clouds, to meet the Lord in the air: and so shall we ever be with the Lord."

It is connected with the coming of Christ.

Paul said in I Corinthians 15:20, "But now is Christ risen from the dead, and become the firstfruits of them that slept."

The firstfruits, I am told, are like a man raising a crop. The firstfruits were the first ears of corn to ripen. The man would carry them in and say, "This is a guarantee that there is a main harvest to follow."

The resurrection of Jesus is a guarantee of our own resurrection. Someday the trumpet will sound, and we will be raised from the dead.

He is all in revelation, all in creation, all in salvation, all in the church, all in the Christian graces, all in our expectation, all in death, and all in resurrection.

7. Christ Is All in Heaven

What is going to be the theme of Heaven? From the book of Revelation, I get the idea it will be Christ. I think Revelation 4 and 5 is a heavenly scene. The saints are in Heaven in 5:9, and they begin to sing: "Thou art worthy...for thou wast slain, and hast redeemed us to God by thy blood out of every kindred, and tongue, and people, and nation."

What will we talk about in Heaven? Jesus! We will never tire of talking about Him—not after ten thousand years. After ten billion years, we will still be singing about Him. After ten trillion years, it will still be Jesus—Jesus—Jesus.

> **There is a name I love to hear,**
> **I love to sing its worth;**
> **It sounds like music in mine ear,**
> **The sweetest name on earth.**

If Jesus Christ is all in revelation, all in creation, all in salvation, all in the Christian graces, all in the church, and all in our expectations in the future, then don't you think He ought to be all in our lives?

I trusted Jesus Christ when I was eleven. I knew so little about salvation. I prayed three hours that night, and for a long time afterward I thought I was saved because I had prayed three hours. After long praying, my eyes were sore and swollen from crying.

I could hardly talk, but I said something like this:

> Dear Jesus. I am just an eleven-year-old boy. I have begged You to save me, and You won't save me. I have cried and prayed. I got on my knees and prayed. I have lain on my stomach and prayed. I have done everything. I have confessed every sin I remember that I have ever committed. And, Lord, there are some I have forgotten about, I know.
>
> I'll tell You one thing, Jesus: this is one little boy that sure did want to go to Heaven. And when I get to Hell, I'm going to look up out of Hell and say, "It's not my fault; it's Yours. I begged You to save me, and You wouldn't."

I didn't realize it, but when I said that, I was completely trusting Christ and putting my salvation in His hands. I didn't know what terminology to use. As a result, I doubted. I was up and down. I thought I was saved because I felt good, until I learned to base my assurance on what the Bible says. Then I felt good because I knew I was saved.

As a boy and a young man, I never heard sermons on the Spirit-filled life, on dedication, on surrender. If I had, I would have surrendered myself to Christ and sought to be filled with the Spirit many years before I was.

But one day I read Romans 12:1, 2:

"I beseech you therefore, brethren, by the mercies of God, that ye present your bodies a living sacrifice, holy, acceptable unto

God, which is your reasonable service.

"And be not conformed to this world: but ye be transformed by the renewing of your mind, that ye may prove what is that good, and acceptable, and perfect, will of God."

I said, "Dear God, I have trusted You as my Saviour. I have tried to run my life too much of the time, but I want to go as far as I can as a Christian. I want to be the best Christian I can be. I give myself to You 100%. I want You to be all in my life."

That was in 1961, and I have never been the same since.

In those verses, Paul is not speaking to unsaved people. He is saying, "You born-again believers, you who are blood-washed, I beg you, in view of all God's mercy, in view of all God has done for you—the air you breathe, the health you enjoy, the clothes you have, the food you eat—give your bodies a living sacrifice to God. Make Him Lord."

As an old lady lay dying, she said, "Bring...." That was all she could say; she was so weak. They brought in the picture album. No, no, she didn't want that. She gained a little strength and again said, "Bring...." They brought in the children one by one. No, no, no. They brought her a glass of water. No, no. Again, "Bring...." They brought a washcloth and bathed her lips. They brought everything they could think of, but she could not finish the sentence. She could only say, "Bring...."

Just before she died, she gained enough strength to sit up in the bed and say, "Bring forth the royal diadem, and crown Him Lord of all."

He is all in revelation. He is all in creation. He is all in salvation. He is all in the church. He is all in the Christian graces. He is all in our expectations. And for God's sake, let us make Him all in our lives while we live for Him and while we are waiting to go to Heaven.

LEE ROBERSON
1909–

ABOUT THE MAN:

When one considers the far-reaching ministries of the Highland Park Baptist Church, Chattanooga, Tennessee, and pauses to reflect upon its total outreach, he has cause to believe that it is close to the New Testament pattern.

In the more than forty-one years—from 1942 when Dr. Lee Roberson first came to Highland Park until his retirement in April 1983—the ministry expanded to include Camp Joy, reaching some 3,000 children annually; World Wide Faith Missions, contributing to the support of over 350 missionaries; 50 branch churches in the greater Chattanooga area; Union Gospel Mission, which feeds and sleeps an average of 50 transient men daily; a Sunday school bus ministry, which covers 45 bus routes; a deaf ministry; "Gospel Dynamite," a live broadcast held daily over 2 radio stations; a church paper, THE EVANGELIST, being mailed free each month to over 73,000 readers; and Tennessee Temple University, Temple Baptist Theological Seminary and Tennessee Temple Academy.

He has preached to thousands, trained preachers, supported the mission cause. Dr. John R. Rice called him "the Spurgeon of our generation."

Dr. Roberson has many fine books in print. These include *Touching Heaven, The Man in Cell No. 1, The Faith That Moves Mountains, Coming to Chattanooga—Soon, Ten Thousand Tears, Disturbing Questions...Solid Answers, The Gold Mine* and *Diamonds in the Rough.*

VII.

The Poor Man's King

LEE ROBERSON

"The book of the generation of Jesus Christ, the son of David, the son of Abraham.

"Abraham begat Isaac; and Isaac begat Jacob; and Jacob begat Judas and his brethren."—Matt. 1:1, 2.

And we read in verses 16 and 17:

"And Jacob begat Joseph the husband of Mary, of whom was born Jesus, who is called Christ.

"So all the generations from Abraham to David are fourteen generations; and from David until the carrying away into Babylon are fourteen generations; and from the carrying away into Babylon unto Christ are fourteen generations."

Now verses 18 to 25:

"Now the birth of Jesus Christ was on this wise: When as his mother Mary was espoused to Joseph, before they came together, she was found with child of the Holy Ghost.

"Then Joseph her husband, being a just man, and not willing to make her a publick example, was minded to put her away privily.

"But while he thought on these things, behold, the angel of the Lord appeared unto him in a dream, saying, Joseph, thou son of David, fear not to take unto thee Mary thy wife: for that which is conceived in her is of the Holy Ghost.

"And she shall bring forth a son, and thou shalt call his name JESUS: for he shall save his people from their sins.

"Now all this was done, that it might be fulfilled which was spoken of the Lord by the prophet, saying,

"Behold, a virgin shall be with child, and shall bring forth a son, and they shall call his name Emmanuel, which being interpreted is, God with us.

"Then Joseph being raised from sleep did as the angel of the

Lord had bidden him, and took unto him his wife:

"And knew her not till she had brought forth her firstborn son: and he called his name JESUS."

When I read Spurgeon's exposition of the Gospel of Matthew, I was attracted by the sane, simple, beautiful way in which he interpreted the Word of God, verse by verse. I could almost sense the speaking of the great Spurgeon. As I read chapter 1 in his book, one special paragraph attracted my attention:

> Our Lord was a "root out of dry ground," a shoot from the withered stem of Jesse. He set small store by earthly greatness. He must needs be of the human race; but He comes to a family of low estate, and there He finds His reputed father, Joseph, a carpenter of Nazareth. HE IS THE POOR MAN'S KING. He will not disdain any of us, though our father's house be little in Israel. He will condescend to men of low estate.

When I read that single paragraph, I underscored the words, "He is the poor man's King."

God ordained that Christ would come into the world in a certain definite fashion. Somewhere in the council chambers of Heaven, when the Father, Son and Holy Spirit met together, this matter was discussed—the coming of our Lord, even from the foundation of the world. It was ordained that Christ would come in a certain way. Here is the fulfillment of it in the coming of Jesus, "the poor man's King!"

I. THE KING BECAME A MAN

Christ, the Son of God, condescended to become a man.

"Let this mind be in you, which was also in Christ Jesus:

"Who, being in the form of God, thought it not robbery to be equal with God:

"But made himself of no reputation, and took upon him the form of a servant, and was made in the likeness of men:

"And being found in fashion as a man, he humbled himself, and became obedient unto death, even the death of the cross.

"Wherefore God also hath highly exalted him, and given him a name which is above every name:

"That at the name of Jesus every knee should bow, of things

in heaven, and things in earth, and things under the earth;

"And that every tongue should confess that Jesus Christ is Lord, to the glory of God the Father."—Phil. 2:5–11.

This is one of the profound portions of the Word of God. The King became a man! The Son of God, the Lord Jesus Christ, the King of Glory, became a man!

Now, this is God's way of salvation—by the Man Christ Jesus. Not by works, not by morality, not by position, not by power, but by Jesus Christ. This is the way whereby sinful mankind comes into the family of God and comes to be made in the likeness of the Son of God.

Again, the way is so simple that *every* person can understand. Some try to make it difficult. Some try to add to it many things that have no part in the way of salvation. Salvation is by the Lord Jesus Christ, the Christ of Calvary, the King who became a man when He came down to this earth.

The way is singular, for Jesus said, "I am *the* way," not by many ways, not by many men, but by one man, the Man Christ Jesus.

II. THE KING RELATED HIMSELF TO POOR MEN

Our Lord came to this earth, born of a human mother, the humble Mary, the lowly virgin. The King of Kings, the Lord of Glory, came down out of Heaven to this earth!

Someone has put it into words like these:

> He was so poor that He said of Himself that He had "not where to lay his head." His only pocketbook was the mouth of a fish. He rode on another man's beast, cruised the lake in another man's boat, was rocked in another man's cradle, was buried in another man's grave; yet He laid aside a purple robe to do it.
>
> He never wrote a book. His words as recorded would hardly make a vest pocket edition; yet if all the words that have been written about Him were brought together, they would fill a thousand Congressional libraries.
>
> Shakespeare has been translated into thirty languages; Thomas à Kempis, into sixty; John Bunyan, into one hundred; but the Book that told us first of this Man has been translated

into more than one thousand languages.

Shakespeare has reached two million copies; *The Pilgrim's Progress*, three million; *In His Steps*, eight million; but the Book that tells of this Man has reached that staggering total nine times over, or more than half a hundred million.

He never founded a college to perpetuate His doctrines; yet His teachings have endured for two thousand years.

He never carried a sword. He organized no army, built no navy; yet He founded an empire in which there are millions who would die for Him today.

He never studied medicine; yet He healed all who came or were brought to Him and refused to take a fee for His service.

When He came, the world would not have Him; yet when He died the sun veiled its face in crepe, and all the heavens put on mourning.

The poverty of our Saviour! The wonder of our Lord Jesus! The King relating Himself to the poorest of men!

Some try to hide their poverty and poor beginnings by elaborate talk. They try to hide the fact that they come from poor parents. They try to forget they did not have anything in the beginning of their lives. Yet, my dear friends, if God brought you into the world by way of poor parents, then rejoice in it, because it may be that this will bring the greatest blessings to your life outside of the Lord and Saviour. Don't hide from poverty.

Many have come to places of affluence and importance and riches, yet I remember when these same folks were barely making a living. These remember too their poor beginning and rejoice in it, and I rejoice that they have this spirit. They are not ashamed of their humble beginning nor forgetting what God has done for them. Some big men have retained a consciousness that everything they have has come from our blessed Lord.

The King became a poor man, and He related Himself to the poor. Read about Jesus and the beggars, Jesus and blind Bartimaeus, Jesus and the lepers, Jesus and the maniac of Gadara, Jesus and Lazarus of Luke 16. See the Son of God, how He identified with the poor.

While I am talking about Jesus' relating Himself to poor people, I must say that salvation is FREE.

"For by grace are ye saved through faith; and that not of yourselves; it is the gift of God:

"Not of works, lest any man should boast."—Eph. 2:8, 9.

The blind, the halt, the lepers came to Him, and He turned none away. Salvation is free—free to the rich and to the poor! All are saved in the same way—by trusting in Jesus Christ.

Not only is salvation free, but salvation is available. The door is open. The Lord said, "Come; for all things are now ready." He invites you to come and partake of the salvation He offers.

Again, when you receive Christ, He comes into your life to guide you, to provide for you, to take your prayers to the Father and to keep you as you surrender yourself to Him. What a glorious and beautiful picture of the King!

III. THE KING ALIGNED HIMSELF WITH SINFUL MEN

In verse 1 of Matthew 1 we read, "The book of the generation of Jesus Christ, the son of David...." This calls to mind the story of David and Bathsheba, Uriah and Solomon. Our Lord Jesus aligned Himself with sinful men. He came to be born of the virgin, but He came from the line of those who were mortal and weak, who had failures but were in the family of God.

Look at verse 5: "And Salmon begat Boaz of Rachab [or Rahab]." Rahab the harlot had a special place when Israel came into the Promised Land, and she was in the line of our Lord Jesus!

In verse 10 we read, "And Ezekias begat Manasses." Manasseh was a sinful one, yet through a line of sinners comes the Lord.

Look at verse 21 again: "And she shall bring forth a son, and thou shalt call his name JESUS: for he shall save his people from their sins." He will save, not only His people, but all people when they trust Christ as Saviour.

The King became a poor man; the King aligned Himself with sinful men that He might be the Saviour of sinners.

The Bible says that we have all sinned and come short of the glory of God. The Bible says, "There is none righteous, no, not one."

It says, "All we like sheep have gone astray; we have turned every one to his own way; and the LORD hath laid on him the iniquity of us all."

The Bible says that all men without Christ are lost. The beautiful and wonderful theme that we want you to see is that Christ came to save sinners. Listen to His Word: "For he shall save his people from their sins." We read, "There is one God, and one mediator between God and men, the man Christ Jesus."

He identified Himself with poor, sinful humanity that we might be saved and that we might be made part of the family of God.

Are you saying, "I would like to know how to be saved"? Well, I will be so happy to tell you.

"But as many as received him, to them gave he power to become the sons of God, even to them that believe on his name."—John 1:12.

"For God so loved the world, that he gave his only begotten Son, that whosoever believeth in him should not perish, but have everlasting life."—John 3:16.

"He that believeth on him is not condemned: but he that believeth not is condemned already, because he hath not believed in the name of the only begotten Son of God."—John 3:18.

"He that believeth on the Son hath everlasting life: and he that believeth not the Son shall not see life; but the wrath of God abideth on him."—John 3:36.

"Neither is there salvation in any other: for there is none other name under heaven given among men, whereby we must be saved."—Acts 4:12.

The Bible speaks so plainly upon this great matter of salvation, so no one need be deceived or troubled. Everyone can see that the way is to come to Jesus, that "the wages of sin is death; but the gift of God is eternal life through Jesus Christ our Lord" (Rom. 6:23).

The poor man's King! Isn't that a beautiful picture? Jesus, the Son of God, the King of Kings, the Lord of Lords, came down from Heaven's glory to be born of a virgin. He came into this world to align Himself with the sinful and lowly; with the poor and the despised. The Son of God died upon Calvary's cross that sinners might be saved and the way of salvation made open to the whole world.

Into the city of Chattanooga staggered a man, dressed in the poorest of clothing. He was a despicable sight. He was a slave to strong drink and a dope addict. I had a part in leading him to Christ. This poor man, this despised man, this man with the dirt and filth of the world upon him, the man who called himself a "bum," came to Christ and was wondrously saved. He followed the Lord in baptism in our church.

That man is now the head of a company in another state. Today he is a prosperous businessman. When I was in his city a short time ago, he was a candidate for an office in the government of his state.

He was in church with his family where I was preaching. I told his story to the congregation. He stood to give a testimony to the saving grace of the Lord Jesus Christ. This man, now a dignified and respected citizen, was saved by the power of God, became a member of the church and is living for Christ.

The poor man's King came down from Heaven's glory that sinners might be saved.

Friend, you need Christ. I have tried to preach as plainly as I know how. I have tried to speak just as positively as the Lord would enable me. I pray that you have seen the picture of the poor man's King. Sinner, you are poverty-stricken, without hope, until you let Jesus into your life. Won't you do that today?

HARRY A. IRONSIDE
1876–1951

ABOUT THE MAN:

Few preachers had more varied ministries than this man. He was a captain in the Salvation Army, an itinerant preacher with the Plymouth Brethren, pastor of the renowned Moody Memorial Church in Chicago, and he conducted Bible conferences throughout the world. Sandwiched between those major ministries, Ironside preached the Gospel on street corners, in missions, in taverns, on Indian reservations, and in other places.

Never formally ordained and with no experience whatever as a pastor, Ironside took over the 4,000-seat Moody Memorial Church in Chicago and often filled it to capacity for 18½ years. A seminary president once said of him, "He has the most unique ministry of any man living." Although he had little formal education, his tremendous mental capacity and photographic memory caused him to be called the "Archbishop of Fundamentalism."

Preaching—warm, soul-saving preaching—was his forte. Special speakers in his great church often meant nothing; the crowds came when he was there. He traveled constantly; at his prime, he averaged forty weeks in the year on the road—always returning to Moody Memorial for Sunday services.

His pen moved too; he contributed regularly to various religious periodicals and journals in addition to publishing eighty books and pamphlets. His writings included addresses or commentaries on the entire New Testament, all of the prophetic books of the Old Testament, and a great many volumes on specific Bible themes and subjects.

In 1951 Dr. Ironside died in Cambridge, New Zealand, and was buried there at his own request.

VIII.

The Unchanging Christ

H. A. IRONSIDE

"And when he had spoken these things, while they beheld, he was taken up; and a cloud received him out of their sight.

"And while they looked stedfastly toward heaven as he went up, behold, two men stood by them in white apparel;

"Which also said, Ye men of Galilee, why stand ye gazing up into heaven? this same Jesus, which is taken up from you into heaven, shall so come in like manner as ye have seen him go into heaven."—Acts 1:9–11.

"Jesus Christ the same yesterday, and to day, and for ever."—Heb. 13:8.

Notice especially those precious words, "This same Jesus." Men often talk of needing a new Christ for a new age.

In a recent book, the writer states that a changing order demands a fresh revelation of God, that we cannot think of any past revelation as "the faith which was once delivered unto the saints." He declares that inasmuch as times change, people change, and our viewpoints change, it is not to be supposed that the Christ of nineteen hundred years ago will meet the needs of men today. God reveals Himself in different ways, and He may have another revelation of Himself which will soon break upon us, making all previous ones obsolete!

It is very common to hear people use that kind of language today, but the blessed Book is God's last word to men.

In the first chapter of the Epistle to the Hebrews, we read:

"God, who at sundry times and in divers manners [in many ways] *spake in time past unto the fathers by the prophets,*

"Hath in these last days spoken unto us by his Son, whom he hath appointed heir of all things, by whom also he made the worlds."—Vss. 1, 2.

The word translated "worlds" there is the customary word for "ages." So that verse may be translated, "By whom also he fitted the ages together."

Christ is the beginning, Christ is the end, and Christ is the center of all the ages.

"Who being the brightness of his glory, and the express image of his person, and upholding all things by the word of his power, when he had by himself purged our sins, sat down on the right hand of the Majesty on high."—Heb. 1:3.

And there He sits today, the same blessed Saviour that He was when on earth.

I. CHRIST THE SAME IN THE ETERNAL YESTERDAY

In the last chapter of this epistle are these wonderful words, "Jesus Christ the same yesterday, and to day, and for ever."

"Jesus Christ the same yesterday" carries us back to the long ages before He became incarnate. You and I began to be when we were born into this world. Not so with our Lord. He did not begin to live when He was born of a virgin; He simply changed His clothing, as it were. He who had been in the form of God, who thought it not robbery to be equal with God, divested Himself of the garments of glory that had been His from all eternity, clothed Himself in a body of flesh and blood, stooped in grace to become a servant; as servant, became not an angel, but a Man, and as Man, humbled Himself and became obedient unto death. And such a death—that of the cross! He was the same in the past eternity.

In chapter 16 of John's Gospel, verse 28, He says, "I came forth from the Father, and am come into the world: again, I leave the world, and go to the Father."

There you have Him in the past. He came forth from the Father; He dwelt in the Father's bosom throughout the interminable ages of the past.

"In the beginning was the Word [when everything that ever had beginning began, "the Word *was,*" not, "the Word *began.*" This was

an unbeginning beginning], *and the Word was with God, and the Word was God.*

"The same was in the beginning with God.

"All things were made by him; and without him was not any thing made that was made.

"In him was life; and the life was the light of men."—John 1:1–4.

Notice the seven things that are predicated of Him in regard to the past, that yesterday of Hebrews 13.

First, His eternal existence—"In the beginning was the Word."

Second, His distinct personality—"the Word was *with* God."

Third, His true and perfect Deity—"the Word *was* God."

Fourth, the unchangeableness of His personal relationship to the Father—"The same was in the beginning with God."

Fifth, His full creatorial glory—"All things were made by him; and without him was not any thing made that was made."

Sixth, all life had its source in Him—"In him was life."

Seventh, all light comes from Him—"the life was the light of men."

This is the One who came in grace into this world, assumed a servant's form, passed angels by, and became a Man for our redemption.

Do we need a different Christ? Where will we find Him? God Himself has already come down to us, and there is none higher than He to come.

> **No angel could our place have taken,**
> **Highest of the high though he;**
> **The loved One, on the cross forsaken,**
> **Was one of the Godhead Three!**

We look for no other Christ; there can be none other. God has been fully told out in Him. I believe that is involved in the expression: "In the beginning was the Word"—"the *Logos.*"

I wonder sometimes whether the Spirit of God did not intend this message, given through John, to be the answer to the yearning cry of Plato and his followers throughout the Greek-speaking world. You remember that Plato, dazed and amazed as he thought of the great mysteries of life, death and eternity, said on one occasion to that little group in Athens discussing these questions: "It may be that someday there will come forth from God a Word, a *Logos*, who will reveal all mysteries and make everything plain." And the Spirit of God, through the Apostle John, says:

"And the Word [the Logos] was made flesh, and dwelt among us, (and we beheld his glory, the glory as of the only begotten of the Father,) full of grace and truth."—John 1:14.

II. CHRIST NOW THE SAME ETERNAL GOD, YET THE BLESSED MAN

Jesus Christ the same yesterday, and Jesus Christ the same today; for having by Himself made purification for sins, He has been raised from the dead by the glory of the Father.

Have you ever noticed that the resurrection of our Lord is attributed to every Person of the Holy Trinity? We read in one instance that the Father raised Him from the dead; we read again that He was quickened by the Spirit; then we hear Him saying, "Destroy this temple, and in three days I will raise it up."

The Father raised Him from the dead, the Spirit raised Him from the dead, and the Son raised Himself from the dead. He says, "I have power to lay it [My life] down, and I have power to take it again." So intimate is the relationship subsisting among the three Persons of the adorable Trinity that the one Person does not act apart from the others.

As Christ walked here on earth, the Father walked here also. Now that He has gone back to the Father, He says, 'I will send the Comforter.' But He also says, "If any man hear my voice, and open the door, I will come in to him, and will sup with him." By the reception of the Holy Spirit, we now receive the Father and the Son.

How wonderfully we are blessed! When our Saviour comes again, God is coming to take control of things in this world, and the Holy Spirit will be poured out upon all flesh.

Father, Son and Holy Spirit in council in the past eternity; Father, Son and Holy Spirit working out our salvation here on earth; Father, Son and Holy Spirit bringing in the glory by and by when the long period of man's trial is over, when the kingdom is fully established and the Lord Jesus Christ abides forevermore the One in whom the

Father and Spirit as well as the Son are fully displayed—for He is the image of the invisible God.

In chapter 17 of John, the Lord is addressing the Father in His great high priestly prayer: "And now, O Father, glorify thou me with thine own self with the glory which I had with thee before the world was" (vs. 5).

He came from that glory into the degradation and humiliation of that which resulted in the cross; now He has gone back to that glory but remains a Man in glory still.

Does your soul get hold of that? Some Christians have lost the blessedness of it; they think Christ is no longer the Man Christ Jesus that He was when here on earth, but Scripture says, "There is one God, and one mediator between God and men, the man Christ Jesus" (I Tim. 2:5). And as the Man in glory, He is seated on the Father's throne, waiting until the day of His triumph when His enemies shall be made His footstool.

> **When He comes, our glorious King,**
> **All His ransomed Home to bring,**
> **Then anew this song we'll sing:**
> **"Hallelujah! What a Saviour!"**

The One coming back is Jesus Christ who is "the same yesterday, and to day, and for ever."

III. THE UNCHANGED JESUS WILL RETURN FOR US

"This same Jesus, which is taken up from you into heaven, shall so come in like manner as ye have seen him go into heaven."

Away with the ridiculous errorists who tell us that Christ will never come back again as a Man; that He only exists now as a part of the all-pervading spirit of the universe!

He who walked on earth as the lowly Man of Galilee, knelt in agony in Gethsemane's garden, cried in anguish from the cross, "My God, my God, why hast thou forsaken me?" later surrendered His spirit in peace to the Father as He exclaimed, "It is finished"!

He who was raised from the dead, walked for forty wonderful days among His disciples, then led them out one day to the Mount of Olives, as far as Bethany, was suddenly parted from them and ascended up and up until a cloud, the royal chariot of Heaven, came down and received Him out of their sight and wafted Him away to the Father's house from which He had come—this same Jesus will be unchanged when He comes back.

When I was a boy, we used to sing in the Sunday school:

> **I think when I read that sweet story of old,**
> **When Jesus was here among men,**
> **How He called little children as lambs to His fold,**
> **I should like to have been with them then.**
>
> **I wish that His hands had been placed on my head,**
> **That His arms had been thrown around me,**
> **And that I might have seen His kind look when He said,**
> **"Let the little ones come unto Me."**

I can remember as well as though it were yesterday how I would say to myself, *My! I wish I had been born eighteen hundred or more years sooner. I wish I had lived when Jesus was here. Those boys in Galilee and Judea had something I will never have. He is so changed now, I will never hear His voice as they did; I will never see those kind eyes as they did; I have been born altogether too late.*

But after I was saved and began to understand this blessed Book of God, I learned that the same precious, adorable Saviour, unchanged and unchangeable, is the One I shall see when He returns. The only difference is that He will come in His kingly robes. He was here on earth in lowly garb, but it is just the outward semblance that is changed. He will be in royal apparel when He returns.

How gladly we will greet Him and bow at His feet when we adore Him as King of Kings and Lord of Lords!

IV. IS THIS UNCHANGING SAVIOUR YOURS?

I wonder if you have trusted this wonderful Saviour. He came the first time to put away sin by the sacrifice of Himself, and on yonder cross the Lord of Glory died. There He bore the judgment that your sins and mine deserved; there as our Surety He took our place.

"He was wounded for our transgressions, he was bruised for our iniquities: the chastisement of our peace was upon him; and with his stripes we are healed."—Isa. 53:5.

Today He lives in Glory, the exalted One, mighty to save, for "God hath made that same Jesus, whom ye crucified," Peter says, "both Lord and Christ." He, the risen One, is inviting sinners to come to Him, inviting weary, burdened souls to find rest at His feet.

> **Millions have fled to His spear-pierced side;**
> **Welcomed they all have been; none were denied.**

If I am speaking to one soul who has never trusted in Him, it is not yet too late; you may come now and know Him as your own personal Saviour.

I close by repeating three stanzas of Madge Rae's poem, "This Same Jesus."

> **"This same Jesus," not another,**
>   **Not a stranger never known—**
> **But the One who went to Calvary,**
>   **Died to make me all His own.**
> **Nineteen hundred years in Glory**
>   **Have not changed Him in the least—**
> **He, the same who raised a Lazarus,**
>   **Deigned to sit at Martha's feast!**
>
> **He it is who cleansed the leper,**
>   **Healed the sick and raised the dead—**
> **Stilled the raging storm-tossed billows,**
>   **And the hungry thousands fed.**
> **HE—I met Him first at Calvary,**
>   **Saw Him standing in my place—**
> **Dying there for me the sinner,**
>   **Oh, what matchless, sovereign grace!**
>
> **May I earthly things hold loosely,**
>   **Counting all but dross for Him—**
> **With my eyes beholding Jesus,**
>   **All beside grows faint and dim.**
> **He is coming, "this same Jesus";**
>   **Sweet the thought that soon the day**
> **With its beams of light shall banish**
>   **Earth's dark shadows far away.**

IX.

My Substitute

H. A. IRONSIDE

Although the word *substitution* is not in the Bible, it stands for a great truth that runs through the Scriptures from Genesis to Revelation. That is the fact that the Lord Jesus Christ in infinite grace took the place of poor, lost, guilty sinners and made it possible for a holy God to reach out in mercy and save all who would come to Him in the name of His beloved Son.

I do not have one particular text in mind, but I have been thinking of five different passages in the New Testament where we get the same expression—He "gave himself"; and I want you to think with me of these Scriptures.

The One who gave Himself was our Lord Jesus Christ, and I should like you to notice what it was for which He gave Himself.

In the Epistle to the Galatians, chapter 2 and verse 20, the Apostle Paul writes:

"I am crucified with Christ: nevertheless I live; yet not I, but Christ liveth in me: and the life which I now live in the flesh I live by the faith of the Son of God, who loved me, and gave himself for me."

Note the individuality of it. Paul, who had been a bitter persecutor of the people of God, who had been an enemy of the cross of Christ, one day had his eyes opened. He suddenly realized that the One who died on that cross went there for him, that He had taken his place, that it was love that led Him to go to that shameful death. From that moment the heart of Saul of Tarsus went out in adoring gratitude to our Lord Jesus Christ. And until the very end of his days, he found his greatest joy in trying to give some evidence, by a life of service, of his love for the One who had thus loved him.

Christ "Gave Himself for Me"

Notice how he speaks of Him: "The Son of God, who loved me, and gave himself for me." There you have the very heart of the

Gospel—"himself for me." That is substitution.

Some people tell us, because we do not find the actual word *substitution* in the Bible, that the truth of it is not there. And so they talk of atonement by other means than by substitution—atonement by example or atonement by reconciling love—that leads men to turn to God adoringly, simply because of the goodness that He showed in seeking them out in the Person of His Son.

But no, the Word of God makes it very definite. The work that took place on Calvary was a substitutionary transaction. It was the Lord Jesus Christ, God's own blessed, eternal Son, who became man for our redemption, giving Himself on our behalf.

"The Son of God, who loved me, and gave himself for me" is the language of faith. When a poor, needy sinner looks at the cross and sees, as it were, the blessed Saviour hanging there, he says, "He was there for me; it was my sins that put Him there; it was in order that I might be fitted for the presence of God that He went into the darkness and endured the judgment of God. He is my Substitute. The Son of God loved me and gave Himself for me."

Christ a Substitute for All

But it is not only for *me*; it is also for *us*. In the Epistle to the Ephesians, chapter 5 and verse 2, we read:

"And walk in love, as Christ also hath loved us, and hath given himself for us an offering and a sacrifice to God for a sweet-smelling savour."

I am so thankful that in my thinking I do not have to limit the gift of God's grace in the Person of His Son to just some little group, as though it were just for a small elect company that Jesus died. 'He gave Himself for us.' I can look out over the whole wide world, whether men are saved or unsaved, and say to them on the authority of the Word of God that 'He gave Himself for us'—for every one of us.

Whether you be Jew or Gentile, whether you be very religious or have no time for religion, I would say to you, "The Son of God gave Himself for us." He saw us in our lost condition, and He went to Calvary's cross in order to redeem us. That is how the Prophet Isaiah puts it. He looked on down through the centuries, and by faith he saw the very scene of Calvary and cried out:

"He was wounded for our transgressions, he was bruised for our iniquities: the chastisement of our peace was upon him; and with his stripes we are healed."—Isa. 53:5.

How Jean Saw It Was for Her

I remember a number of years ago I went over to a town in Minnesota to hold some meetings. My wife and our eldest son, just a little child at the time, went with me.

When we got there, a big, burly Highland Scotsman met us. He said, "Now you come along with me; I am going to take you to my house. We are going to sleep you there, and then across the way at the McKenzies they will eat you."

Of course I knew he didn't mean anything cannibalistic, and I was glad to accept the provision made.

We went to his house and settled ourselves and then went over to the McKenzies for our meal.

I remember one Sunday we left to go down to the meeting in the afternoon, and it happened that there was one daughter in the family who had not yet received the Lord Jesus Christ as her Saviour. The mother said, "Will you pray for Jean? She knows the way, but somehow she doesn't seem to want to come. She says she is young yet, and she wants to have her fling before she settles down."

Well, we did pray for her, and someway or other as I preached that afternoon in the big tent, I couldn't help seeing Jean way in the back, eagerly listening to the message. When it was over, I thought she might be one who would move to the front when the invitation was given; but instead of that, I saw her get up and hurry away. I felt a disappointment.

When I finished speaking with those who had come forward, I went on home. There I found, as I opened the front door, my wife sitting with an open Bible and Jean beside her. My wife turned to me and said, "Come and join us. I am trying to show Jean that Christ died in our place, but someway or other she can't seem to grasp it."

I sat down with them and said something like this: "Jean, you know the Gospel, don't you?"

"Yes," she said, "I think I do."

"What is the Gospel?"

"Well, it is that Christ died for our sins according to the Scriptures."

My wife said, "I have been showing her Isaiah 53."

The Bible was open at that chapter so I said, "Look, you have it right here: 'But he was wounded for our transgressions, he was bruised for our iniquities: the chastisement of our peace was upon him; and with his stripes we are healed.' Don't you see, Jean? Christ died for you; He took your place; He bore God's judgment against your sins."

"I see what is written there," she replied, "but somehow I can't get hold of it for myself. It doesn't seem to mean me."

So we got down on our knees and prayed that the Spirit of God Himself might make the great truth of the substitutionary work of the cross real to her. Then I said to her, "Jean, while we are here on our knees, I want you to read the words for yourself, and we will pray that the Holy Spirit will open them up to you."

She read them: "But he was wounded for our transgressions, he was bruised for our iniquities: the chastisement of our peace was upon him; and with his stripes we are healed."

Then she said, "Yes, I see it, but I don't seem to be able to make it my own."

"Perhaps it would be different now if you will just read it again and change the pronoun, putting it into the first person singular. Read it like this: 'He was wounded for *my* transgressions'; because you see, Jean, it really means that. He was wounded for the transgressions of all of us, yours and mine. Read it that way."

She started to read: "He was wounded for *my* transgressions." She stopped as the tears began to flow. She wiped them away and read on: "He was bruised for *my* iniquities," and again she stopped. Then she read, "The chastisement of *my* peace was upon Him," and then she fairly shouted, "Oh, I see it! With His stripes *I am* healed."

In a moment the light had shone into her darkened heart. She saw that the Lord Jesus was *her* substitute; He had taken *her* place.

We gave thanks, and then she said that she must go and tell her "Mither." She didn't know that all the while her mother had been standing outside the window and had heard the whole thing.

Out the front door she went and down the garden path and around to the side, and she ran right into that mother's arms. "O Mither, Mither, I'm saved; by His stripes *I am* healed."

What joy that brought to the mother's heart, and what a happy time of rejoicing we all had then!

You see, that is substitution. That is the very pith and marrow of the Gospel.

A poor old woman was asked once, "Dinah, you are always talking about being saved through the atonement of Christ, but do you know what the word *atonement* means?"

She looked up and said, "Honey, indeed I understand the word *atonement*. It just means He die, or I die. He die, so I not die."

"The Son of God, who loved me, and gave himself for me." He gave Himself for our sins.

In a Special Sense, Christ Gave Himself for the Church, the Saved

Next, we do have a special group mentioned for whom He gave Himself. In the last part of the fifth chapter of Ephesians, in verse 25, we read:

"Husbands, love your wives, even as Christ also loved the church, and gave himself for it."

When we get home to Glory, when we who have been redeemed to God by His precious blood are presented faultless in the presence of our heavenly Bridegroom, we shall look up into His face, and we shall be able to say, "The Son of God loved the church and gave Himself for it."

You remember the story that is told of one of the generals of Cyrus the Great, king of Persia, the one who overthrew, in God's providence, the mighty Babylonian Empire. One of his generals came home from a campaign and was shocked to find that in his absence his own wife had been arrested and was languishing in prison, charged with treachery against her country.

The trial was to be held that very day. The general hastened to the court of Cyrus, and the guards brought in his own beloved wife. She, poor woman, pale and anxious, tried to answer the charges brought against her, but all to no avail.

Her husband, standing near, heard the stern voice of the Persian ruler pronounce the death sentence. In a moment, as they were about to drag her away to behead her, he ran forward and threw himself down at the feet of the emperor. "O sire," he cried, "not she but me. Let me give my life for hers. Put me to death but spare my wife."

As Cyrus looked down upon him, he was so touched by his deep devotion and his love for his wife that his heart was softened. He remembered too how faithful this servant had been, and he gave command that the wife should go free. She was fully pardoned.

As her husband led her out of the room he said to her, "Did you notice the kind look in the eyes of the emperor as he pronounced the word of pardon?"

She said, "I did not see the face of the emperor. The only face I could see was that of the man who was willing to die for me."

Oh, when we get Home, when we see the face of the Man who did die for us, how our hearts will praise Him! How we will rejoice in His presence as we say, "The Son of God, who loved me, and gave himself for me."

Our Substitute Can Deliver Us From the Power of Sin

We need to realize that He died not only to deliver us from the judgment due to our sins, but He died for us in order that we might be delivered from the power and pollution of sins right here and now in this life.

In Galatians 1:3,4, we have these words:

"...our Lord Jesus Christ,

"Who gave himself for our sins, that he might deliver us from this present evil world, according to the will of God and our Father."

He gave Himself for our sins, not simply that we might have our past sins forgiven, nor that we might stand justified before Him as to the future, but in order that the power of sin might be broken in our lives, that we might no longer be subject to Satan's authority, that we might be free men and women, living here to the glory of the Lord Jesus.

This is one of those truths that I do want to press upon you who have but recently been brought to a saving knowledge of Christ. Dear young Christian, do not be satisfied to know that you are saved from Hell, blessed as that is; but oh, go on day by day to a fuller walk with God, that you may be saved from sin and that your whole life may be lived to His praise and to His glory.

After all, somebody might raise the question: "Well, it is perfectly true that it says He gave Himself for us, and He gave Himself for the church, and He gave Himself for our sins; but are you really sure that it applies to everybody? May He not, after all, have had just some particular elect company in view when He thus gave Himself? And if we do not belong to that company, what right have we to come to Him at all and to expect Him to do anything for us?"

For answer, will you look at the First Epistle to Timothy, chapter 2, verses 5 and 6:

"For there is one God, and one mediator between God and men, the man Christ Jesus;
"Who gave himself a ransom for all, to be testified in due time."

O dear friends, do not allow anything to narrow down your conception of the inclusiveness of the work of our Lord Jesus Christ. He "gave himself a ransom for *all.*" Do not try to read into that what it does not say.

Some people say, "Well, of course, you know we must understand the words *the elect* to come in there. He gave Himself a ransom for all *the elect.*"

Oh no. God does not need you and me to help Him out. He knows what to say, and He means what He says. When He writes, He "gave himself a ransom for all," He means us to understand the words exactly as they are written.

You May Take Christ as Your Substitute

They used to tell a story about a certain professor of theology at Princeton Seminary in the days when Princeton was pretty rigid as to what they called "a limited atonement." One day one of the students asked, "Professor, just what is our stand in this seminary on the atonement?"

The teacher replied, "Well, we stand with Dr. _____; we preach the theology of Dr. _____, and he taught a limited atonement—that Christ died only for the elect."

Then the student said, "And over at New Haven, Connecticut [at that time New Haven was a very sound seminary], what do they teach there? What is Dr. Taylor's theology?"

The professor said, "Over there they teach that 'God so loved the world, that he gave his only begotten Son, that whosoever believeth in him should not perish, but have everlasting life.'"

"Oh," said the student, "well, I'll accept that, because that is what the Bible says. That is not just Dr. Taylor's theology or New Haven doctrine; that is the Word of God."

And so we say to you, whoever you may be, the Lord Jesus gave Himself a ransom for all. On Calvary's cross He put away sin by the sacrifice of Himself. In other words, when He presented Himself there as a substitute for guilty humanity, He finished the work that satisfied every righteous demand of the throne of God and met all the claims of His holy nature; so that on the basis of the substitutionary work of our Lord Jesus Christ, any poor sinner in all the world who comes to Christ and puts in his claim will be saved. That is the doctrine of the atonement as we have it in the Bible. There is no other in this blessed Book.

And so we put the question to you: Have you put in your claim? There are a lot of people who know all about it, but they have never believed and acted upon it.

You remember the incident of the veteran of the Civil War who was found living in wretched poverty. The city authorities found him in such a deplorable state that they thought all they could do was to take him to the county poor farm.

One of them happened to notice something on the wall. It wasn't exactly a picture; it looked more like a document of some kind. He took it down, looked at it, then asked, "What is this, my friend?"

The poor old man replied, "That was sent to me by Abraham Lincoln himself, and I kept it because it has his signature on it."

It turned out to be a check. I forget the amount, but it was really a pension check signed by the president and sent to this man years before. Instead of cashing it, the poor man had kept it all the time and had framed it and hung it there on the wall. In the meantime, he got poorer and poorer, until he was a candidate for the county farm.

They found that the government at Washington would still honor the check, although it was years old, and they had enough to take care of the man comfortably until he died.

Oh, do not be content just to have the statement of the substitutionary work of the Lord Jesus, but come to Him for yourself. Trust Him as your own Saviour. Cash in on it. He "gave himself a ransom for *all*."

(From the book, *Great Words of the Gospel*, of the Moody Press Colportage Library, Chicago)

DWIGHT LYMAN MOODY
1837–1899

ABOUT THE MAN:

D. L. Moody may well have been the greatest evangelist of all time.

In a forty-year period, he won a million souls, founded three Christian schools, launched a great Christian publishing business, established a world-renowned Christian conference center, and inspired literally thousands of preachers to win souls and conduct revivals.

A shoe clerk at seventeen, his ambition was to make a hundred thousand dollars. Converted at eighteen, he uncovered hidden gospel gold in the hearts of millions for the next half century. He preached to twenty thousand a day in Brooklyn and admitted only nonchurch members by ticket!

He met a young song leader in Indianapolis and said bluntly, "You're the man I've been looking for for eight years. Throw up your job and come with me." Ira D. Sankey did just that; thereafter it was "Moody will preach; Sankey will sing."

He traveled across the American continent and through Great Britain in some of the greatest and most successful evangelistic meetings communities have ever known. His tour of the world with Sankey was considered the greatest evangelistic enterprise of the century.

It was Henry Varley who said, "It remains to be seen what God will do with a man who gives up wholly to Him." And Moody endeavored to be, under God, that man; and the world did marvel to see how wonderfully God used him.

Two great monuments stand to the indefatigable work and ministry of this gospel warrior—Moody Bible Institute and the famous Moody Church in Chicago.

Moody went to be with the Lord in 1899.

X.

"What Think Ye of Christ?"

D. L. MOODY

"What think ye of Christ? whose son is he? They say unto him, The son of David."—Matt. 22:42.

I suppose there is no one here who has not thought, more or less, about Christ. You have heard about Him, read about Him and heard men preach about Him. For eighteen hundred years men have been talking and thinking about Him. Some have their minds made up about who He is, and doubtless some do not. And although all these years have rolled away, this question comes up, addressed to each of us today, "What think ye of Christ?"

I do not know why it should not be thought a proper question for one man to put to another. If I were to ask you what you think of any of your prominent men, you would already have your mind made up about him. If I were to ask you what you think of your noble queen, you would speak right out and tell me your opinion. If I were to ask about your prime minister, you would tell me freely what you had for or against him.

Then why should not people make up their minds about the Lord Jesus Christ and take their stand for or against Him? If you think well of Him, why not speak well of Him and range yourselves on His side? And if you think ill of Him and believe Him to be an impostor and that He did not die to save the world, why not lift up your voice and say you are against Him?

It would be a happy day for Christianity if men would just take sides—if we could know positively who are really for and who against Him.

It is of very little importance what the world thinks of anyone else. The queen and the statesmen, the peers and the princes must soon be gone. Yes, it matters little, comparatively, what we think of them. Their lives can only interest a few, but every living soul on the face of the earth is concerned with this Man.

The question for the world is, "What think ye of Christ?" I do not ask you what you think of the Episcopal church, or of the Presbyterians, or the Baptists, or the Roman Catholics. I do not ask you what you think of this minister or that, of this doctrine or that. But what do you think of the living Person of Christ?

I would like to ask, Was He really the Son of God—the great God-Man? Did He leave Heaven and come down to this world for a purpose? Was it really to seek and to save?

I should like to begin with the manger and follow Him up through the thirty-three years He was here upon earth. I should ask you what you think of His coming into this world and being born in a manger when it might have been a palace; why He left the grandeur and glory of Heaven, the royal retinue of angels; why He passed by palaces, crowns and dominions, and came down here alone.

I should like to ask what you think of Him as a *Teacher*. He spake as never man spake.

I should like to take Him up as a *Preacher*. I should like to bring you to that mountainside, that we might listen to the words as they fall from His gentle lips. Talk about the preachers of the present day! I would rather a thousand times be five minutes at the feet of Christ than listen a lifetime to all the wise men in the world.

He used just to hang truth upon anything.

Yonder is a sower, a fox, a bird, and He just gathers the truth 'round them, so that you cannot see a fox, a sower or a bird without thinking what Jesus said.

Yonder is a lily of the valley; you cannot see it without thinking of His words, "They toil not, neither do they spin."

He makes the little sparrow chirping in the air preach to us.

How fresh those wonderful sermons are! How they live today! How we love to tell them to our children, and how the children love to hear! "Tell me a story about Jesus"—how often we hear it; how the little ones love His sermons! No storybook in the world will ever interest them like the stories that He told. And yet how profound He was. He puzzled the wise men. The scribes and the Pharisees could never fathom Him! Oh, do you not think He was a wonderful Preacher?

I should like to ask you what you think of Him as a *Physician*. A man would soon have a reputation as a doctor if he could cure as Christ did. No case was ever brought to Him but what He was a match for. He had but to speak the word, and disease fled before Him.

Here comes a man covered with leprosy. "Lord, if thou wilt, thou canst make me clean," he cries. "I will," says the Great Physician, and in an instant the leprosy is gone. The world has hospitals for incurable diseases, but there were no incurable diseases with Him.

Now we see Him in the little home at Bethany binding up the wounded hearts of Martha and Mary; tell me what you think of Him as a *Comforter*. He is a husband to the widow and a father to the fatherless. The weary may find a resting-place upon that breast, and the friendless may reckon Him their friend.

He never varies; He never fails; He never dies. His sympathy is ever fresh; His love is ever free. O widows and orphans, O sorrowing and mourning, will you not thank God for Christ the Comforter?

But these are not the points I wish to take up. Let us go to those who knew Christ and ask what they thought of Him. If you want to find out what a man is nowadays, you inquire about him from those who know him best. I do not wish to be partial; we will go to His enemies and to His friends. We will ask them, "What think ye of Christ?"

If we only went to those who liked Him, you would say, "Oh, he is so blind; he thinks so much of the Man that he can't see His faults. You can't get anything out of him, unless it be in His favor; it is a one-sided affair altogether."

So we shall go in the first place to His enemies, to those who hated Him, persecuted Him, cursed and slew Him. I shall put you in the jury box, and call upon them to tell us what they think of Him.

WITNESSES

1. Pharisees: First among the witnesses, let us call upon the Pharisees. We know how they hated Him. Let us put a few questions to them: "Come, Pharisees, tell us what you have against the Son of God. What do *you* think of Christ?"

Hear what they say: *"This man receiveth sinners."*

What an argument to bring against Him! Why, it is the very thing that makes us love Him. It is the glory of the Gospel. He receives sinners. If He had not, what would have become of us? Have you nothing more to bring against Him than *this*? Why, it is one of the greatest compliments that was ever paid Him.

Once more, when He was hanging on the tree, you had this to say of Him: *"He saved others; himself he cannot save."* And so He did save others, but He could not save Himself and save us too. So He laid down His own life for yours and mine. Yes, Pharisees, you have told the truth for once in your lives! He saved others. He died for others. He was a ransom for many; so it is quite true what you think of Him—*"He saved others; himself he cannot save."*

2. Caiaphas: Now, let us call upon Caiaphas. Let him stand up here in his flowing robes; let us ask him for his evidence. "Caiaphas, you were chief priest when Christ was tried; you were president of the Sanhedrin; you were in the council chamber when they found Him guilty; you yourself condemned Him. Tell us: What did the witnesses say? On what grounds did you judge Him? What testimony was brought against Him?"

"He hath spoken blasphemy," says Caiaphas. "He said, 'Hereafter shall ye see the Son of Man sitting on the right hand of power, and coming in the clouds of heaven.' When I heard that, I found Him guilty of blasphemy, so I rent my mantle and condemned Him to death."

Yes, all they had against Him was that He was the Son of God; and they slew Him for the promise of His coming for His bride.

3. Pilate: Now, let us summon Pilate. Let him enter the witness box. "Pilate, this Man was brought before you; you examined Him, talked with Him face-to-face: What think ye of Christ?"

"I find no fault in Him," says Pilate. "He said He was the King of the Jews [just as he wrote it over the cross]; but I find no fault in Him." Such is the testimony of the man who examined Him!

And as He stands there, the center of a Jewish mob, there comes along a man elbowing his way in haste. He rushes up to Pilate and, thrusting out his hand, gives him a message. He tears it open; his face turns pale as he reads, "Have thou nothing to do with that just man: for I have suffered many things this day in a dream because of him." It is from Pilate's wife—her testimony to Christ.

You want to know what His enemies thought of Him? You want

to know what the heathen thought? Well, here it is: "no fault in him"; and the wife of a heathen, "that just man"!

4. Judas: And now, look—in comes Judas. He ought to make a good witness. Let us address him. "Come, tell us, Judas, What think ye of Christ? You knew the Master well; you sold Him for thirty pieces of silver; you betrayed Him with a kiss; you saw Him perform those miracles; you were with Him in Jerusalem. In Bethany, when He summoned up Lazarus, you were there. What think ye of Him?"

I can see him as he comes into the presence of the chief priests; I can hear the money ring as he dashes it on the table—*"I have betrayed the innocent blood"!* The man who betrayed Him—this is what he thinks of Him!

Yes, my friends, God has made every man who had anything to do with the death of His Son put his testimony on record that He was an innocent Man.

5. The Centurion: Let us take the centurion who was present at the execution. He had charge of the Roman soldiers. He had told them to make Him carry His cross; he had given orders for the nails to be driven into His feet and hands, for the spear to be thrust in His side. Let the centurion come forward.

"Centurion, you had the charge of the executioners; you saw that the order for His death was carried out; you saw Him die; you heard Him speak upon the cross. Tell us, What think you of Christ?"

Hark! Look at him. He is smiting his breast as he cries, *"Truly, this was the Son of God"!*

6. The Thief: I might go to the thief upon the cross and ask what he thought of Him. At first he railed upon Him and reviled Him. But then he thought better of it. *"This man hath done nothing amiss,"* he says.

7. The Devils: I might go further. I might summon the very devils themselves and ask them for their testimony. Have they anything to say of Him?

Why, the very devils called Him the Son of God! In Mark we have the unclean spirit crying, *"Jesus, thou Son of the most high God."*

Men say, "Oh, I believe Christ to be the Son of God, and because I believe it intellectually, I shall be saved." I tell you, the devils did that. And they did more than that—they trembled.

8. His Friends: Let us bring in His friends. We want you to hear their evidence. Let us call that prince of preachers. Let us hear the forerunner, the wilderness preacher, John. Save the Master Himself, none ever preached like this man—this man who drew all Jerusalem and all Judaea into the wilderness to hear him; this man who burst upon the nations like the flash of a meteor. Let John the Baptist come with his leathern girdle and his hairy coat, and let him tell us what he thinks of Christ.

His words, though they were echoed in the wilderness of Palestine, are written in the Book forever: *"Behold the Lamb of God, which taketh away the sin of the world."* This is what John the Baptist thought of Him. "I...bare record that this is the Son of God."

No wonder he drew all Jerusalem and Judaea to him, because he preached Christ. And whenever men preach Christ, they are sure to have plenty of followers.

Let us bring in Peter, who was with Him on the Mount of Transfiguration, who was with Him the night He was betrayed. "Come, Peter, tell us what you think of Christ. Stand in the witness box and testify of Him. You denied Him once. You said with a curse you did not know Him. Was it true, Peter? Don't you know Him?"

"Know Him!" I can imagine Peter saying, "It was a lie I told them. I *did* know Him." Afterwards I can hear his charging home their guilt upon these Jerusalem sinners. He calls Him *"both Lord and Christ."* Such was the testimony on the day of Pentecost. "God hath made that same Jesus,...both Lord and Christ."

And tradition tells us that when they came to execute Peter, feeling he was not worthy to die in the way his Master died, he requested to be crucified with his head downwards. So much did Peter think of Him!

Now let us hear from the beloved disciple John. He knew more about Christ than any other man. He had laid his head on his Saviour's bosom. He had heard the throbbing of that loving heart. Look into his Gospel if you wish to know what he thought of Him.

Matthew writes of Him as the Royal King come from His throne. Mark writes of Him as the Servant; and Luke, as the Son of Man.

John takes up his pen and with one stroke forever settles the question of Unitarianism. He goes right back before the time of Adam. "In the beginning was the Word, and the Word was with God, and the Word was God." Look into Revelation. He calls Him "the bright and morning star." So John thought well of Him—because he knew Him well.

We might bring in the doubting disciple. "You doubted Him, Thomas? You would not believe He had risen, and you put your fingers into the wound in His side. What do you think of Him?"

"My Lord and my God!" he answers.

9. Decapolis: Then go over to Decapolis, and you will find Christ has been there casting out devils. Let us call the men of that country and ask what they think of Him. *"He hath done all things well,"* they say.

10. Persecuting Saul: But we have other witnesses to bring in. Take the persecuting Saul, once one of the worst of His *enemies*. Breathing out threatenings, he meets Him. "Saul, Saul, why persecutest thou me?" says Christ; and He might have added, "What have I done to you? Why do you treat Me thus, Saul?"

And then Saul asks, "Who art thou, Lord?"

"I am Jesus of Nazareth, whom thou persecutest." You see, He was not ashamed of His name, although He had been in Heaven: "I am *Jesus of Nazareth."*

What a change did that one interview make to Paul! A few years after we hear him say, *"I have suffered the loss of all things, and do count them but dung, that I may win Christ."* Such a testimony to the Saviour!

11. The Angels: But I shall go still further. I shall go away from earth into the other world. I shall summon the *angels* and ask what they think of Christ. They saw Him in the bosom of the Father before the world was. Before the dawn of creation, before the morning stars sang together, He was there. They saw Him leave the throne and come down to the manger. What a scene for them to witness! Ask these heavenly beings what they thought of Him then.

For once they are permitted to speak; for once the silence of Heaven is broken. Listen to their song on the plains of Bethlehem: "Behold, I bring you good tidings of great joy, which shall be to all people. For unto you is born this day in the city of David *a Saviour, which is Christ the Lord."*

He leaves the throne to save the world. Is it any wonder the angels thought well of Him?

12. The Redeemed Saints: Then there are *the redeemed saints*—those who see Him face-to-face. Here on earth He was never known, no one seemed really to be acquainted with Him; but He was known in that world where He had been from the foundation. What do they think of Him there?

If we could hear from Heaven, we should hear a shout which would glorify and magnify His name. We are told that when John was in the Spirit on the Lord's Day, and being caught up, he heard a shout around him, ten thousand times ten thousand, and thousands and thousands of voices: *"Worthy is the Lamb that was slain to receive power, and riches, and wisdom, and strength, and honour, and glory, and blessing"!*

Yes, He is worthy of all this. Heaven cannot speak too well of Him. Oh, that earth would take up and join with Heaven in singing, "WORTHY...to receive power, and riches, and wisdom, and strength, and honour, and glory, and blessing"!

13. God the Father: But there is yet another witness, a higher still. Some think that the God of the Old Testament is the Christ of the New. But when Jesus came out of Jordan, baptized by John, there came a voice from Heaven. *God the Father spoke.* It was His testimony to Christ: *"This is my beloved Son, in whom I am well pleased."*

Ah, yes! God the Father thinks well of the Son. And if God is well pleased with Him, so ought we to be. If the sinner and God are well pleased with Christ, then the sinner and God can meet. The moment you say as the Father said, 'I am well pleased with Him' and accept Him, you are wedded to God.

Will you not believe the testimony? Will you not believe this witness, this last of all, the Lord of hosts, *the King of Kings Himself?* Once more He repeats it so that all may know it. With Peter and James and John on the Mount of Transfiguration He cries again: "This is my beloved Son,...hear ye him." And that voice went echoing and reechoing through Palestine, through all the earth from sea to sea; yes, that voice is echoing still, *"Hear ye Him. Hear ye Him"!*

WHAT THINK *YOU* OF CHRIST?

My friend, will you hear Him today? Hark! What is He saying to you?

"Come unto me, all ye that labour and are heavy laden, and I will give you rest.

"Take my yoke upon you, and learn of me; for I am meek and lowly in heart: and ye shall find rest unto your souls.

"For my yoke is easy, and my burden is light."—Matt. 11:28–30.

Will you not think well of such a Saviour? Will you not believe in Him? Will you not trust in Him with all your heart and mind? Will you not live for Him? If He laid down His life for us, is it not the least we can do to lay down ours for Him? If He bore the cross and died on it for me, ought I not to be willing to take it up for Him?

Oh, have we not reason to think well of Him? Do you think it is right and noble to lift up your voice against such a Saviour? Do you think it is just to cry, "Crucify Him! Crucify Him"?

Oh, may God help all of us to glorify the Father by thinking well of His only begotten Son.

WILLIAM EDWARD BIEDERWOLF
1867–1939

ABOUT THE MAN:

Presbyterians produced some of the most noteworthy evangelists of the late 1800s and early 1900s—and a notable among them was William E. Biederwolf.

After his conversion, he continued his education at Princeton, Erlangen and Berlin universities, and at the Sorbonne in Paris.

Biederwolf's first church was the Broadway Presbyterian Church of Logansport, Indiana, the state where he was born. Then he became a chaplain in the Spanish-American War and then entered evangelism—a ministry he was to serve for thirty-five years.

In conjunction with his evangelism, Dr. Biederwolf was associated with the world-renowned Winona Lake Bible Conference for forty years.

In 1929, he became pastor at the storied Royal Poinciana Chapel in Palm Beach, Florida, a position he held until his death.

Biederwolf's ministry was mighty. Perhaps his greatest campaign was in Oil City, Pennsylvania in the bitter winter of 1914. Thousands thronged the tabernacle. Twice it was enlarged. His messages were pungent and powerful.

His kind of preaching caused men and women from every walk of life to come in deep contrition for their sins—the mayor of the city, physicians, lawyers and men from the factories, young people from the schools; and the whole city and county were mightily stirred in deep concern about the things of God.

He was the author of several books.

XI.

Why Christ Came

W. E. BIEDERWOLF

"What think ye of Christ? whose son is he?"—Matt. 22:42.

Many want us to believe that it makes no difference about the parentage of Christ—no difference whose Son He is. But it does make a difference. They say it is not important. But it is important. They tell us, "The virgin birth is not to be accepted as an historic fact," and want us to "spend our energy on something that really matters." But it does matter.

If the attack upon the miracle of His birth goes unchallenged, they will next attack the miracle of His resurrection and everything else supernatural about Him; then they will end their attack upon His cross, and we shall be without a Christ altogether.

I. SON OF JOSEPH, OR SON OF GOD?

If Jesus was not conceived by the Holy Ghost, as the Bible says He was, then Mary was not a good woman; for the Bible says in just so many words that Joseph found Mary great with child "before they came together" (Matt. 1:18).

If Mary was great with child through Joseph, why did she say to the angel, "How shall this be, seeing I know not a man?" (Luke 1:34).

If Mary was great with child through Joseph, then why did Joseph want to put her away, for he was a just man? (Matt. 1:19).

If Mary was great with child through Joseph, why did God have to explain to him through an angel how it had all come about before he would take her back? (Matt. 1:20–25).

Back in Christ's own day His enemies said He was the son of Joseph; but they at least had sense enough or were honest enough to admit the awful charge their insinuation carried with it.

Driven at last into a corner in controversy, they turned on Him and spit out their vile insinuation—this unholy charge and sacrilegious slander that has found an echo in the heart of the so-called modernist or self-styled "intellectual ecclesiastic." They said to Him with a sneer,

"We be not born of fornication." But Jesus, with holy indignation, resented their infamous imputation and said, "Ye are of your father the devil" (John 8:44); "I proceeded forth and came from God" (vs. 42).

"What think ye of Christ? whose son is he?" The hardest proposition the infidel crowd has ever been up against is to answer that question. Isaiah said, "His name shall be called Wonderful" (Isa. 9:6). And there is no better name to describe Him. He is the world's one great wonder. No one else ever approached Him. He is in a class by Himself.

If He were only a man, then by every law of evolution and by every code of common sense, this twentieth century ought to produce a better one. It is one thing to proclaim His natural birth; it is quite another thing to explain on the same ground the mystery of His personality and life.

Let the evolutionist, the psychologist, the agnostic account for this! Apart from His supernatural birth, He is the world's one great mystery; and the only clue you will ever find to that mystery is to be found in the first chapter of Luke's Gospel, where when Mary asked, "How shall this be, seeing I know not a man?" the angel replied:

"The Holy Ghost shall come upon thee, and the power of the Highest shall overshadow thee: therefore also that holy thing which shall be born of thee shall be called the Son of God."—Vs. 35.

Now this is what we mean when we talk about the incarnation. When Jesus Christ came into this world He came with two natures—a human nature and a divine one—and this was brought about by the miraculous manner of His birth.

"But," you say, "the thing seems so utterly impossible."

Nothing is impossible with God! If God could perform one miracle, He could perform a hundred miracles just as hard or harder—if anything could be hard with God.

What kind of God does the modernist want us to worship anyhow? a God who can't do this and can't do that and can't do the other thing, or who, if He can do it, must not do it because it seems so much more rational to do it some other way?

I believe in a God who can do anything, and I am ready to believe anything and everything the Word of God says He did do. Why not?

"But," you say, "the whole thing seems so unnecessary."

It takes an infinite amount of conceit for little, finite, erring individuals like you and me to say what was necessary and what was not necessary in so stupendous an event as bringing into the world the only begotten Son of God. If Christ was to offer Himself a sacrifice for your sins and mine, He had to be sinless Himself; and it was the miracle of His birth that precluded the possibility of moral taint from the earliest moment of conception.

"But," you say, "why are there not more witnesses to it in the Bible?"

Well, how many witnesses does God require to establish His Word as true? It is recorded by the prophets before His birth and by two of the evangelists after His birth and is supported by the question of Mary to the angel and by the conduct of Joseph, as we have already seen, and all of this in language too clear to be denied.

"But," you say, "if it were true, the other writers would have known about it, and their silence therefore implies their denial of it."

But you are far from the truth here. Their silence implies their acceptance of it, or they would have made correction where the others had gone into error.

If, however, silence on the part of one or more means denial, then there is altogether little indeed in the whole New Testament that can be relied upon; e.g., the first three Gospel writers are silent about the resurrection of Lazarus; therefore, it never took place.

John makes no reference to the Transfiguration; therefore, there was none, although Matthew, Mark and Luke say John was one of the three who saw it.

Matthew and John say nothing about His ascension; therefore, it never occurred.

Mark and John say nothing at all about His birth; therefore, He was never born. These two evangelists begin with His public ministry, and so there was no occasion to say anything about His birth, virgin or otherwise. But they both specifically called Him the Son of God, and John repeatedly spoke of Him as the "only begotten Son of God."

What does *beget* mean? It means "to generate." It means "to bring into existence." Did John mean "begotten of Joseph," or did he mean "begotten of God"?

"What think ye of Christ? whose son is he?" Is He the son of Joseph?

The prophets say, "No!"
Matthew says, "No!"
Mark says, "No!"
Luke says, "No!"
John says, "No!"
Mary says, "No!"
Joseph says, "No!"
Jesus says, "No!"
God says, "No!"
The modernist says, "Yes!"

And all I can say is, God pity the man who, with the Word of God open before him, lends himself to this sacrilegious but futile attempt to snatch from the blessed brow of Jesus this masterpiece of the incontrovertible evidence of His glorious Godhood.

"The Word was made flesh, and dwelt among us" (John 1:14). I thank God that Jesus came. He might have come some other way, but I can think of no more beautiful way or more sensible way He could have come than by the way the Bible says He did come—through His supernatural virgin birth.

II. CHRIST CAME TO DESTROY THE WORKS OF SATAN

But here is another question just as important and, from a certain standpoint, even more so. Why did He ever come at all? What was the real meaning of the incarnation? What was its purpose?

Well, there was more than one purpose. Let us see what the Word of God says.

In I John 3:8 we are told, "For this purpose the Son of God was manifested, that he might destroy the works of the devil." Is it not a bit of the most glorious news you ever heard? You know what the works of the Devil are: murder, lying, lust and everything else born in Hell.

There is only one thing in God's world that I am afraid of, and that is sin. No man ever played with sin that sin didn't get the better of him.

Don't try to play with sin. If you must play with something dangerous, then go out into the field and pick up a rattlesnake and let it play in your bosom. Go down to the electric road and play with the third rail. Reach up into the skies and play with God's forked lightning; but for God's sake and your soul's sake, don't play with sin.

Two little Italian lads of New York City were returning from a swim. Pietro had picked up a piece of copper wire and thought he would have a little fun with the third rail of the New York Central track along which they were walking.

He poked away around the wooden covering of the rail, but nothing happened. "That's funny," he said. "I guess I didn't touch the right spot." Then he pushed the point of his wire down underneath the covering. There were a flash of blue flame and a shriek of pain as 11,000 volts of electricity shot through the wire. In a moment or less, his clothing was on fire, and his hair and eyebrows were burned off. He tried to drop the wire as it hissed and sputtered at white heat, but it wouldn't let go. He tried to pull it away, but it stuck to the rail as if it were soldered there.

When his little friend tried to pull him away, he was hurled to the ground with a terrific shock. The brave little fellow then threw his rubber coat around Pietro and pulled him loose. Pietro started to run but fainted and fell. They took him to the hospital. The doctor said, "One chance in a thousand to recover."

The two boys said they knew there was something dangerous about that rail—they had heard older people say so—but they thought it wouldn't hurt any to play with it a little.

And so sin scorches and burns and kills like a live third rail. People know it, yet they will trifle with sin.

Maybe you, my friend, have played with your sin so long that to you your case seems hopeless; but thanks be to God, sin never took anyone so low, it never bound anyone so tightly that Christ Jesus, the God-Man, couldn't reach down as low, snap the fetters, and set him free. That is why He was manifested; that is why He came—to destroy the works of the Devil.

And so I come to you with this message: No matter what your past has been nor what you have done nor where you have gone, Jesus works just as powerfully today as He did in the days of old; and if you will turn to Him, He will set you free, destroy the works of the Devil in you and give you victory.

"Well," you say, "that is very fine, and I need that kind of power in my life; but hold on. Oh, I'm already burdened with a sense of guilt; I've sinned enough already to lose my soul a thousand times over; the burden of guilt is like a thousand millstones, and it seems to press my soul downward toward Hell."

Yes, that is so; but I have another piece of good news for you.

III. CHRIST CAME TO TAKE AWAY OUR SINS

In I John 3:5 God's Word says, "Ye know that he was manifested to take away our sins."

The man who knows his sin and loathes it; the man who hates the memory of his sin; the man whose soul is lashed with the whips of a guilty conscience—to this man the sweetest story ever told, the sweetest song ever sung, the sweetest message ever delivered is the glad news that in some mysterious way which he can never quite fully comprehend, Jesus Christ puts Himself underneath his sin, underneath all that is foul and vile in the experience of the past, lifts it up and off from his soul and takes it away. That is what He came to do.

You may say, "My thoughts have been dirty and impure." But the message rings out, "It's all taken away." 'I will remove thine iniquities from thee as far as the east is from the west' (Ps. 103:12).

You say, "I've cursed and blasphemed and profaned." But the word rings back, "It's all taken away." "For thou hast cast all my sins behind thy back" (Isa. 38:17).

You say, "I've led a double life. I have a virtuous wife, but I've not been true to her." The glad news leaps out from the pages of God's Word, "It's all taken away." "Thou wilt cast all their sins into the depths of the sea" (Mic. 7:19).

You say, "I've been a crook and a liar and a thief." God's answer is, "It's all taken away." "I have blotted out, as a thick cloud, thy transgressions, and, as a cloud, thy sins" (Isa. 44:22).

But you say, "I took a man's life in cold blood." Yes, and you've done something worse than that. You have crucified the Son of God. Your sin wove the crown of thorns and pressed it down on His brow. Your sin fastened Him to the cross. Your sin drove the spear into His side. And it was your sin that broke His heart.

But I can hear the angels shouting down from Heaven, "It's all taken away." "I will forgive their iniquity, and I will remember their sin no more" (Jer. 31:34).

He was manifested to take away sins. Oh, I wish I could paint a picture of Jesus on the cross that would break your heart and bring you to Him. The wonder to me is that the whole mob around the cross, instead of one poor penitent thief, didn't become a band of penitents and sob out their sorrow for the sins they had committed.

IV. CHRIST CAME TO REVEAL THE FATHER

"Oh," I hear you say, "all this is too good to be true."

Well, that is because you don't know God. And here comes the other purpose of the incarnation—He was manifested to reveal the Father. In John 14:9 Jesus says, "He that hath seen me hath seen the Father."

You have had an idea that God is a vindictive God and that He delights in blood and likes to punish and takes pleasure in letting a man go to Hell. But you do not know God, if that is your idea of Him.

The only perfect revelation God ever made of Himself, He made in Jesus Christ; and if you will look at Him through Jesus Christ, you will know what kind of God He is. "He that hath seen me hath seen the Father."

The old hymn runs, "God is reconciled." But I don't like it. When I took my concordance the other day and looked up the word *reconciled*, I found many places where it talked about our being reconciled to God; but I could not find any place where it said God was reconciled to us.

Jesus revealed God as a Father, and as a Father He does not need to be reconciled. He is waiting for you to come and be reconciled to Him. The only place in the Bible where God is represented as running is in the story of the Prodigal Son, where the father runs out to meet his penitent, returning child.

The story is told by a man whose name is Brown, an honored evangelist now in Glory. He had conducted a meeting in one of the towns of Wisconsin. He went away, and a little later he got a letter from an old man by the name of Stewart, telling him that his boy had left home saying he would come back, but he did not know when. The letter stated: "Mr. Brown, you travel a good deal; if you ever see my boy, tell him his father loves him and that his mother is dying to have him come home."

Two years later Mr. Brown went back to that town. The first

man he saw when he stepped off the train was old Mr. Stewart. On this cold, raw day, Mr. Brown asked, "Mr. Stewart, what are you doing here?"

The old man replied, "My son."

Said Mr. Brown, "Hasn't he come yet?"

"No," answered the father, "but I'm sure he will. I've met every train since he went away."

After eleven years, Mr. Brown again went to the same town. As he stepped from the platform, the first person he saw was old Mr. Stewart. His hair was white as snow, his brow was wrinkled, and his form was bent. Mr. Brown said, "Good morning, Mr. Stewart."

The old man had forgotten him, and he asked, "Who are you?"

Mr. Brown made himself known and asked him why he was there.

The old man said, "I'm waiting for my boy."

"Why, hasn't he come yet?"

"No," said the old man, "we haven't heard anything; but I'm sure he's coming, and I thought he might be here this morning."

"Just then," said Mr. Brown, "I saw a stalwart young man coming down the steps of the car. I said to myself, *If I were not sure the boy was dead, I would say that was the son.* But other eyes had seen him too; and the old man dropped his cane and ran as fast as his tottering limbs would let him, and in less time than I can tell it, the boy was in his father's arms."

The old white-haired man sobbed out, "O my son! Thank God, you've come!" Then turning to Mr. Brown, he said, "Mr. Brown, I would have waited until I died."

Something like that is God's love for you. A yearning something like that is what God has in His heart for you. He has been waiting for some of you now thirty, forty, fifty, sixty years, and you haven't come yet. But if Christ was made flesh and dwelt among us for the reasons we have seen, and if God loves you like a father and is a God like the God we know Him to be, I think if I were you, I would not keep Him waiting longer.

TOM MALONE
1915–

ABOUT THE MAN:

Tom Malone was converted and called to preach at the same moment! At an old-fashioned bench, the preacher took his tear-stained Bible and showed Tom Malone how to be saved. He accepted Christ then and there. Arising from his knees in the Isbell Methodist Church near Russellville, Alabama, he shook the circuit pastor's hand; and this bashful nineteen-year-old farm boy announced: "I know the Lord wants me to be a preacher."

Backward, bashful and broke, Tom borrowed five dollars, took what he could in a cardboard suitcase and left for Cleveland, Tennessee. Immediately upon arrival at Bob Jones College, Malone heard a truth that totally dominated his life and labors for the Lord ever after—soul winning!

That day he won his first soul! The green-as-grass Tom, a new convert himself, knew nothing of soul-winning approaches or techniques. He simply asked the sinner, "Are you a Christian?" No. In a few minutes that young man became Malone's first convert.

Since that day, his experiences in personal evangelism have been countless.

Mark it down: Malone began soul winning his first week in Bible college. And he has never lost *the thirst* for it, *the thrill* in it nor *the task* of it since. Pastoring churches, administrating schools, preaching across the nation have not deterred Tom Malone from this mainline ministry.

It is doubtful if young Malone ever dreamed of becoming the man he is today. He is now Doctor Tom Malone, is renowned in fundamental circles for his wise leadership and great preaching, is pastor of the large Emmanuel Baptist Church of Pontiac, Michigan, founder and president of Midwestern Baptist Schools, and is eagerly sought as speaker in large Bible conferences from coast to coast.

Dr. John R. Rice often said that Dr. Tom Malone may be the greatest gospel preacher in all the world today!

XII.

Why Jesus Became a Man

TOM MALONE

"...Christ Jesus:
"Who, being in the form of God, thought it not robbery to be equal with God:
"But made himself of no reputation, and took upon him the form of a servant, and was made in the likeness of men:
"And being found in fashion as a man, he humbled himself, and became obedient unto death, even the death of the cross."—Phil. 2:5–8.

Two phrases in this passage I wish to call to your attention. Philippians 2:7,8 has these two expressions: "made in the likeness of men" and "being found in fashion as a man."

Some may want to distinguish between the virgin birth of Jesus and His incarnation. In a sense there is a difference, yet these two are closely related.

The virgin birth involves that miraculous act of God whereby the Lord Jesus was conceived, without man, in the body of a pure virgin maiden named Mary. The incarnation is the divine act of God whereby Jesus was manifest in human flesh.

Many passages speak of the virgin birth. Matthew 1:18–20 says:

"Now the birth of Jesus Christ was on this wise: When as his mother Mary was espoused to Joseph, before they came together, she was found with child of the Holy Ghost.

"Then Joseph her husband, being a just man, and not willing to make her a publick example, was minded to put her away privily.

"But while he thought on these things, behold, the angel of the Lord appeared unto him in a dream, saying, Joseph, thou son of David, fear not to take unto thee Mary thy wife: for that which is conceived in her is of the Holy Ghost."

Other passages such as those in our text deal specifically with the incarnation of Jesus.

"And the Word was made flesh, and dwelt among us, (and we beheld his glory, the glory as of the only begotten of the Father,) full of grace and truth."—John 1:14.

"And without controversy great is the mystery of godliness: God was manifest in the flesh, justified in the Spirit, seen of angels, preached unto the Gentiles, believed on in the world, received up into glory."—I Tim. 3:16.

If one attacks the virgin birth of our Lord, he also attacks the incarnation of Jesus.

In recent years especially, there has been a blatant, insidious attack by rationalists, modernists and infidels against the virgin birth and incarnation of Jesus. For instance, some say that the word *virgin* found in the English translation of the Bible does not necessarily mean a chaste, pure, young woman. Some contend that the Hebrew word *almah* does not mean virgin but young woman; that is, any kind of young woman. This is not true.

Let us read Isaiah 7:14:

"Therefore the Lord himself shall give you a sign; Behold, a virgin shall conceive, and bear a son, and shall call his name Immanuel."

Virgin here definitely means a pure, chaste woman who has not known man. This is its meaning in Genesis 24:43 when Rebekah is called a virgin; this is its meaning in Proverbs 30:19 and also in Psalm 68:25. In Matthew 1:23 God quotes Isaiah 7:14 and in the Greek New Testament says "virgin."

The birth mentioned in Isaiah 7:14 was to be a miraculous sign to the house of David and to all the world. How could the natural birth of a baby boy be a special sign? Hasn't this happened millions of times? No. In order to be a sign, it must be a birth by a virgin who had not known man.

There are three general names of Jesus in the Bible: Son of David, Son of God, Son of Man.

Son of David is His Jewish, racial name. All of us know that nearly every book in the Bible was written by a Jew. Jesus came from the tribe of Judah, the family of David, so He was a Jew.

Then, Son of God is His divine name.

But there is another name—Son of Man. Eighty times in the Word of God, Jesus is spoken of as Son of Man.

We'll look at some of those verses, but I want you to think of Jesus Christ as a man, in a human body just like yours and mine. Jesus was perfect, divine, but He had a human body.

Many times Jesus is called a man, a human being. We read, for instance, in Hebrews 2:14, "Forasmuch then as the children are partakers of flesh and blood, he also himself likewise took part of the same." Jesus took part of "flesh and blood."

The humanity of Jesus is of vast importance. I've heard great scholars and Bible teachers say that the humanity of Jesus needed to be emphasized in our preaching and teaching just as much as His deity.

The woman at the well who got gloriously saved went back into the city and said, "...a man, which told me all things that ever I did" (John 4:29). When she viewed Jesus sitting on the well there in Samaria, she recognized Him to be in the form of a man.

On many occasions Jesus spoke of Himself as having flesh and blood. In John 6:53, 54 He said:

"Except ye eat the flesh of the Son of man, and drink his blood, ye have no life in you.

"Whoso eateth my flesh, and drinketh my blood, hath eternal life."

Jesus claimed that He was a man, claimed that He had flesh and blood.

In connection with all the great things He did, many times Jesus referred to Himself as the Son of Man.

When talking to Nicodemus that night in John, chapter 3, He said:

"And as Moses lifted up the serpent in the wilderness, even so must the Son of man be lifted up:

"That whosoever believeth in him should not perish, but have eternal life."—Vss. 14, 15.

When Jesus talked of Calvary, redemption, the cross and the shedding of His blood for the salvation of the world, He referred to Himself as the Son of Man.

He had just saved Zacchaeus, and people wondered that He was such a wonderful friend of sinners. Jesus said in Luke 19:10, "For the Son of man is come to seek and to save that which was lost." So we see His humanity connected with His divine purpose in coming into the world.

Again Jesus spoke of Himself as the Son of Man when He spoke of the resurrection:

"For as Jonas was three days and three nights in the whale's belly; so shall the Son of man be three days and three nights in the heart of the earth."—Matt. 12:40.

When Jesus spoke of the second coming, He spoke of Himself as being the Son of Man:

"But as the days of Noe were, so shall also the coming of the Son of man be."

"For in such an hour as ye think not the Son of man cometh."—Matt. 24:37,44.

Lest you think I am emphasizing something that Jesus did not emphasize or something the Word of God does not emphasize, I remind you that no fewer than eighty times Jesus was referred to in the Bible as the Son of Man. Son of God—yes, but Son of Man just as surely and distinctively.

It is said that one stormy night a little girl in her bedroom began to cry. She was afraid of the thunder, lightning, wind and rain. Mother went up and tried to comfort her. "Now, honey, you are not alone. You know God is in our hearts and in our home."

As she started to leave the room, the little girl continued to weep. When the mother went back to the bed, the child said, "I know the Lord is with me, but, Mother, I want somebody with skin on." In other words, she wanted someone she could feel and touch, someone she could see.

Jesus came in visible form. He humbled Himself and lived on earth in the fashion of a man.

Why was it necessary for Jesus Christ, the Son of God, the member of the Trinity, from the very beginning, the preexistent, the eternally existing Son of God, to become a man?

I. HE BECAME A MAN THAT HE MIGHT SUBJECT HIMSELF TO THE LIMITATIONS OF THE HUMAN BODY

First, He subjected Himself to childlike obedience to His parents. Think of that little Babe born in a manger that night; that little Babe snuggled in a mother's arms; that little Baby nursing from a mother's breast; that little Baby carried about, taken care of and cleansed. That little Baby in human form is Almighty God.

See Him at the age of twelve. When His parents journeyed homeward, they missed Him. Coming back to the temple, they found Him. He said, 'What? know you not that I must be about My Father's business?' Then they went on their way. This was Jesus at twelve years of age, the blessed Son of God, in the body of a little Boy; "And he went down with them, and came to Nazareth, and was subject unto them" (Luke 23:51).

Jesus Christ subjected Himself to childlike obedience. He obeyed His parents. He honored His mother and father. He subjected Himself to all the limitations of a human body.

Jesus knew what it was to be tired. That body became fatigued with many hours of labor.

One day amidst a storm, Jesus is in the boat. The storm is raging. Mark 4:38 tells us that Jesus "was in the hinder part of the ship, asleep on a pillow" and the disciples awoke Him.

The Son of God got so tired from toiling, laboring, ministering, speaking, loving and weeping over people that His body became worn out. Tired and sleepy, He lay on the deck of a vessel on a borrowed pillow. He had to be awakened even in the midst of a storm. The body of Jesus was subject to fatigue.

Jesus knew what it was to be hungry. Mark 11:12 says, "And on the morrow, when they were come from Bethany, he was hungry."

When you think of Jesus, don't think of Him as always working a miracle. Think of Him as being in a human body, subject to limitations such as you and I have.

Jesus subjected Himself not only to childlike obedience, fatigue and hunger, but to thirst. He knew what it was to crave water. See Him as a Stranger sitting on a well in that hot noontime of the day, saying to a woman, "Give me to drink."

Jesus perspired. He got dusty as He walked along the road. He asked for something to drink. Almost the last thing He said on the cross was, "I thirst." That human body knew fever, pain and suffering, and it wanted water.

Jesus' body was subjected to deprivation. He knew what it was to want some things that He couldn't have because He came in the form of a man, to walk among men. One time He said, "The foxes have holes, and the birds of the air have nests; but the Son of man hath not where to lay his head" (Matt. 8:20).

Jesus was deprived. He owned no home. "And every man went unto his own house. Jesus went unto the mount of Olives." When others said, "I'm going home," Jesus said, "I'll go to the garden and pray," or "I'll go to the mountain and pray." The Son of Man had nowhere to lay His head. Jesus Christ was subjected to all the limitations of the human body.

The Bible says He "was in all points tempted like as we are, yet without sin" (Heb. 4:15). And Hebrews 2:18 says, "For in that he himself hath suffered being tempted, he is able to succour them that are tempted."

When you become thirsty and tired, hungry and deprived, remember, Jesus in His human body was also thirsty, hungry and tired. He subjected Himself to the limitations of a human body.

We are aware of it when we observe the Lord's Supper, the ordinance of communion. In I Corinthians 11:24 Paul quotes Jesus, "Take, eat: this is my body, which is broken for you." The word *broken* was inserted. It should read, "Take, eat: this is my body, which is for you."

Jesus took upon Himself a body. Why? That was God's way for Christ to be revealed and manifested in a human body and subject to all the limitations of a human body.

II. HE BECAME A MAN THAT HE MIGHT SUBJECT HIMSELF TO MAN'S SINS

Jesus became a Man so that He might assume the penalty of man's sin. The penalty for sin is given in Romans 6:23: "The wages of sin is death." Ezekiel 18:4,20 reminds us that "the soul that sinneth, it shall die." You and I have sinned. The penalty is death, spiritual death, to be cut off from God.

In I Corinthians 15:3 we read, "Christ died for our sins according to the scriptures." We read in II Corinthians 5:21 more about Jesus' being subjected to man's sin: "For he [God] hath made him [Jesus] to be sin for us, who knew no sin; that we might be made the righteousness of God in him."

God made Him a sin-offering. God made Him in the form of a man that we might be made the righteousness of God in Him.

Have you ever wondered if Jesus, as a man, ever identified Himself with our sins?

I read something recently that I had never seen—the statement of Jesus recorded in Matthew 27:46 where, dying on the cross midst the darkness, He cried, "My God, my God, why hast thou forsaken me?" Many times I have read that. Many times I have repeated it. Many times it has gone through my mind. "My God, my God...." I realized that Jesus had never called His Father that before. He always called Him "My Father"—"I and my Father are one"; "He that hath seen me hath seen the Father"; "I do always those things that please him [the Father]." But on the cross He cries, "My God, my God, why hast thou forsaken me?" Why?

Psalm 22 answers the question:

"My God, my God, why hast thou forsaken me? why art thou so far from helping me, and from the words of my roaring?

"O my God, I cry in the daytime [when it is light], *but thou hearest not; and in the night season* [when it is dark], *and am not silent."*—Vss. 1, 2.

Now verse 3 answers the question that Jesus asked:

"But thou art holy, O thou that inhabitest the praises of Israel."

Hear it! That is why God turned His face away when Jesus became a sin-offering on the cross.

We read in Habakkuk 1:13, "Thou art of purer eyes than to behold evil, and canst not look on iniquity." When Jesus was identified with your sin and my sin, God the Father turned His face away.

No wonder yonder sun refused to shine. No wonder the blessed Saviour cried, "My God, my God, why hast thou forsaken me?" In that crucial hour when the Son of Man was lifted up that He might redeem us from all iniquity, your sin and my sin were upon Him.

Oh, listen! He became a man that He might subject Himself to the penalty of man's sin.

Isaiah 53—that mountain peak of Bible prophecy, that great chapter of the Gospel in the book of Isaiah; some twenty-four times in Isaiah 53 we are shown of another One taking our place. Forty-eight times there are personal pronouns used in these twelve verses.

"Who hath believed our report? and to whom is the arm of the LORD revealed? [Jesus is the Arm of the Lord to do His bidding, to execute His will, to accomplish His work.]

"For he shall grow up before him as a tender plant, and as a root out of a dry ground: he hath no form nor comeliness; and when we shall see him, there is no beauty that we should desire him.

"He is despised and rejected of men; a man of sorrows, and acquainted with grief: and we hid as it were our faces from him; he was despised, and we esteemed him not.

"Surely he hath borne our griefs, and carried our sorrows: yet we did esteem him stricken, smitten of God, and afflicted.

"But he was wounded for our transgressions, he was bruised for our iniquities: the chastisement of our peace was upon him; and with his stripes we are healed.

"All we like sheep have gone astray; we have turned every one to his own way; and the LORD hath laid on him the iniquity of us all."—Vss. 1-6.

Yes, Jesus was in the form of man that He might subject Himself to man's sin.

Dr. H. A. Ironside was a great Bible teacher. His interpretation of the Bible always led to Christ. Everything he said pointed to Jesus: what He did, who He was, and what He came to do.

Dr. Ironside told one time of a sheep ranch that he visited down in Texas. He said there he saw one of the greatest demonstrations of the righteousness of God imputed to us because Jesus, as a man, died on the cross.

He saw something he couldn't figure out. It looked like a sheep, but it had four front legs, four back legs and two heads. It looked like a deformed little animal.

He asked the sheep rancher, "What in the world is this?"
The rancher replied:

> Preacher, this is a story that you will probably tell the rest of your life. We had a little lamb to die and a mother sheep to die. The lamb left a mother without a baby, and a mother left a lamb without a mother.
>
> We took the little lamb without a mother and put it in the pen of the mother without its baby. The mother didn't want the baby. She would lower her head and push it away.
>
> Some of the helpers here got the idea that if the mother thought that little lamb was really hers, she would adopt it, nurse it and raise it. So they took the skin off the little dead lamb, put it around the little orphan lamb and tied it on. That is why you see four front feet, four back feet and what looks like two heads.
>
> When it was covered, we put it in the pen with the mother. She loved and cared for it. There is nothing horrible looking about it to her. She has accepted it because it is clothed in the garments of her own.

Dr. Ironside commented: "What a perfect illustration of orphaned sinners with no Father and no Saviour! But robed in the righteousness of God, we are accepted in the Beloved."

That is the result of Jesus' becoming a Man and identifying Himself with man's sins.

III. HE BECAME A MAN THAT HE MIGHT SUBJECT HIMSELF TO MAN'S DEATH AND THE GRAVE

All men, save one generation of Christians who will be alive when Jesus comes, are subject to death. From the first family, Adam and Eve, to this hour, none have escaped the great reaper of Death.

The Word of God tells us many times about man's being subject to death. We don't get very far in the book of Genesis until some eight times we read, "...and he died"; "...and he died"; "...and he died." Some men lived nearly a thousand years, but the summary of their lives was: "...and he died." All men are subject to death.

If Jesus should tarry, every man, every woman, every boy, every girl must walk through the chilly waters of Death, cross from time to eternity. Even Jesus went to the grave.

A good man, Joseph, lived in a town called Arimathaea, not too far from Jerusalem. He is spoken of in the Bible as Joseph of Arimathaea.

"This man went unto Pilate, and begged the body of Jesus.

"And he took it down, and wrapped it in linen, and laid it in a sepulchre that was hewn in stone, wherein never man before was laid."—Luke 23:52, 53.

What a picture! This man one day hewed out of the side of a rock a great tomb. He said to his family, "Here are graves for two adults and one child—our family plot. When I die, this is where I will be buried."

The substitutionary love of God and Christ is seen on nearly every page of the Bible. Not Joseph of Arimathaea was laid in that grave, but the body of the Son of God.

A huge stone closed the door and sealed it off. His enemies stood there and declared, "We will see that forever He is a victim of the grave. We will see that that body of flesh and blood will rot in this soil because Death has Him now!"

They were wrong. But Jesus Christ was made in the likeness of men so He might subject Himself to man's grave.

We read in Isaiah 53:9, "And he made his grave with the wicked, and with the rich in his death."

"With the wicked"—that is, between the two thieves on the cross.

"With the rich"—that is, Joseph and Nicodemus, who begged His body and buried Him.

It will be seven hundred years before Jesus will come to Bethlehem's manger. The Word of God says that He is to have a grave. He is to know what it means to be buried. He is to know, like all men know, what it is to die in a human body. He is to taste and experience death. That is why He became a man.

Oh, when I think of death and the victory God has given those who believe on Him, I feel like Paul in I Corinthians 15. Here you see the resurrection of believers and of Christ discussed from five different views. I don't think Paul ever gave a more wonderful shout of victory than this: "O death, where is thy sting? O grave, where is thy victory?"

Then he went on to declare that Christ has taken the sting out of Death and victory from the grasp of the Grave. Why? Because He became a man and died like all men will have to die.

I thank God there has been One in the grave before me, One whom I love, One who loves me with an eternal, unbounded, everlasting love. He has walked that way and left a light in the tomb for me. He was made a man that He might know what it means to die.

A little girl and her mother were picking flowers. The child became alarmed when a bee was getting closer and buzzing around. "Mother, I'm afraid of the bee," she whined. So she stayed close to her mother.

But in a short while she said again, "Mother, I'm afraid the bee will sting me."

The mother said, "No, honey, that bee can never sting you."

"Mother, how do you know that bee isn't going to sting me?"

As the mother scratched at the swollen place on her own arm to find the stinger, she said, "Because it has already stung me. The stinger is in Mother's arm. So the bee can never harm you now."

So when I hear Paul cry, "O death, where is thy sting? O grave, where is thy victory?" I can say, "In the body, the human body of the Son of God, is the sting."

When the Christian dies, it is a triumph, a moving to a glorious land, the land where living waters flow. It is a change of address; moving out of an old tent which rots and decays, into a house eternal, not made with hands, prepared for those who love the Lord.

So He became a man that He might be subject unto man's death and the grave.

IV. HE BECAME A MAN THAT HE MIGHT SUBJECT HIMSELF AS A MAN TO ADAM'S CURSE

We are children of Adam, and Jesus took upon Himself Adam's curse. God said to Adam in Genesis 3:17, 18, "...cursed is the ground for thy sake;...Thorns also and thistles shall it bring forth." The curse of Adam is thorns.

Matthew 27:29 says:

"And when they had platted a crown of thorns, they put it

upon his head, and a reed in his right hand: and they bowed the knee before him, and mocked him."

That crown of thorns represented the thorns in Adam's curse. But what about that reed? Remember God said to Adam in Genesis 3:18, "Thou shalt eat the herb of the field." He was saying to Adam, "Out among the grass and weed and herbs of the field, you will wring your living from the soil by the sweat of your brow."

There is a crown of thorns on His head, a reed in His hand, and man is mocking the Son of God.

Paul wrote to the Galatians:

"Christ hath redeemed us from the curse of the law, being made a curse for us: for it is written, Cursed is every one that hangeth on a tree."—Gal. 3:13.

A song I have thought so much of in recent days starts like this:

> **I saw One hanging on a tree,**
> **In agony and blood;**
> **He fixed His languid eyes on me,**
> **As near His cross I stood.**

Another verse says:

> **A second look He gave, which said,**
> **"I freely all forgive:**
> **This blood is for thy ransom paid.**
> **I died that thou may'st live."**

The chorus of another song says:

> **He's looking on you!**
> **He's looking on you!**
> **Oh, ever were love and compassion,**
> **Love and compassion so true.**
> **He's looking on you!**
> **He's looking on you!**
> **He's looking, looking on you!**

Thank God, the curse is gone! To those who believe, it is lifted.

Yes, He subjected Himself to the body of a man that He might assume man's curse.

V. HE BECAME A MAN THAT WE MIGHT BE MADE IN THE LIKENESS OF GOD

What beautiful truth! He was made like man that we may be made like God. First John 3:1,2 says:

"Behold, what manner of love the Father hath bestowed upon us, that we should be called the sons of God: therefore the world knoweth us not, because it knew him not.

"Beloved, now are we the sons of God, and it doth not yet appear what we shall be: but we know that, when he shall appear, we shall be like him; for we shall see him as he is."

Romans 8:29 declares the whole purpose of this salvation story: "For whom he did foreknow, he also did predestinate to be conformed to the image of his Son."

Folks argue that some are predestinated to be saved and some are predestinated to be lost. But neither is true. Certainly no one is predestinated to be lost, for God loves the whole world. The Bible never teaches any such thing as a person elected or predestinated to go to Heaven. Those who are saved are predestinated and foreordained to be like Christ. "For whom he did foreknow, he also did predestinate to be conformed to the image of his Son" (Rom. 8:9).

"When he shall appear, we shall be like him." Oh, I've tried for these many years to grow more like Him. What a sweet truth this phrase to my needy heart! When the Lord comes, I'll be like Him in full redemption, not only in soul but in body.

Speaking of the first Adam, I Corinthians 15:49 says, "And as we have borne the image of the earthy, we shall also bear the image of the heavenly." We will be like Jesus.

The psalmist of old said, "I shall be satisfied, when I awake, with thy likeness" (Ps. 17:15).

Many times in the Bible this beautiful truth is set forth. For instance, in Philippians 3 we are told He was made in the likeness of men so we could be made like Him.

Paul wrote Philippians 3:20,21 from his prison cell:

"For our conversation [citizenship] is in heaven; from whence also we look for the Saviour, the Lord Jesus Christ:

"Who shall change our vile body, that it may be fashioned like unto his glorious body."

The same expression is found, "...made in the likeness [fashion] of a man."

What is He going to do when He comes?

"...change our vile body, that it may be fashioned like unto his glorious body, according to the working whereby he is able even to subdue all things unto himself."

That I'm going to be like Jesus is the longing of my heart.

Paul wrote of it:

"Behold, I shew you a mystery; We shall not all sleep, but we shall all be changed,

"In a moment, in the twinkling of an eye, at the last trump: for the trumpet shall sound, and the dead shall be raised incorruptible, and we shall be changed."—I Cor. 15:51,52.

Changed, and like Jesus! "Oh, to be like Him!" is the heart-cry of every true believer!

He was made in the likeness of a man so that I might be made in the likeness of Christ.

ROBERT GREENE LEE
1886–1978

ABOUT THE MAN:

R. G. Lee was born November 11, 1886, and died July 20, 1978.

The midwife attending his birth held baby Lee in her black arms while dancing a jig around the room, saying, "Praise Gawd! Glory be! The good Lawd done sont a preacher to dis here house. Yas, sah! Yes, ma'am. Dat's what He's done gone and done."

"God-sent preacher" well describes Dr. Lee. Few in number are the Baptists who have never heard his most famous sermon, "Payday Someday!" If you haven't heard it or read it, surely you have heard some preacher make a favorable reference to it.

From his humble birth to sharecropper parents, Dr. Lee rose to pastor one of the largest churches in his denomination and head the mammoth Southern Baptist Convention as its president, serving three terms in that office. Dr. John R. Rice said:

"If you have not had the privilege of hearing Dr. Lee in person, I am sorry for you. The scholarly thoroughness, the wizardry of words, the lilt of poetic thought, the exalted idealism, the tender pathos, the practical application, the stern devotion to divine truth, the holy urgency in the preaching of a man called and anointed of God to preach and who must therefore preach, are never to be forgotten. The stately progression of his sermon to its logical end satisfies. The facile language, the alliterative statement, the powerful conviction mark Dr. Lee's sermons. The scholarly gleaning of incident and illustration from the treasures of scholarly memory and library make a rich feast for the hearer. The banquet table is spread with bread from many a grainfield, honey distilled from the nectar of far-off exotic blossoms, sweetmeats from many a bakeshop, strong meat from divers markets; and the whole board is garnished by posies from a thousand gardens.

"Often have I been blessed in hearing Dr. Lee preach, have delighted in his Southern voice, and have been carried along with joy by his anointed eloquence."

XIII.

Christ "Above All"

R. G. LEE

(Sermon preached in 1972 at Sword of the Lord Conference,
Highland Park Baptist Church, Chattanooga, Tennessee)

In John's Gospel, the third chapter and the thirty-first verse, we have these words upon which I ask you to pitch your mental tents worshipfully, prayerfully, and around which I ask you to gather the meditation of your heart this morning:

"He that cometh from above is above all: he that is of the earth is earthly, and speaketh of the earth: he that cometh from heaven is above all."

Those are the words of John the Baptist, the great wilderness preacher who descended upon the iniquities of his day with a torch in one hand and a sword in the other.

John the Baptist, who for Jesus was a bright and burning light.

John the Baptist, concerning whom Jesus said, 'A greater hath never been born of woman.'

John the Baptist, to whom was given the very delicate task of interpreting the voice of betrothal as a friend of the Bridegroom.

John the Baptist, who spoke nearly always in judicial tones, and his words were sharp arrows that pierced the hearts of prating formalists, artful hypocrites, skeptical Sadducees, and the materialistic-minded, money-greedy, money-grabbing men of his day.

John the Baptist, who never visited a haberdasher's shop, and I suppose he would have a hard time getting a call to any Baptist church in our nation today because of the way he dressed. And I don't think the ladies of the missionary societies would want him for lunch, because they wouldn't know how to make grasshopper salad for Baptist preachers.

John the Baptist, who buried Jesus in the rolling tides of the Jordan River at which time the heavens were opened unto Jesus, and the Holy Spirit in the form of a dove descended and abode upon Him, and a voice from Heaven said, "This is my beloved Son, in whom I am well pleased."

John the Baptist, who pointed out Jesus as the Lamb of God.

John the Baptist, who said about Jesus as he spoke in the power of the Holy Spirit, "He that cometh from above is above all...he that cometh from heaven is above all."

Of course, when men set their minds and mouths and pulpits and pens and printing presses to portray fully all that Jesus was, is, and evermore will be in His glory, His greatness, His goodness and His grace—they set themselves to tasks that put men and angels to an eternal nonplus.

Can one little coal of fire warm a thousand cold hearthstones? Can one little rosebud perfume the stifling atmosphere of a city? Can one little cup of water cleanse a thousand dirty hands? Can any musician play Beethoven's *Ninth Symphony* on a tin whistle?

You say no. I say, no more can all the words of the wisest of men set forth Jesus as He deserves to be set forth in His greatness, His glory, His goodness and His grace.

Today Jesus is Heaven's bread for earth's hunger; Heaven's water for earth's thirst; Heaven's light for earth's darkness; Heaven's glory for earth's shame; Heaven's grace for earth's guilt; Heaven's beauty for earth's ugliness; Heaven's wisdom for earth's folly; Heaven's peace for earth's strife; Heaven's justification for earth's condemnation; Heaven's salvation for earth's damnation. Oh, who can really paint Him!

Let the sweetest tones that ever trembled on the harps of Heaven be discord; let the shining seraphim, whose anthem is eternity, be dumb while wonder, praise, adoration melt into muteness as they see their Christ—the one and only Perfection, the one eternally "above all."

And Jesus was "above all" in His source. Jesus and the prayer He prayed are recorded in John 17. It said that He had glory with God before the world was and was loved by the Father before the foundation of the world. Meaning what? Meaning that He was coexistent, coessential, coeternal, and coequal with God. And Jesus said, "I and my Father are one."

CHRIST "ABOVE ALL"

O-N-E—one! No husband has ever been so *one* with the wife of his bosom. No wife has ever been so *one* with the husband of her heart. No child has ever been so one—O-N-E—with his mother from the moment of his conception as was Jesus with God in the glory They had and the love They had with and for each other before this world ever was.

No beams of light ever came so brightly from the sun, no fragrance ever issued so sweetly from flowers, no crystal streams ever came so purely clear from crystal fountain, as did the delights of the Holy, Holy Father's heart with a thrice Holy Son and the love They had, and the glory They had, with and for each other before this world ever was; from which love and glory the blessed Holy Spirit Himself was never excluded.

JESUS, CREATOR OF ALL THINGS, IS "ABOVE ALL"

And Jesus is "above all" in His relation to this physical, this material universe in which we now live.

I look upon this material universe as a vast autograph album with its pages made up of mountains, molecules, moats, atoms, prairies, forests, oceans, seas, rivers and all other things you can find in that vast and mysterious kingdom of nature.

No matter where you look, you will find the signature of Jesus Christ. Sometimes so small that you have to take a microscope to see it; sometimes so large—and being so far away, being large, you have to take a journey of a billion miles on telescopic lens to see it. But you see the signature of Jesus everywhere.

He is the Designer behind all the designs of this universe; the Lawmaker behind all its laws; the great Creator behind all creation. How do I know this? I know it from this blessed, inspired, infallible, inerrant Word of God—regenerative in its power, inexhaustive in its adequacy, the miracle Book of diversity and unity, of harmony and infinite complexity. What does it say?

John 1:3: "All things were made by him; and without him was not any thing made that was made."

And Paul, writing to the Christians at Colosse:

"For by him were all things created, that are in heaven, and

that are in earth, visible and invisible, whether they be thrones, or dominions, or principalities, or powers: all things were created by him, and for him:

"And he is before all things, and by him all things consist [hold together]."—Col. 1:16,17.

Notice those wonderful "all things" there.

And you have another "all things" in the first of Hebrews:

"God, who at sundry times and in divers manners spake in time past unto the fathers by the prophets,

"Hath in these last days spoken unto us by his Son, whom he hath appointed heir of all things, by whom also he made the worlds."—Vss. 1,2.

He is "above all" in His relation to this universe because He conceived it by His wisdom and created it by His power.

Who was it that put the sun yonder in its tabernacle in the heavens?

Who was it that planned the garden of the stars?

Who was it that made the moon to blossom like a huge yellow jonquil in that garden of the stars?

Who was it that sent out the first ray of light like some flaming archangel with garments afire?

Who was it that poured out from the crystal chalices of eternity all the rivers of this earth?

Who was it that put the song in the throat of a mockingbird, which I call the Beethoven of the Boughs, and the lyric in the throat of the lark, which I call the Mendelssohn of the Meadows?

There is only one answer to all these questions—Jesus Christ, Son of Man without sin, and Son of God with power. He is above all.

1. Jesus "Above All" in His Incarnation

I love to think how He is "above all" in the way He came into the universe. He was conceived by His wisdom and was physically created by His power and became a human being without any sin.

In eternity, Jesus rested on the bosom of the Father without any mother; and in time, He rested on the bosom of a mother without any earthly father. And God, who in Eden's Garden took from the body of a man a motherless woman, in Bethlehem's cow stall took from the body of a woman a fatherless Man—Jesus, the Son of God!

Did you ever hear of a baby being just as old as its father? You say, Of course not. But Jesus was just as old as His Heavenly Father. He was coexistent, coessential, coeternal, and His goings forth were of old, even from everlasting.

Did you ever hear of a baby being a hundred years older than its mother? You say, Of course not. But Jesus was ages older than His mother Mary, proving that He was a great Unique—the One unlike in all the worlds.

Yes, and Jesus, who created all the angels of Heaven, was made lower than these angels. Jesus, who created all the thrones in Heaven, left His throne in Heaven for the place of the skull, where He bore our sins in His own body on the tree.

And this Word of God tells us that Jesus said, "Before Abraham was, I am," and He was born two thousand years *after* Abraham.

This Word says that God sent forth His Son made of a woman, made flesh. When did God send forth His Son made of a woman and made flesh? He was made of a woman and made flesh when a little Jewish virgin, who had never touched a man, never known a man, with child by the Holy Ghost, went down into that mysterious land of motherhood; and when she came back she was holding in her arms the only Baby who never had an earthly father.

His every muscle was purely divine—this One. His every nerve was divine handwriting. His every bone was divine sculpture. His every heartbeat was a heartbeat of deity. His every breath was a whisper of deity.

He was God's will, God's thought, God's purpose for all mortality. He was a Light God had seen, the Word God heard, the Life God felt. He is "above all" in the way He became a human being without any sin.

2. Jesus "Above All" as Revealing the Father

I love to think how He is "above all" as revealing God. John 1:18 says:

"No man hath seen God at any time; the only begotten Son,

which is in the bosom of the Father, he hath declared him."

He hath exegeted God. He is the exegesis of God, in other words.

One day Philip said to Jesus:

"Lord, shew us the Father, and it sufficeth us [satisfies us]*."*—John 14:8.

And I think Jesus had rebuke and sorrow in His voice when He answered Philip:

"Have I been so long time with you, and yet hast thou not known me, Philip? he that hath seen me hath seen the Father; and how sayest thou then, Shew us the Father?"—Vs. 9.

In other words, "Philip, you have seen Me walk, and you have seen the Father walk. You have see Me work, and you have seen the Father work. You have heard Me speak, and you have heard the Father speak. Why do you have to see the Father? He that hath seen Me hath seen the Father."

In Jesus, the silence of God broke into full voice. Jesus was God manifested in the flesh. And what Jesus was in the days of His flesh on this earth to the prodigal, to the publican, the harlot, the hypocrite, the saint, the sinner, the disciples, the devils, the rich, the poor, the men, the women, the boys, the girls, to pagans and philosophers, to beggars, kings and queens—that is God always, everywhere, to everybody.

God was in Christ Jesus. Jesus was God manifested in the flesh. Never forget that truth!

3. Jesus "Above All" in Power

I love to think how Jesus is above all in His supernatural power. His power is above all the powers that men know anything about. He said, "All power" (I don't like that translation that says "all authority." I say it means "all power") "is given unto me in heaven and in earth."

We have a little old sinful race that can strut sitting down, boasting about its power—bombs of power, satellites of power, ships of power, motors of power, armies of power and navies of power.

Power, power, power. We do have power.

I gave my lecture on "Achievements and Limitations of Science" in Chicago to a group of scientists and physicists and chemists. I don't know how many of them were Christians, but they heard about Jesus that day! I never address a civic club that I don't bring in Jesus as the climax of my message. You leave Jesus out, and you haven't said anything worthwhile at a civic club!

One of these scientists asked me out to lunch. He was very sober-minded. I said to this Christian scientist:

> Sir, I go up and down this country and talk to a lot of young people, some of them getting married and will have children, and some of them already married and have their children. Tell me one thing to tell them as to what sort of universe they will live in from the scientific and nuclear viewpoint, and rear their children in.

He said:

> O sir, right now we are in danger of global cremation! Tell these young people to trust Christ, to love Christ, to serve Christ, to go in the direction He points, and to be obedient to His will; then if they die in a cloud of atomic dust, nothing can take away their salvation or make the influence of their lives null and void.

Now I am trying to tell that to young people all up and down this country.

Yes, we have power, and I love to think that Jesus used His power to help, not to hurt, people.

There was only one miracle that Jesus wrought that was a miracle of destruction, and that was when He blighted the barren fig tree. You might want to call it a miracle of destruction when He gave the devils in the young man permission to get in the hogs, and the hogs ran down a steep cliff and committed "hogicide."

Years ago I was in Cocoa, Florida. I was invited to speak to the students in the university at Gainesville. I always enjoy speaking to students. An old country boy took me in an old Model-A Ford across about twenty miles of sandy roads until we got to the beautiful highway. On the sandy roads, I looked to my right and I looked to my left. I saw little animals that reminded me of animated corkscrews.

I asked, "What are those things?"

"Razorbacks," he answered.

"What are they good for?"

"Sausage."

"How do you know when to kill them to get sausage?"

"We pick them up by their ears. If the snout drapes, they ain't ready. If the hindquarters drape, they're ready."

I said, "Young man, you've caused me to change my subject. I'm going to talk to the students when I get over there on 'The Devil's Second Choice—the Razorback.'"

After my message I gave an invitation. A big, handsome young fellow came and shook hands with me. It was almost like shaking hands with the tail of a live trout. He said, "Who told you about me?"

I said, "Nobody told me about you, but if you were in that room where my guns were turned, don't blame me for your getting hit."

He talked loud as he said, "Well, all these folks know me. I plead guilty, sir. I've been giving guest room in my lighthouse to the Devil and my body to the Devil whose second choice is a hog. But I'm promising God and my parents and my fiancée and everybody else who wants to hear my promise, that never again will I give guest room in my body or in my lighthouse, as you express it, to the Devil whose second choice is a razorback."

Other students came and made the same promise that morning, and we had a blessed, heavenly hour. (I wish we could have more hours like that in our state universities.)

Yes, Jesus used His power to bless folks.

He never met a blind man that He didn't give sight.

He never met a deaf man that He didn't make hear.

He never met a dumb man but that He melted the frozen fountains of his speech and filled his mouth with laughter, language and song.

He never met a man with a withered hand that He didn't send home with a super hand.

He never met a crazy man but that He restored his reason.

He never met a foul leper that He didn't cleanse.

He never met an outcast woman that He didn't lift up and put back into the path of the chaste life.

He never faced a storm that He didn't calm.

He never met a human need that He didn't supply.

He never came in touch with a broken heart that He didn't heal.

He never went into a sick room but that He healed the sick.

He never met a funeral procession that He didn't break up.

He never went into a cemetery but that He raised the dead.

Teaching us what? That in this universe there's Someone to whom all power over everything and everybody is given. And in His glorified body in Heaven today, Jesus, with one touch of His finger, could have more power in it than all the nuclear bombs men could ever explode in a hundred years!

He is "above all" in His power, above everything and everybody. Thank God for that truth!

4. Jesus "Above All" as a Teacher

I love to think of how Jesus is "above all" as a Teacher. These authorities, these hypocritical religious authorities, sent some officers one day to take Him (in our language today, arrest Him). When they came back without taking Him, without arresting Him, these authorities asked, "Why didn't you bring Him?"

They were told, "Never man spake like this man." In other words, "We heard Him teach."

As a Teacher, Jesus stands out above all teachers as a great palm tree in the desert of mediocrity. He shines above all teachers as a thousand-bulb chandelier above a little cluster of feeble and flickering candles. He flows among all teachers as a deep, crystal-clear river amid a little shallow, babbling and sometimes muddy brook.

He is the greatest Teacher the world has ever had, can ever have, or will ever have. And He said some things to us that we need to do and obey.

He taught in paradoxes. He taught us to live by dying. He taught us to get up by getting down, to win by losing, to hold on by letting go, to find our lives by losing our lives, to become rich by becoming poor, to be wise by being foolish in the eyes of the world. Have we learned that yet?

What are some of the things He said?

"*Judge not, that ye be not judged.*

"*For with what judgment ye judge, ye shall be judged: and with what measure ye mete, it shall be measured to you again.*

"*And why beholdest thou the mote that is in thy brother's eye, but considerest not the beam that is in thine own eye?...*

"*Thou hypocrite, first cast out the beam out of thine own eye; and then shalt thou see clearly to cast out the mote out of thy brother's eye.*"—Matt. 7:1-5.

Do we do that? Do we have a will to do His will?

Jesus said that "a man's life consisteth not in the abundance of the things which he possesseth." How many people believe that today? Just grab and get, get and grab; get all you can and can all you get. Get, get, get. There we go—old grabbers and getters, with absolute aloofness to the command of Jesus.

I ate breakfast in Oklahoma not so long ago with a man who has a four-thousand-acre ranch. I knew him when he was a ten-year-old boy in the first little church where I was pastor. Then he went to Oklahoma and became a several-times millionaire.

As we talked, he just talked money. I said, "Fred, do you ever talk about anything except money?"

His wife said, "Dr. Lee, I wish you would land on him. He goes to bed talking money, gets up talking money, and talks money all day."

He said, "Yeah, I talk money and I make money—a lot of it."

I said, "Fred, how much of this ground of these four thousand acres of your ranch is it going to take to bury you in? A whole acre to bury you?"

He looked at me rather startled.

I said, "Answer my question. How much of this ground of these four thousand acres is it going to take to bury you when you die? How much are you going to hold in your hands when you die?"

I startled him.

Yet a lot of people don't believe what Jesus said—"A man's life consisteth not in the abundance of the things which he possesseth."

Rich folks don't have anything on me. A rich man can wear but one suit at a time, and I can do that. He can ride in but one automobile at a time, and I can do that. He can fly in but one plane at a time, and I can do that. He can eat but one meal at a time, and I can do that. He can take but one bath at a time, and I can do all that.

Jesus said something about Hell. Some today don't believe there is a Hell, but Hell is just as much a part of God's love plan for His moral and spiritual universe for time and eternity as a sewage system and a cemetery are a part of the health plan of Chattanooga.

What did Jesus say?

"If thine eye offend thee, pluck it out: it is better for thee to enter into the kingdom of God with one eye, than having two eyes to be cast into hell fire [real fire]:

"Where their worm dieth not, and the fire is not quenched."— Mark 9:47, 48.

What did Jesus say?

"If thy hand offend thee, cut it off: it is better for thee to enter into life maimed, than having two hands to go into hell, into the fire [real fire] *that never shall be quenched."*—Vs. 43.

What did Jesus say?

"If thy foot offend thee, cut it off: it is better for thee to enter halt into life, than having two feet to be cast into hell, into the fire [real fire] *that never shall be quenched."*—Vs. 45.

I have never forgotten what I heard Dr. Torrey, that marvelous evangelist, say on one occasion:

> A man's usefulness or uselessness depends upon what he believes and the stand he takes on the facts of Hell. But a man who accepts that part of the Bible which he wants to accept and which he calls agreeable to his thinking, and rejects that part which he does not want to accept, in plain, unvarnished language, is a fool!

That's what I believe too.

An old grouch went up to Billy Sunday once and said, "I don't believe in a Hell."

Billy Sunday said, "You won't be there two minutes until you believe in one!"

Jesus said something else: "Bless them that curse you." How much do we put that into practice? "Do good to them which hate you." How often do we practice that? "Pray for them which despitefully use you." How often do we put Jesus' teaching as to that into practice?

I'm so glad that in Jesus' teaching they've never put any question marks after His blessed Word. The Old Testament Scriptures of our day were practical Old Testament Scriptures of His day. And knowing the end from the beginning, He knew what the New Testament would be, when it should be written under the power of the Holy Ghost, by men whom God moved with the Holy Ghost to write it. And He said, "Sanctify them through thy truth: thy word is truth." And He said, "Search the scriptures; for in them ye think ye have eternal life: and they are they which testify of me...for he [Moses] wrote of me."

Take Jesus out of this Book, and it's like taking heat out of fire, melody out of music, numbers out of mathematics, mind out of metaphysics, facts out of history, truth out of literature, brains out of the skull and expecting intelligence, and blood out of the body and expecting health.

He is the Theme of this Book! He never questioned any miracles of it.

He never said that Mary mistook the Angel Gabriel for a passing stranger, like some of these liberal teachers and preachers say today.

He never said that Methuselah's long age was incompatible with the physical structure, like some folks are taught to believe today.

He didn't say of Uzzah when he reached out his hand to touch the ark, which was carried on an oxcart (not the way to carry it), and was struck dead, "Maybe he died of a heart attack, or probably the cart turned over and crushed him"; as these modernists say.

I wrote a book, *Lord, I Believe,* when I was pastor of the First Baptist Church of New Orleans.

Some of the Tulane University students used to come hear me preach. Then they began to ask me up to what they called their student forum. They would let me talk only twenty minutes. Now that is a hard thing for me to do. They had a man with a stop watch, and if I went one second over twenty minutes, an old Chinese gong went bong, bong, bong, bong! They would shoot questions at me, and sometimes they kept me there an hour asking questions.

My book, *Lord, I Believe*, gives some of the questions asked me by those Tulane University students and the actual answers that I gave them.

They wanted to know where Cain got his wife. I told them I didn't know and didn't care. If she suited Cain, she suits me.

Then one beautiful, auburn-haired, green-eyed girl, very serious, said, "Dr. Lee, do you really believe a whale swallowed Jonah?"

I said, "Well, the Bible tells us that God prepared a big fish to swallow His runaway preacher. And if God can make a preacher, He can make a fish big enough to swallow him. And I want to tell you, if that fish had to hold down some of your professors for three days, it could never do it!"

I never make fun of anybody's face. But there was one young man with the biggest nose I had ever seen on a human face, and a tiny Hitler mustache beneath it. Of course, the mustache was small, because nothing can grow in the shade!

He came up to me with a supercilious sneer on that little Hitler mustache beneath the big nose and said, "Now, man-to-man, honest-to-God, do you believe Balaam's ass talked?"

I said, "Yes, I believe Balaam's ass talked. Being a female of the species, she had the advantage to start with." I continued: "Did you ever hear Madam Schumann-Heink sing?"

"No sir."

I said, "I did. I paid five dollars to hear her." It was worth more than five dollars to hear her sing "Silent Night" in German and English.

I asked, "Did you ever hear Caruso sing?"

"No sir."

"I did. I took my sweetheart to hear Caruso, that marvelous tenor, sing." I said, "I can take you to my house, and I can touch a little spring and start a white disk rolling, and we can hear Madam Schumann-Heink and Caruso come out of that wax just singing."

I told those students this incident:

While in New York in a Bible conference, I read in the paper where they were having a commemorative concert out at Alton Park. We went out to the park and sat there in a worshipful attitude. Nobody was hawking "Peanuts, peanut, peanuts...lemonade, lemonade," and such stuff.

You know what we did? We sat there for an hour and a half in a commemorative concert held in behalf of Mr. Caruso. And in that worshipful attitude, we heard a man who had been dead for thirty years sing for an hour and a half! And he was buried three thousand miles from where we were sitting!

Now, if a man can compress Caruso into the microscopic point of a needle, and make him sing an hour and a half thirty years after he is dead, do you think God Almighty would have any trouble making an old, flop-eared, water-eyed, Democratic donkey talk!

All of this Book I believe. Not some of it, not most of it, not a part of it, but *ALL* of it! Inspired in totality, the Miracle Book of diversity and unity of harmony and infinite complexity!

5. Jesus "Above All" in His Atoning Suffering

Jesus is "above all" in what He suffered on our behalf.

My favorite verse in the New Testament is II Corinthians 5:21: "For he hath made him to be sin for us, who knew no sin; that we might be made the righteousness of God in him."

Him—that is Jesus, who knew no sin—did God make to be sin in our behalf that we might become the righteousness of God in Him.

Meaning what? That on the cross Jesus became for us everything that God must judge, that we through faith and repentance might become everything that God cannot judge. He on the cross, Jesus, the perfect, the righteous One, was judged as unrighteous; that we, the unrighteous ones, through repentance and faith, might be judged as righteous.

It means that Jesus stood before God with *all* of our sins upon Himself that we through repentance and faith might stand before God with none of our sins upon ourselves.

It means that God ordered sin to execution in the body and soul of His own Son in our behalf that we might become what? cultured? educated? refined? No, "...the righteousness of God in him."

Think of drunkards, adulterers, thieves, liars becoming the righteousness of God. You can't tell a congregation any greater truth than this!

That Man suffered with two deaths on Calvary—physical death in His body; and spiritual death—absence from God. Yes, Jesus died two deaths for me—the physical death of the earthly body and the spiritual death when God turned His back on Him.

Jesus "above all" at the death. They never did stop until they killed Him. Old Death grabbed Him and wrote *Ichabod*—"Thy glory has departed"—above every claim that Jesus made.

Oh, this thing called death! Death! Death, whose only flowers are faded garlands on coffin lids. Death, whose only music is the sob of broken hearts. Death, whose only pleasure is found in the falling tears of the world.

Death entered my house last year and took from it its light. It made me know the loneliness of an empty house. It made me know the heartache of a vacant chair at the table. It made me know the loneliness of life—that sweet woman with whom I had lived for fifty-seven years.

And Death laid hold upon Jesus, but Death couldn't hold Him!

> **Up from the grave He arose,**
> **With a mighty triumph o'er His foes:...**
> **Hallelujah! Christ arose!**

Jesus said, "I am he that liveth, and was dead; and, behold, I am alive for evermore...and have the keys..."! And He does. And what He locks, nobody can unlock; and what He unlocks, nobody can lock. He is "above all"!

Let us put Him "above all" in our living, in our love, in our service. Let us put Jesus "above all"—the One to whom God has given "a name which is above every name"! Let's not just talk about it; let's do it. Let's put Him "above all."

BASCOM RAY LAKIN
1901–1984

ABOUT THE MAN:

On June 5, 1901, a baby boy was born to Mr. and Mrs. Richard Lakin in a farmhouse on Big Hurricane Creek in the hill country of Wayne County, West Virginia. Mrs. Lakin had prayed for a "preacher man" and had dedicated this baby to the Lord even before he was born.

Lakin was converted in a revival meeting at age 18. Following his conversion, he became a Baptist preacher. With a mule for transportation, he preached in small country churches in the mountains and hills of West Virginia and Kentucky. The transportation changed as well as the size of his congregations.

In 1939, he became associate pastor of Cadle Tabernacle, Indianapolis, and upon the death of founder Cadle, became pastor of that once great edifice of evangelism that seated 10,000 and had a choir loft of 1,400. Lakin preached to over 5,000 on Sunday mornings and half that many on Sunday nights.

Cadle Tabernacle had no memberships. It was a radio-preaching center broadcasting from coast to coast. In those fourteen years there, Ray Lakin became a household word across America.

In 1952, he entered full-time evangelism. His ministry carried him around the world, resulting in an estimated 100,000 conversions, and legion the number entering the ministry.

He was the preacher's friend, the church's helper, the common man's leader, and for sixty-five years, God's mighty messenger.

He was one of the most sought-after gospel preachers in America. On March 15, 1984, the last of the old-time evangelists took off for Glory. He would soon have been 83.

XIV.

The Lamb of God

B. R. LAKIN

"Behold the Lamb of God, which taketh away the sin of the world."—John 1:29.

John the Baptist's challenge, "Behold the Lamb of God," is universal and timeless. It was not just a command to the few hundred people gathered on the banks of the Jordan where John was baptizing; its challenge is just as fresh and clear today. The clarion voice of John echoes down the corridors of time and challenges men and women to 'Behold Him!'

Let us consider the subject of "The Lamb of God" under three divisions: The Work of the Lamb; The Worth of the Lamb; and The Wrath of the Lamb.

I. THE WORK OF THE LAMB

The substitutionary death of Christ on the cross was the world's greatest tragedy and Heaven's greatest triumph.

It was tragic that His trial was so unfair; that His arraignment was executed by an enraged, prejudiced mob; that the court was cowed and moved by the violence of mob psychology; that man's sin was so great that it demanded the sacrifice of the best that Heaven had for the worst that earth had.

But it was a triumph that Christ's death on the cross wrought redemption for the race, reconciled man to God, and bridged the gulf that separated earth from Heaven.

The death of the Lamb of God on the cross was not an accident but was foreordained of God and was an absolute *necessity*. He was "the Lamb slain from the foundation of the world" (Rev. 13:8). Before the world was formed, Christ agreed, at the request of God, to give His life for transgressors in the eventuality of sin in the proposed created world.

Had mankind never sinned, Christ would not have had to die. But sin came swiftly and surely to the race, and the Lamb of God was sacrificed upon the altar of Golgotha to atone, not for one man, not just a few men, but for the sins of the whole world.

But why did Jesus have to die? Study the Scriptures, and you will find three reasons why His death was a *necessity*.

1. It Was the Only Cure for Sin

Had there been any other way of removing sin from the race, God would not have allowed His only Son to die.

"All we like sheep have gone astray; we have turned every one to his own way; and the LORD *hath laid on him the iniquity of us all."*—Isa. 53:6.

It was the transgression of Israel that led them into bondage, but it was the Passover Lamb that brought about their deliverance. It is the age-old story of blundering, sinning man and a merciful, loving God. The necessity of Christ's death reveals the hideousness of sin.

Sin is universal. It lurks in the closets of the rich; it dwells in the filth-ridden houses of the poor. It makes its indelible mark upon the learned and leaves its stain upon the ignorant. It motivates the murderer, enslaves the addict and activates the alcoholic. It is the enemy of the home, the school and the church; and it seeks, by intrigue, to destroy them.

It courts the company of youth but having robbed them of their virtues, rejects them in old age. Its power is death-dealing, its purpose is to destroy, and its intent is to demolish.

It is a malignant growth in the mind of man, a cancer of the heart and leprosy of the soul. If neglected, the victim becomes morally weak, mentally unsound and spiritually dead.

It is the Mr. Hyde, dissipating the character. It is the voice of the sirens, luring the unsuspecting soul upon the rocks of destruction. Sin is radioactive, blighting and killing all with whom it comes in contact.

It was because of the destructive power of sin that Christ, the Lamb, had to die. God, in His infinite mercy and love, simply could not stand idly by and see mankind ravaged by sin. His only recourse was the Lamb; His only remedy was the blood; and His only alternative was to give His only Son.

2. It Was the Only Means of Reconciliation

"That he might be a merciful and faithful high priest in things pertaining to God, to make reconciliation for the sins of the people."—Heb. 2:17.

Christ, the Lamb, was the great Arbitrator, settling by His own death, forever, the differences between God and man. With His hands stretching out in two opposite directions, He brings wayward man and an estranged God together.

His triumphant death upon Calvary canceled forever the power of sin to damn humanity, for there He took upon Himself the penalty that belonged to mankind.

"But he was wounded for our transgressions, he was bruised for our iniquities: the chastisement of our peace was upon him; and with his stripes we are healed."—Isa. 53:5.

A condemned man sits in his cell awaiting the fateful day of his execution. He hears the clank of the steel door as the warden permits a stranger to enter the cell. "We haven't time to lose," says the stranger. "I am the king's son, and I have heard of your plight. My heart goes out in pity for you, for you have a family who need you. I have come to exchange clothes and places with you. You are a free man; I will die in your place."

The prisoner, bewildered, almost believing it to be a dream, quickly obeys the command of the prince. In the attire of the prince, he walks out of the death house a free man, and the prince dies upon the gallows that were built for him.

This story, perhaps inadequate in many ways, shows in a small way what Christ did when He took our place upon the cross. He died the death that belonged to us. He carried the cross that belonged to Barabbas, the condemned murderer and thief. Since the law says that a penalty for sin can only be exacted once, we, through His death, are free men—reconciled to God.

3. It Was the Only Method of Redemption

"For thou wast slain, and hast redeemed us to God by thy blood."—Rev. 5:9.

Redemption is the purchase price of a slave. Humanity, lured by the deceptive devices of Satan, had passed from the merciful watchcare of God to the diabolical bondage of Satan. The race which God had created for His own fellowship had fallen, by error, into the possession of the Devil. A great price was demanded, much greater than man could pay, but not greater than God could provide. It was then that "he gave his only begotten Son, that whosoever believeth in him should not perish, but have everlasting life."

The forces of sin, of which Satan is the head, and the forces of righteousness, which God commands, are waged in gigantic combat.

In war there is a device known as an "exchange of prisoners." Oftentimes an officer of high rank is exchanged for scores, or perhaps hundreds, of ordinary soldiers who are held by the enemy.

Christ, the Captain of our salvation, was turned over to the forces of Satan during His trial and death on Calvary, and Satan was allowed to do with Him what he would.

He was spat upon, mocked, beaten, cursed and finally killed. But in exchange for that, Satan was compelled to release all who looked upon Him as Saviour. It was the exchange of the One for the many, the sacrifice of the "worthy Lamb" for the erring race.

And it was a redemption prompted by love. The Word says, "God commendeth his love toward us, in that, while we were yet sinners, Christ died for us."

So great was that love that even the fluent language of the eloquent Paul was beggared to describe it. But we see it etched in the deep furrows of pain in the Saviour's face. We see it written in the sand at the base of the cross where the blood formed the letters of red. We see it written upon the dark clouds in letters of jagged lightning as Christ's life ebbed slowly away upon the cross.

Yes, it was redemption in process as the Saviour paid the purchase price for the ransom of Satan's slaves at the counter of divine sacrifice.

"For if the blood of bulls and of goats, and the ashes of an heifer sprinkling the unclean, sanctifieth to the purifying of the flesh:

"How much more shall the blood of Christ, who through the eternal Spirit offered himself without spot to God, purge your

conscience from dead works to serve the living God?"—Heb. 9:13,14.

II. THE WORTH OF THE LAMB

"Worthy is the Lamb that was slain to receive power, and riches, and wisdom, and strength, and honour, and glory, and blessing."—Rev. 5:12.

No other person in Heaven or earth was qualified to 'take away the sin of the world' but Jesus, the Lamb of God.

He was morally worthy, for He was a Lamb without spot or blemish. His immaculate life was tangible proof of His virgin birth. His sinless perfection qualified Him to be the perfect Saviour of sinners. Even His most severe critics, the Pharisees, said, "Never man spake like this man." Pilate, His civil judge, said, "I find no fault in this man."

He was worthy in His power. The winds and the waves obeyed His authoritative commands and nestled meekly, like subdued slaves, at His feet. The water at the marriage feast at Cana blushed red when He looked upon its face, and was transformed into wine at His command. Disease fled before Him as wild beasts before a safari. Demons were subject unto Him, and they recognized His authority by calling him Son of God.

He was worthy in His wisdom. He amazed the scholars of His time with His profound reasoning and answers to their difficult questions. He confounded the Pharisees who sought to confuse Him with their trick questions. His wise words have been preserved for the centuries, and no man born of woman is worthy to be compared to Him in His wisdom.

Isaiah said of Him: "And the spirit of the Lord shall rest upon him, the spirit of wisdom and understanding, the spirit of counsel and might, the spirit of knowledge and of the fear of the Lord" (Isa. 11:2).

He was worthy in His compassion. "When he saw the multitudes, he was moved with compassion on them, because they fainted, and were scattered abroad, as sheep having no shepherd" (Matt. 9:36).

The word *compassion* carries a meaning far greater than sentimental love. The word comes from two Latin words: *cum*, meaning "with," and *passio*, meaning "to suffer." Hence, *compassion* means "to suffer with."

We have all been moved by emotions akin to compassion. When we stand beside a friend who has lost a loved one, words come hard as our hearts bleed for him. When we see a helpless child with a broken arm or broken leg, and his face is twisted in agony, we long to share that suffering as we have compassion upon him. It is an entering into the suffering of another.

The miracles of healing performed by Jesus were not mere "showy" efforts to prove His divinity but demonstrations of His compassion.

He had compassion upon the multitudes and fed them.

He had compassion upon the leper and healed him.

He had compassion upon the widow of Nain who had lost her son, and He raised her son from the dead.

He loved Lazarus who had died, and at His command Lazarus came forth from the grave.

It was His compassion for the lost which caused Jesus to give His life upon Calvary.

Paul wrote: "And walk in love, as Christ also hath loved us, and hath given himself for us an offering and a sacrifice to God for a sweetsmelling savour" (Eph. 5:2).

"Worthy is the Lamb," is the theme of Revelation. "Worthy is the Lamb that was slain to receive...." He was the great Giver of life, light, healing and hope; but in the day of "his appearing," He will be the Receiver. He, and He alone, is worthy to receive power, riches, wisdom, strength, honor, glory and blessing. All of these He bestowed upon others; in the day of reward they will all be given unto Him.

III. THE WRATH OF THE LAMB

"And [they] said to the mountains and rocks, Fall on us, and hide us from the face of him that sitteth on the throne, and from the wrath of the Lamb:

"For the great day of his wrath has come; and who shall be able to stand?"—Rev. 6:16, 17.

We are living in the day of grace. It affords opportunity for all to be saved by looking to the Lamb of God.

But there is another day on God's calendar which is sure to come—the day of wrath. It is an unpleasant truth to a "stiffnecked" generation, but it is a truth that cannot be lightly ignored, for it is just as surely woven into the warp and woof of God's Word as the doctrine of His love.

Unrequited love may be spurned, ignored and insulted until its patience is exhausted and its tender love is transformed into justified wrath.

Rationalists, humanists and modernists have tried to discredit the doctrine of judgment and divine retribution, but the Bible anticipated the efforts of such:

"Let no man deceive you with vain words: for because of these things cometh the wrath of God upon the children of disobedience."—Eph. 5:6.

Jesus spoke graphically of the day of wrath:

"And when the king came in to see the guests, he saw there a man which had not on a wedding garment:

"And he said unto him, Friend, how camest thou in hither not having a wedding garment? And he was speechless.

"Then said the king to the servants, Bind him hand and foot, and take him away, and cast him into outer darkness; there shall be weeping and gnashing of teeth."—Matt. 22:11-13.

The Lamb, who was worthy to be slain, has provided the white robes of righteousness for all who trust Him. And those who do not have the robes of acceptance will be subject to His wrath in that awful day.

"These are they which came out of great tribulation, and have washed their robes, and made them white in the blood of the Lamb."—Rev. 7:14.

> **Have you been to Jesus for the cleansing pow'r?**
> **Are you washed in the blood of the Lamb?**
> **Are you fully trusting in His grace this hour?**
> **Are you washed in the blood of the Lamb?**

"Behold the Lamb of God"! Look to Him! Believe on Him! He alone can take away the sin of the world. Your excuses, alibis and apologies will not avail in the day of His wrath. Now is the accepted time. Today is the day of salvation.

The prayer of those who reject the Lamb in that day will be a godless prayer:

"And [they] said to the mountains and rocks, Fall on us, and hide us from the face of him that sitteth on the throne, and from the wrath of the Lamb."—Rev. 6:16.

"The same shall drink of the wine of the wrath of God, which is poured out without mixture into the cup of his indignation; and he shall be tormented with fire and brimstone in the presence of the holy angels, and in the presence of the Lamb:

"And the smoke of their torment ascendeth up for ever and ever."—Rev. 14:10, 11.

But those who have made their robes white in the blood of the Lamb:

"They shall hunger no more, neither thirst any more; neither shall the sun light on them, nor any heat.

"For the Lamb which is in the midst of the throne shall feed them, and shall lead them unto living fountains of waters: and God shall wipe away all tears from their eyes."—Rev. 7:16, 17.

The reward is great for those who accept God's estimate of their sin and His Substitute, the Lamb of God, as their Saviour from sin. But the wrath of God will rest upon those who reject the Lamb.

As the Word says:

"He that believeth on the Son hath everlasting life: and he that believeth not the Son shall not see life; but the wrath of God abideth on him."—John 3:36.

ROBERT L. MOYER
1886–1944

ABOUT THE MAN:

Dr. Moyer was an evangelist from 1915 to 1920, then became pastor of the United Brethren Church in Minneapolis. Later Dr. W. B. Riley asked him to become his assistant at First Baptist Church, Minneapolis. When Dr. Riley retired from the pastorate in 1942, Dr. Moyer then became pastor and served in that capacity until his death.

Dr. Moyer was long dean of Northwestern Bible School, and the author of several books.

Dr. H. A. Ironside said:

> Few men have the winsomeness and tenderness combined with sound scriptural teaching that characterizes the ministry of my esteemed friend and fellow-laborer, Dr. Robert L. Moyer.

XV.

Our Solitary Saviour

ROBERT L. MOYER

"He was...alone."—Matt. 14:23.

Our Saviour is none other than Emmanuel—"God with us." Nineteen hundred years ago God walked and talked with men as Jesus Christ. There is no question concerning the deity of Jesus Christ. Of Him it is written, "This is the true God" (I John 5:20).

But Jesus Christ is also man. We read of Him, "The Word was God," and "The Word was made flesh, and dwelt among us" (John 1:1,14). He became a partaker of flesh and blood; He took upon Himself our nature; He became one of us (Heb. 2:14–18).

The incarnation was by way of the virgin birth. God sent forth His Son, made of a woman, to be born in a stall and cradled in a manger. He was a baby, a boy, a man. He was subject to all the sinful infirmities of the human race. He slept, He walked, He ate, He drank, He worked, He sorrowed—just as we do.

In the text it is stated that "he was...alone." This has reference to Him alone in the mountain, praying. But that text might be written over the whole of His earthly life, for He was lonely, solitary. That is one of the peculiarities of His humanity. Someone, in commenting on it, said, "His was the solitude of the royal stranger who tarries for a night."

In this study we shall see that from the manger to the cross He was alone; that through His whole life there ran a deep, silent, sad undercurrent of loneliness.

I. HE WAS SOLITARY IN HIS SINGULARITY

Jesus Christ is unique. He is the only One of His kind. There has been and there is none other like Him. There has never been, nor will there ever be, another incarnation. There has been but one God-Man.

It is not right to say that Jesus Christ was a good man, a great man, a great leader, a great teacher. He was all that, of course, but more. He was human, yet He was God. There was in Him a duality of nature, yet a singleness of person. Two persons did not dwell in one body—make no mistake about that. There were two natures, not two persons. Into union with His divine personality, God took a human nature, to become the Solitary One; for He was never paralleled by any created person. He is far separated from the human race. He was in the midst of death, the Living One. He was in the midst of darkness, the Light of the World. He was in the midst of sin, the Holy One.

It is possible to be surrounded by human beings and still be alone.

On my first visit to New York City, I went alone. In that city I was surrounded by five or six million people—yet I was alone. (Sometimes folk laughingly say, "Well, if I do go to Hell, I'll have lots of company." Yes—and you'll be alone.)

I saw a Chinese man on the streets today—a man in the midst of men, yet solitary. He was away from his land, away from his home and away from his kind. He was alone.

But what can a finite illustration do to bring to us the thought of Christ surrounded by man, yet alone; alone, because no other being of His kind ever existed?

II. HE WAS SOLITARY IN HIS SINLESSNESS

Someone has described Jesus Christ as a "white Rose in the midst of a bed of scarlet poppies."

Isn't that a vivid picture of our Saviour in the midst of the sinful men of this world? He had nothing in common with them. It was true then, as now, that "the whole world lieth in wickedness." How His sensitive soul must have shrunk from the blasphemy, sin and hypocrisy of His day! His stainless purity could have no fellowship with the wrongs, sins, impurities and shames of this earth. His own disciples wounded Him again and again. In a very true sense of the word, He had no companions.

Men could not be His companions, for they were impure, while He is pure; their aspirations were unholy, while His are always holy; their hearts were full of hate, while His is full of love.

Think how lonely a saint would be in Hell! Yet loneliness such as that is not comparable to the loneliness of our Lord while on earth. He was alone in His sinlessness.

III. HE WAS SOLITARY IN HIS LOVE

Jesus Christ loved men, but they did not love Him. "They hated me without a cause," was His declaration. He called to men, "Come unto me," but "He came unto his own, and his own received him not." The leaders of His nation—His own nation—derided Him and cried out, 'It is not fit that such a fellow should live. Away with Him! Crucify Him!' His own denied Him, forsook Him and sold Him.

I have often imagined Christ walking the highways and byways of His own land, His eager eyes scanning each face that He met for some sign of recognition. But He was in the world, and the world knew Him not.

When my boy was a baby, I came home every two or three weeks from some evangelistic trip. I remember how I walked to the crib where he was lying—my boy—to look down into those blue eyes, longing for some sign of recognition. He was my own, yet he gave no sign of recognition whatsoever. How often I turned away from that crib to say, "Oh, he doesn't know me." He was my own, but he didn't know me. That brings grief to the heart of a man.

There isn't anything more depressing or that makes a heart heavier than to long for those whom you love, only to find them beyond reach or out of touch.

This was impressed upon me recently when I went into the home of a man over ninety years of age who had, just a few months before, buried away from his sight, like Abraham of old, the wife of his bosom. She had been a wife to him. She had made a home for him. She had been a companion to him. Now she was gone.

He was ill. In weakness he sat in his chair that day and said to me, "Brother Moyer, I don't want to stay." Then in his weakness he broke into tears and, unable to speak, pointed with a shaking finger to the wall where hung her picture.

I knew that he longed to be with the one he loved. His heart reached out after her, but she was beyond his reach.

Yet never in all the history of the race did one yearn after a loved one as Christ yearned after men. Full of loneliness is that wail, that sad, sad wail, 'O Jerusalem, Jerusalem! How oft I would have gathered you together, but you would not!'

The very men whom He loved, instead of coming to Him, instead of loving Him, spat upon Him, smote Him, thorn-crowned Him, mocked Him and crucified Him. Oh, the heartache of it! How lonely He was!

And He has the same yearning over men today. He still calls to men, "Come unto Me," and men still refuse to come.

Is His heart still yearning for you? Is He still the solitary Saviour, the lonely Lord, as far as you are concerned?

IV. HE WAS SOLITARY IN HIS MISSION

There was a dullness of the human intellect, a deadness of the human heart with reference to the mission of our Saviour. He knew His mighty task, but no one else seemed to comprehend it. When He was born they called His name Jesus, because He was to save His people from their sins, but that seemed to men nothing, even to His dear ones.

All through His life His eye was on the cross. When He spoke of His "Father's business," He referred to the cross. When He mentioned "mine hour," He had in mind the cross. From the beginning He knew the awful climax of His earthly career: that of agony, anguish, shame, pain beyond human description.

If some of us knew the future, the responsibility would break us; we would be overwhelmed; some would go insane. The only hope for us, did some of us know the future, would be in the companionship and fellowship of those who love us. But He had no one who understood. He was alone. His heart must have yearned for sympathy, but He found none.

He was misunderstood at every step. His own people were blind to His mission. They thought only of temporal glory, not of redemption. They knew that their Scriptures declared of their Messiah, "The government shall be upon his shoulder" (Isa. 9:6). He would "dash them [His enemies] in pieces like a potter's vessel" (Ps. 2:9).

But here was this Man Jesus, called the Christ, 'tis true, yet walking through the dust of the land while the enemy rode in chariots, with nowhere to lay His head while the enemy dwelt in palaces. So they laughed Him to scorn and cried out, "Away with Him!" Finally they condemned Him as an impostor and nailed Him to the cursed tree.

Even His own disciples were disappointed in Him. They shared the hopes of their people and expected Him to go to the throne of David in the overthrow of Rome. Then when He told them that He must suffer, that He must be killed, Peter rebuked Him and cried out, "Be it far from thee, Lord: this shall not be unto thee" (Matt. 16:22).

And beyond this, even His mother, who knew of His supernatural birth and sinless years, did not seem to understand His course. It seems that she joined with others in considering Him "beside himself" (Mark 3:21).

It was all of this misunderstanding and rejection, this loneliness, which culminated in the cross, which inspired the poet to write, "He died of a broken heart."

V. HE WAS SOLITARY IN HIS SUFFERING

Go to Gethsemane. See Him in the travail of His soul. See the agony and bloody sweat. Hear Him cry out to His Father. Oh, how He needed sympathy that night! How He longed for the disciples to watch with Him for a little while! And they were asleep! He was alone. They did not comprehend the agony which shook His soul. He was alone.

Then, when He stepped out from beneath the shadow of the olive trees, He was betrayed by one of His familiar friends—betrayed with a kiss! Then they all forsook Him and fled! And then Peter—Peter!—took an oath that he had never known this Man Jesus!

What a scene! The Friend of men stood without a friend! He was alone. He stood alone before the high priest, with no one to protest the indignities offered Him. He stood alone before Pilate, with not a single one to speak a single word in His defense. Oh, one did carry His cross, but only because he was compelled to do so.

Then when they nailed Him to the tree, what friendly hearts there may have been were lost in the crowd, and He was confronted on every hand by the face of a foe. The crowd milled round the cross—the priests wagging their heads, the rabble mocking and reviling, the multitude shouting—all with hard, unmoistened faces waiting to see the end, watching to see Him die. There was no cry of sympathy anywhere. He was alone.

Oh! if that were all, it might not be so bad, for others have endured pain, agony and persecution. But—He was forsaken of God! That is the meaning of that strange cry that pierced the air, "My God, my God, why hast thou forsaken me?" (Matt. 27:46). Even God forsook Him.

No angel came to help Him. Earth clenched her fist at Him. And Heaven was shut up against Him. There was no look of love, no word of hope, no hand to help from either earth or Heaven. Around about, enemies shouted hatred at Him; above, God turned away from Him. He was alone. The dense darkness that came at midday seemed to declare and intensify His loneliness, for it cut Him off from everyone, from everything. He was left to Himself.

There has never been, in all the annals of the human race, such solitude as this.

When the three Hebrew children were thrust into the fiery furnace, the king saw walking with them in the flame the Son of God. They were not alone.

An early Christian martyr was taken by the cruel hands of torture, to have flesh rent and bones broken, in an effort to make him deny his faith. When he was left, he was a mass of bleeding flesh and broken bones. Yet he endured all the suffering without a single cry. When his dear ones found him and sobbed over him, they said, "How did you stand it all without a single cry or complaint?" He answered simply, "Jesus was with me." He was not alone.

But our Lord on the cross was denied the comforting presence of God. He was alone. He wrestled, prayed, sorrowed, suffered and died alone.

AND OUR SIN MADE IT SO. The sinless One on the cross was made to be sin for us. He "bare our sins in his own body on the tree." He was made a "curse for us." He was there "smitten of God, and afflicted" in our room and stead. He bore what we deserved. He alone died for us because He alone could do it. Hebrews says, "When he had by himself purged our sins"—and it must be "by himself," for it could be by no other one. No other person could do it, not even the one who loves you most.

That is why He was alone in the work of redemption. He alone bore our iniquity. He alone bore the curse of God. He alone bore the wrath against sin. He alone could do it, so He was alone in it.

VI. HE IS NOT NOW SOLITARY

We believe that now our Saviour is in Heaven, surrounded by multitudes of men and women who are absent from the body and at Home with Him—because He died alone. Isaiah may have meant something like this when he wrote of the time when "he shall see his seed." Paul tells of the bringing of many sons unto glory. God has always desired to surround Himself with men.

A blessed intimacy existed between God and man in Eden—an intimacy marred by sin. God dwelt in the midst of His people Israel in the Tabernacle and later, in the temple. God dwelt in the midst of men in the day of His flesh. He will dwell again in the midst of His people in the millennium.

God's purpose will one day be *fully realized* and *gratified* in the eternal state, in that day when all Heaven and earth shall be gathered round Him, and when He shall be all in all. That purpose might be expressed in the words:

"The tabernacle of God is with men, and he will dwell with them, and they shall be his people, and God himself shall be with them, and be their God."—Rev. 21:3.

> **It was alone the Saviour prayed**
> **In dark Gethsemane;**
> **Alone He drained the bitter cup**
> **And suffered there for me.**
>
> **It was alone the Saviour stood**
> **In Pilate's judgment hall;**
> **Alone the crown of thorns He wore,**
> **Forsaken thus by all.**
>
> **Alone upon the cross He hung**
> **That others He might save;**
> **Forsaken then by God and man,**
> **Alone, His life He gave.**
>
> **Can you reject such matchless love?**
> **Can you His claim disown?**
> **Come, give your all in gratitude,**
> **Nor leave Him thus alone.**

JOHN R. RICE
1895–1980

ABOUT THE MAN:

Preacher...evangelist...revivalist...editor...counselor to the thousands...friend to millions—that was Dr. John R. Rice, whose accomplishments were nothing short of miraculous. Known as "America's Dean of Evangelists," Dr. Rice made a mighty impact upon the nation's religious life for some sixty years, in great citywide campaigns and in Sword of the Lord Conferences.

At age nine, after hearing a sermon on the Prodigal Son, John went forward to claim Christ as Saviour. In 1916, with only $9.35 in his pocket, he rode off on his cowpony toward Decatur Baptist College. He was now on the road to becoming a world-renowned evangelist, although he was then totally unaware of God's will for his life.

There was many a twist and turn before Rice rode through the open door into full-time preaching—the army, marriage, graduate work, more seminary, assistant pastor, pastor—then FINALLY, where God planned to use him most—in full-time evangelism.

Dr. Rice and his ministry were always colorful (born in Cooke County in Texas, December 11, 1895, he was often called the "Will Rogers of the Pulpit" because of their likeness and mannerisms)—and controversial. CONTROVERSIAL—and correctly so—because of his intense stand against modernism and infidelity and his fight for the fundamentals.

Dr. Rice lived and died a man of convictions—intense convictions. But like many other strong fighters for the Faith, Rice was also marked with a sincere spirit of compassion. Those who knew him best knew a man who loved them. In preaching, in prayer and in personal life, Rice wept over sinners and with saints. But there is more...

Less than seventy-one hours before the dawning of 1981, one of the most prolific pens in all Christendom was stilled. Dr. John R. Rice left behind a legacy in writing of more than 200 titles, with a combined circulation of over 61 million copies. And through October of 1981, a total of 24,058 precious souls reported trusting Christ through his ministries, not counting those saved in his crusades nor in foreign countries where his literature has been translated.

And who but God knows the influence of THE SWORD OF THE LORD magazine which he started and edited for forty-six years!

And while "Twentieth Century's Mightest Pen"—and man—has been stilled, thank God, the fruit remains! Though dead, he continues to speak.

XVI.

Facing the Pierced Jesus

JOHN R. RICE

When the Lord Jesus died on the cross, the soldiers thrust a spear into His side, and there came out blood and water. And thereby hangs a tale, with tender and profound and beautiful lessons from the Word of God.

In John 19:30–37 the story is told as follows:

"When Jesus therefore had received the vinegar, he said, It is finished: and he bowed his head, and gave up the ghost.

"The Jews therefore, because it was the preparation, that the bodies should not remain upon the cross on the sabbath day, (for that sabbath day was an high day,) besought Pilate that their legs might be broken, and that they might be taken away.

"Then came the soldiers, and brake the legs of the first, and of the other which was crucified with him.

"But when they came to Jesus, and saw that he was dead already, they brake not his legs:

"But one of the soldiers with a spear pierced his side, and forthwith came there out blood and water.

"And he that saw it bare record, and his record is true: and he knoweth that he saith true, that ye might believe.

"For these things were done, that the scripture should be fulfilled, A bone of him shall not be broken.

"And again another scripture saith, They shall look on him whom they pierced."

Men are guilty of the death of Christ. In their wicked hearts they hated Him and planned to kill Him, and did.

Peter said in Acts 2:23, "Him, being delivered by the determinate counsel and foreknowledge of God, ye have taken, and by wicked hands have crucified and slain."

Again in Acts 3:15 Peter said that they had "killed the Prince of life."

But it was significant that in Acts 5:30 Peter again said that God raised up Jesus, "whom ye slew and hanged on a tree."

Actually they killed Jesus before they crucified Him. They were guilty of His death long before He died.

Yet, in a sense, nobody killed Jesus. He Himself "gave up the ghost." Jesus could not die without His own consent. Many a time they had tried to kill Him but could not. Jesus said:

"I lay down my life, that I might take it again.

"No man taketh it from me, but I lay it down of myself."—John 10:17, 18.

So when the time came, Jesus said, "It is finished," and gave up the ghost.

It was finished. Jesus had suffered the torment of the damned soul who cannot see the face of God. Fulfilling the prophecy of Psalm 22:1, Jesus had cried, "My God, my God, why hast thou forsaken me?" Yet He knew why God had forsaken Him. It was because all the sins of the world were piled upon Him, and He was tasting death for every man. Now at last the Father's face was averted no more! Divine justice had been satisfied completely; now God the Father could turn and smile at His own Son again!

Suffering as a lost sinner ought to suffer in Hell, Jesus had addressed God as "My God, my God." But now that the price was paid, now that the veil of the temple was rent in the midst, opening fully the way from man to God, Jesus had spoken to God again. But this time He called Him "Father": "Father, into thy hands I commend my spirit: and having said thus, he gave up the ghost" (Luke 23:46). Divine wrath had smitten its target, divine justice had been satisfied, and Christ could again call God "Father." It was finished!

In some sense, the wrath of man is finished. Even the Pharisees and scribes who hated Jesus with pitiless hatred have had enough. For six hours they have seen Him suffer. They saw Him beaten with a Roman scourge, saw Him nailed to a Roman cross after the common rabble had spit in His face and plucked out His beard, blindfolded Him and slapped Him until His face was so marred that He did not look like a man.

They had seen the mocking crown of thorns on His head; seen

the agony of the long hours of torture. When Jesus said, "I thirst," someone smeared bitter gall and vinegar upon the parched lips and bruised face.

They knew no other way to make Him suffer. Even man's horrible hatred for Christ had done all it knew to do. It was finished!

Now Jesus, with a loud cry, dropped His head upon His breast and gave up His spirit. The stupendous tragedy now was done, except for a last detail. "Without shedding of blood is no remission"; so the blood of the God-Man, the Lamb of God that taketh away the sin of the world, must be poured out for man's sin.

A soldier, not knowing what he did nor why, took a spear and thrust it into His side, into the very heart of Jesus; and there poured out a saving flood of blood and water.

Now with reverent hearts and unshod feet, let us consider two great themes in this Scripture: first, the piercing of Jesus, why it was and what it meant; second, who will face the pierced Saviour. Remember, the text said, "They shall look on him whom they pierced."

I. THE PIERCING OF JESUS

These short verses have much to tell us. How weighty they are with meaning!

1. Christ must be taken down from the cross, for the High Sabbath began at sundown. These scribes, elders and Pharisees who demanded the crucifixion of Jesus and watched Him die were scrupulously religious. They did not mind crucifying the Son of God, the Saviour of the world, but they must strictly observe their ceremonial laws!

Many today will not eat meat on Friday or during Lent, yet they trample under their feet the blood of Christ by not accepting Him as personal Saviour! Many have been christened and confirmed and go to church on Easter who have never repented of their sins nor been born again! Many attend mass or confession but are as certainly unconverted, as certainly rejecters of Jesus Christ, as these same religious Pharisees who crucified Him!

"We have had our vengeance," they seemed to say; "now break the legs of Jesus and those of the two thieves. It will be as painful a way as possible to finish them off. We must have them off the crosses by sundown, for sundown begins our annual High Sabbath. We cannot have that great day defiled by the public display of these hated men with bloody and flyblown backs, with inflamed wounds and tortured faces. Break their legs and get them down!"

The day when Jesus was crucified "was the preparation," that is, the day of preparation for the Passover feast. It was the fourteenth day of Nisan, the first month of the Jewish calendar, when every family in the nation (or two small families together) were to kill the Passover lamb and prepare it for eating in the evening. (Read the story in Exodus, chapters 12 to 18.)

When Jesus died, the Jewish nation had been observing this annual Passover feast for fifteen hundred years. Every year on the fourteenth day of Nisan, whatever the day of the week, each family would kill its Passover lamb in midafternoon. The lamb would be roasted whole with fire and eaten that night with bitter herbs in memory of the Passover night when the children of Israel came out of Egypt, and looking forward to the coming Saviour, God's Passover Lamb, who would deliver all who would trust Him from the bondage of sin and Satan.

The Jewish day began at sundown. Sundown would begin the fifteenth day of Nisan. The Passover lamb would be eaten, and that evening would begin the seven days' feast of unleavened bread.

That approaching fifteenth day of Nisan was a High Sabbath; that is, not a weekly Sabbath, Saturday, but an annual Sabbath.

"And this day shall be unto you for a memorial; and ye shall keep it a feast to the LORD throughout your generations; ye shall keep it a feast by an ordinance for ever."—Exod. 12:14.

Seven days they were to eat unleavened bread.

"And in the first day there shall be an holy convocation, and in the seventh day there shall be an holy convocation to you; no manner of work shall be done in them, save that which every man must eat, that only may be done of you."—Vs. 16.

It was a Sabbath day; that is, a day of rest—the annual Sabbath when the Passover lamb would be eaten and when the feast of unleavened bread would begin. Hence, the Jewish leaders demanded that Christ and the two thieves should be taken down from the crosses.

It becomes clear that Christ Himself did not eat the Passover lamb. Jesus ate a certain Passover meal with them, as we read in Luke 22:8,15. But it was simply a preliminary meal of the day of preparation, which began at sundown, the day before Jesus was crucified. In that meal they ate bread and drank wine or grape juice and did not eat the Passover lamb.

The reason Jesus did not eat the Passover lamb was that He *was* the Passover Lamb, and He had to die at the very time appointed for the slaying of the Passover lambs throughout the nation.

For fifteen hundred years all the Jews had been following the clear instructions of the Lord that the Passover lambs should be slain on the fourteenth day of Nisan. How strange it would be if God had sent this prophecy down for so many centuries, then had His Son, His Passover Lamb, die on the wrong day! God forbid!

No, that midafternoon when Jesus died, it was the very time for the slaying of Passover lambs, the time foretold in prophecy, the time observed for fifteen centuries.

That leads me to say further that the fourteenth day of Nisan, when Jesus died, must have been Wednesday afternoon. Our Catholic friends think Jesus was crucified on Friday because it is said that the next day was a Sabbath day. But I believe they are mistaken. The Sabbath here mentioned in John 19:31 was not the weekly Sabbath on Saturday, but the annual Sabbath, which, this year, I think, came on Thursday.

Jesus Himself had foretold:

"For as Jonas was three days and three nights in the whale's belly; so shall the Son of man be three days and three nights in the heart of the earth."—Matt. 12:40.

I am familiar with all the arguments; but I do not see how, if Jesus were crucified on Friday and in the grave only two nights and one day, this Scripture could have been fulfilled.

Dr. R. A. Torrey has so well explained that Jesus could be in the grave some more than seventy-two hours and fulfill the prophecy that He was "three days and three nights in the heart of the earth," but it seems impossible that He could fulfill the Scripture in less than seventy-two hours.

Hence, we believe that Christ died Wednesday afternoon. Sometime Wednesday night—allowing for the cleansing of the body, anointing with spices and wrapping in fine linen, and the solemn interment in Joseph's new tomb—Jesus was buried. Then Thursday and Friday and Saturday Jesus was in the grave—three days and three nights—and then He arose, fulfilling the Scripture to the letter.

The only reason men can ever believe He was crucified on Friday is that the following day is said to have been a Sabbath. But since it was the annual Sabbath, which would come on a different day each year, there is no reason to suppose the crucifixion was not on Wednesday, which would fulfill the Scriptures to the letter.

Besides, if Jesus were crucified on Friday, there is no account in the Gospels of His activities on certain days of that week.

The anxious haste of the Pharisees to get Him down from the cross led to the piercing of the Saviour which was foretold in prophecy.

2. Why were His bones not broken, as the Jewish leaders intended? "The Jews, therefore...besought Pilate that their legs might be broken."

I suppose the soldiers took the Roman battle-ax and chopped at the propped-up knees and thighs of the two tormented thieves, until they were broken. And those thieves, perhaps with curses on the one hand and moans on the other hand, died of the shock and agony and the loss of blood.

Then the soldier turns to the Saviour on the middle cross to do the same task. Will they desecrate further the holy body? Perhaps Mary sobs afresh; the lips of John the beloved move in stony misery. Even the gaping crowd, strangely moved, watches to see them break the bones of the Lamb of God.

Surely all the angels in Heaven look on with trembling horror as they start to break His legs. I think that demons in the air or fallen angels in Hell are grinning in anticipation. The weight of all the souls in the universe, for a moment, depends upon that gleaming ax—for if they break the bones of Jesus, then He cannot save anybody. There will be no Gospel to preach, the Scripture has not been fulfilled, God's plan has failed, and there is no Saviour for sinners! Long ago it had been prophesied of the Saviour that "a bone of him shall not be broken." If Christ's legs are broken, He is not the promised Messiah; His death is not according to the Scriptures.

The twelfth chapter of Exodus and the ninth of Numbers give many detailed commands about the Passover lamb, which pictured Christ. It must be a male lamb, since Christ is man. It must be a lamb of the first year, in its prime, since Christ died about the age of thirty-three. It must be without spot or blemish to picture the sinless Saviour. It must be roasted with fire without water, because Christ had no water when He was thirsting on the cross. The rich man in Hell could not get even a drop of water to cool his tongue; and there is no alleviation of the torments of the damned which Christ tasted for all. The roasted lamb was to be eaten with bitter herbs picturing Christ's sufferings.

Then Numbers 9:12 commands, "They shall leave none of it unto the morning, nor break any bone of it." Now for fifteen centuries the Israelites had roasted their lambs whole—head, legs and all—and not a bone could be broken and maintain the type. Now if Jesus has His bones broken, He is not the promised Passover Lamb, and all of God's plans for saving the world through Him would fall through.

Oh, how eagerly all the hosts of Heaven must have looked down when the soldiers started to break the legs of the Lord Jesus!

What is the Gospel by which we are saved? It is not simply that Christ died for us; that is good news, but that is not all of it. It is that He died and rose again. The Gospel that Paul preached is given in the inspired language of I Corinthians 15:3,4:

"That Christ died for our sins according to the scriptures;

"And that he was buried, and that he rose again the third day according to the scriptures."

Oh, when Jesus died, it must be *according to the Scriptures!* If He died any other way, then He cannot be the Saviour of lost sinners.

John 19:36 tells us, "For these things were done, that the scripture should be fulfilled, A bone of him shall not be broken."

When Jesus first preached at Galilee after having been filled with the Spirit, the people "were filled with wrath, And rose up, and thrust him out of the city, and led him unto the brow of the hill whereon their city was built, that they might cast him down headlong."

If they had succeeded, had Christ died there, He would not have been our Saviour. The only way the death of Christ could do a sinner any good was that He die "according to the scriptures."

Humanly speaking, it is surprising that the wicked Pharisees and Sadducees did not stone Him to death as they stoned the martyr Stephen a little later. In fact, nothing would have pleased them better than to accuse Him of blasphemy and crush and batter His body into the dust with cruel stones. We know that "the Jews sought the more to kill him" (John 5:18); and again, "the Jews sought to kill him" (John 7:1). In fact, they tried to stone Him: "Then took they up stones to cast at him" (John 8:59).

Had one stone fractured His skull or a rib or broken any bones, that would prove forever that Jesus was not the Son of God and block His plan for saving sinners. Christ must not have a bone broken. His death must be "according to the scriptures."

Just last night it was—that sad, bitter, desolate night—that Jesus went out of the Upper Room, gave the disciples the teachings of chapters 14, 15 and 16 of John, prayed the prayer of John 17, and then went into the Garden of Gethsemane. Just last night it was that "being in an agony he prayed more earnestly." And as the Saviour mopped the sweat that poured profusely from His face, He found His handkerchief bloody red! Jesus was literally dying from sorrow.

He begged the disciples to pray with and for Him, saying, "My soul is exceeding sorrowful, even unto death." If God did not strengthen Him, if He did not get help from Heaven that night, Jesus would die, and all the plans for the redemption of sinners would be thwarted. A Saviour dying in the Garden of Gethsemane could not save anyone. He must die "according to the scriptures."

He must be hanged on a cross, for "Cursed is every one that hangeth on a tree" (Gal. 3:13). Otherwise, He could not bear the curse of man's sin.

He must have the stripes on His back, for "with his stripes we are healed" (Isa. 53:5).

The soldiers must cast lots for His garments (Ps. 22:18).

The wicked must surround Him like bulls of Bashan and gnash on Him with their teeth (Ps. 22:12).

Jesus must have His hands and feet pierced with the nails, according to Psalm 22:16.

And He must die at the time of the slaying of the Passover lambs.

Oh, when you consider the intricate details of prophecy that Jesus fulfilled in His death, it becomes overwhelmingly certain that He is God's own promised Saviour, the Lamb of God that takes away the sin of the world! Only the calloused and ignorant, only the willfully perverted who do not want to know the truth, doubt that Jesus is the Son of God who died for our sins. He did die "according to the scriptures."

So in the Garden of Gethsemane, when Jesus was about to die prematurely, when sin had broken His heart, when the capillaries were bursting open, when His soul was sorrowful even unto death, Jesus prayed that He might live until the morrow; prayed that He might die according to the Scriptures and so fulfill the plan of God.

For what did Jesus pray? Some have thought He prayed to be spared the crucifixion. Some have thought that after agreeing to die for man's sins, planning it with the Father even before the world began, that now Jesus would avoid it! Some have thought that Jesus was here praying against the Scriptures, contrary to the will of God. Some have thought that even now Jesus supposed there might be some other way to save lost sinners.

God forbid! No, no! Jesus was praying in the will of God, not contrary to the will of God. And He got what He asked. To understand this prayer of Jesus, twice-repeated, see the explanation of it in Hebrews 5:7:

"Who in the days of his flesh, when he had offered up prayers and supplications with strong crying and tears unto him that was able to save him from death, and was heard in that he feared."

Jesus prayed in Gethsemane to the Father who "was able to save him from death" that night, save Him from the unscriptural death in the Garden of Gethsemane, and spare Him for the scriptural death on the cross tomorrow.

Jesus did not ask that the bitter cup of death be avoided and taken away. Rather, He prayed that it should pass from Him for the time being, that He might not die that night, "and [He] was heard in that he feared."

God the Father granted that prayer. Jesus prayed in the Father's will, not contrary to it. In fact, in the prayer itself, Jesus had said He was not asking for His own will but according to the Father's will. He said, "Nevertheless not as I will, but as thou wilt" (Matt. 26:39).

That was not a prayer of sad resignation to a duty He did not want to perform. Rather, it was a fervent prayer that the Father would help Him live until tomorrow so He could die according to the Father's own plan.

Thank God, the Saviour's prayer was heard! Jesus had said, "I knew that thou hearest me always" (John 11:42). So an angel was sent to strengthen Him, and Jesus lived to die on the cross "according to the scriptures."

Certainly Satan would have rejoiced to see them break the bones of Jesus before they took Him down from the cross! Satan had done everything he could do to keep Christ from dying "according to the scriptures." If Christ had died in Gethsemane the night before it was planned that He should die, or if Christ had been hit with a stone so as to fracture a bone, as He was often threatened, or if He had had His legs broken in the last hour on the cross, He would not be dying "according to the scriptures."

Numbers 9:12 had commanded of the Passover lamb that they should leave none of it until morning nor "break any bone of it." For fifteen hundred years that command, picturing the coming Saviour in the Passover lamb, has been observed by Israel.

Psalm 34:20, referring, I think, to Christ, states, "He keepeth all his bones: not one of them is broken." Satan was thwarted again, and our beloved Saviour died "according to the scriptures" without a bone broken. And they thrust the spear into His side to make doubly sure He was dead.

3. Jesus must be pierced with a spear because it was foretold in prophecy. Our text in John 19:37 says, "And again another scripture saith, They shall look on him whom they pierced."

How meticulously careful God was to fulfill all His promises in Christ! Many times in the life story of Jesus as told in the

Gospels we find words like these: "That the scripture might be fulfilled which saith...."

So not only was it imperative that the bones of the Saviour must not be broken if He were the Son of God, but it was equally imperative that the spear should pierce His side. The Scripture had said it; therefore, God would fulfill it!

We are told that at Christ's second coming, He will appear at Jerusalem to be seen and recognized by the Jews: "and they shall look upon me whom they have pierced" (Zech. 12:10).

Any careful student must be profoundly impressed with the thoroughness God used in proving that Jesus was the promised Messiah: born of a virgin, of the house of David, of the tribe of Judah, in Bethlehem; dying on the appointed day, hands and feet pierced with nails after having been betrayed by a friend (fulfilling the picture of Psalm 22 perfectly), with soldiers casting lots for His garments, the elders mocking Him—fulfilling every detail of prophecy.

Then when He gave up the ghost, a soldier, surely not knowing what he did, took the spear and pierced His side! The Scripture was fulfilled. Thus, "they shall look upon me whom they have pierced."

4. "And forthwith came there out blood and water" when the spear pierced the Saviour's side. We miss much blessing when we pass over thoughtlessly any statement of the Word of God.

I confess that for years I preached on the blood and never preached on the water that came from the Saviour's side. Then I became convicted and prayed for God to open my heart to the truth He meant to reveal by this double flow from Calvary.

Oh, may we never forget to preach the blood! That is a fulfillment of all the prophecies! Here comes to an end that stream of blood that has trickled down through the centuries, when millions of animals gave their innocent blood to picture the coming Lamb of God! Oh, it is true that "without shedding of blood is no remission." So the blood of Jesus Christ must be poured out.

Mary Baker Eddy, who founded that heathen, anti-Christian religion falsely called "Christian Science," said that the blood of Christ was no more effective when poured out on Calvary than when it was in the veins of the living Jesus.

But that is a lie, a terrible untruth. For the life was in the blood.

And for centuries it had been foretold by the pictured prophecy of the sacrifices that the blood must be poured out. Not blood in the veins, but blood that is *shed*, could pay for man's sin.

Oh, picture it! The spear was placed against the naked body of Jesus, the soldier lunged, and the head of the spear was plunged up into the very heart—that broken heart—of the Son of God! And the blood poured out—that blood without ever a taint of sin—like the gurgling blood of a slaughtered animal. If there was a loincloth, it was soaked in red. The white thigh of the Saviour was covered with the crimson flow. It flowed on down His leg and dripped on the ground. And the cursed nature that cried out for vengeance over the innocent blood of Abel must have cried out to God that all man's sins are paid for!

> **What can wash away my sin?**
>   **Nothing but the blood of Jesus;**
> **What can make me whole again?**
>   **Nothing but the blood of Jesus;**
>
> **Oh, precious is the flow**
>   **That makes me white as snow;**
> **No other fount I know,**
>   **Nothing but the blood of Jesus.**

Or, as another poet has put it:

> **There is a fountain filled with blood**
>   **Drawn from Immanuel's veins;**
> **And sinners, plunged beneath that flood,**
>   **Lose all their guilty stains.**

The blood of Christ is an offense to some. Some say they will have none of this "slaughterhouse religion." But, oh, may it always be the praises of those who love the Lord Jesus!

It is by the blood that I am saved. That is the ransom for my soul! Such is the Gospel I preach, a Gospel of salvation by the blood. And that Gospel I will preach, God helping me, until I die; and then in Heaven I will praise Him forever who died for me! Oh, let us never forget the blood of Calvary!

But when Jesus died, "forthwith came there out blood and water." In John 7:37–39 is this pointed Scripture:

"In the last day, that great day of the feast, Jesus stood and

cried, saying, If any man thirst, let him come unto me, and drink.

"He that believeth on me, as the scripture hath said, out of his belly shall flow rivers of living water.

"(But this spake he of the Spirit, which they that believe on him should receive: for the Holy Ghost was not yet given; because that Jesus was not yet glorified.)"

Are you thirsty? Then you are invited to come to Jesus and drink. "He that believeth on me, as the scripture hath said, out of his belly shall flow rivers of living water." Then we are told, "This spake he of the Spirit, which they that believe on him should receive."

The promise is for the indwelling of the Spirit. Yes, and more. The indwelling of the Spirit is the heritage of every born-again one, but he may also have the Holy Spirit's fullness and power. Out from the heart and life of a Christian may flow a stream of the water of life to dying souls.

So if the blood is for salvation, the water that poured out of the side of Jesus is for the power of the Holy Spirit. Salvation was purchased for us at Calvary, but the marvelous power to do His will in the fullness of the Spirit was also bought for us there.

This twofold meaning of Calvary is pictured by the Saviour again in John 20:19–22. There Jesus came to the disciples the same day He was risen from the dead and said, "Peace be unto you." Then He showed them His hands and side. That is the peace of salvation, of sins forgiven, bought by the blood poured out on Calvary.

The Saviour said to them again, "Peace be unto you; as my Father has sent me, even so send I you." Then "he breathed on them, and saith unto them, Receive ye the Holy Ghost."

A joy, a peace of salvation is illustrated by the wounded hands and side of the Saviour. But, bless God, there is also the peace that a Christian can have in the fullness of joy and the fullness of power wrought in a Christian by the Holy Spirit.

Someone may ask, "Do you believe in a second blessing?" I do not believe in the kind of second blessing some believe in, claiming that the carnal nature is eradicated. But I certainly believe that a Christian can have something far beyond conversion. He can be filled with the Holy Ghost. He can have the power, the joy, the fruitfulness which Bible Christians had, wrought by the Holy Ghost.

Remember that Jesus said, "I am come that they might have life, and that they might have it more abundantly" (John 10:10). "Life" in that promise no doubt refers to salvation bought by the blood; but the promise, "and that they might have it more abundantly," is surely pictured by the water poured out.

This double lesson of Calvary was pictured in the death of the Passover lamb and the feast of unleavened bread in Exodus, chapter 12. The Passover lamb was killed and eaten in one meal. That pictures the salvation wrought by the blood. We take Christ, and He is ours, and our sins are paid for. Only once does one need to be born again.

So the children of Israel ate the Passover lamb. If any was left, it was burned. Not a piece was to remain until morning. But that was not the end of the blessing! They began that night the feast of unleavened bread, and it continued for seven days.

Six is a picture of man's life on earth, and the seventh day includes perfection and Heaven. So Christians may take of Christ just once to the saving of the soul. That is pictured by the blood poured out and by the Passover lamb. But the same Christian then begins the happy feeding on Christ, the Bread of Life, and that he can continue throughout this life and have the same joyful privilege throughout eternity!

Isaiah 44:3 reads:

"I will pour water upon him that is thirsty, and floods upon the dry ground: I will pour my spirit upon thy seed, and my blessing upon thine offspring."

Christian, if you have the blood, why not have the water also? If you are thirsting, drink and drink! And oh, may the Holy Spirit be in you a well of water springing up unto everlasting life and flowing out to all those near you with a stream of salvation!

Again, Isaiah 12:3 says, "With joy shall ye draw water out of the wells of salvation." Dip in your bucket, brother!

Multitudes know about the blood of Christ and have been redeemed, but few know the power of the Holy Ghost. You have the blood that poured from the wounded side of Jesus on the cross; now make sure you have the water, symbolizing the fullness of the Holy Spirit, the birthright of every Christian.

II. WHO WILL FACE THE PIERCED JESUS?

We have been studying how and why Jesus was pierced with a spear and its precious meaning. But the text says, "They shall look on him whom they pierced." Just as certainly as Jesus was pierced with a spear, that certainly people must face the pierced Jesus.

Let us consider, then, who must face the crucified Saviour, and how and when.

1. The Jews must face Jesus, their rejected Messiah. The last chapters of Zechariah tell of the return of Christ in glory to fight the battle of Armageddon, deliver Jerusalem and the Jews from their enemies, and set up His kingdom on earth. Zechariah 12:10 says:

"And I will pour upon the house of David, and upon the inhabitants of Jerusalem, the spirit of grace and of supplications: and they shall look upon me whom they have pierced, and they shall mourn for him, as one mourneth for his only son, and shall be in bitterness for him, as one that is in bitterness for his firstborn."

This is a picture of the beginning of the greatest revival the world will ever see! The remnant of Jews left alive on the earth will see their Messiah. Many Jews even today look for His coming, not believing that He has already come.

But when He comes in power and destroys the Antichrist and his armies, defends Jerusalem and regathers the Jews, God will "pour upon the house of David, and upon the inhabitants of Jerusalem, the spirit of grace and of supplications." Then they will see Jesus and recognize Him as the Messiah that He is! Today there is a blindness on the hearts of Israel, but when Jesus comes, that blindness will be removed.

Romans 11:25–27 has this sweet promise about the conversion of Israel:

"For I would not, brethren, that ye should be ignorant of this mystery, lest ye should be wise in your own conceits; that blindness in part is happened to Israel, until the fulness of the Gentiles be come in.

"And so all Israel shall be saved: as it is written, There shall come out of Sion the Deliverer, and shall turn away ungodliness from Jacob:

"For this is my covenant unto them, when I shall take away their sins."

All of Israel left alive on the earth will be converted. Zechariah 13:1 says, "In that day there shall be a fountain opened to the house of David and to the inhabitants of Jerusalem for sin and for uncleanness." That speaks not of what happened at Calvary so much as what will happen when Jesus comes. Christ has already died, and salvation is free to Jew and Gentile alike; but when the Jews see the pierced Jesus with their own eyes, what a mourning, what a grieving over their sins, and what a great turning to their Messiah and Saviour!

Zechariah 13:6 describes the conscience-stricken inquiry of a Jew at that time:

"And one shall say unto him, What are these wounds in thine hands? Then he shall answer, Those with which I was wounded in the house of my friends."

I wish I could have heard Moody preach. I have wished I could have been in some of the marvelous revivals he led. Oh, if I could have been at Mount Carmel when the nation Israel turned back to God! Or by the river Jordan when John the Baptist preached and they went out from all Jerusalem and Judaea and were baptized by him in the river Jordan, confessing their sins. Or if I could have seen the power of the Holy Ghost shake wicked Jerusalem so that three thousand were saved in a day at Pentecost. But I shall see a greater revival.

Some foolishly say that the day of great revivals is past. No! Instead, the greatest revival is yet to come, when the nation Israel in one day will turn to the Lord Jesus, when they will look on Him whom they pierced! Glad day for Israel when they see the crucified Saviour as He is, and love Him and trust Him!

2. All Christ-rejecting sinners will face the crucified Saviour, bow the knee to Him in condemnation and despair. The promise in Zechariah 12:10, "...they shall look upon me whom they have pierced" (quoted again in John 19:37), referred primarily to the Jews. But many Scriptures make clear that all the unconverted dead must face the pierced Jesus. With what grief, shame and terror they will meet Him!

"Behold, he cometh with clouds; and every eye shall see him, and they also which pierced him: and all kindreds of the earth shall wail because of him. Even so, Amen."—Rev. 1:7.

This is when He returns bodily to reign on the earth. This will be a time of terror, when "all kindreds of the earth shall wail because of him."

Will the unconverted who are already in Hell face Jesus Christ? Yes.

First, the very ones who crucified Jesus—members of the Sanhedrin, the high priests, the Roman soldiers, Pilate and Herod—all who combined in that sin will face the Saviour and give an account to Him!

When the high priest said to Jesus, "I adjure thee by the living God, that thou tell us whether thou be the Christ, the Son of God" (Matt. 26:63), Jesus answered, "Thou hast said: nevertheless I say unto you, Hereafter shall ye see the Son of man sitting on the right hand of power, and coming in the clouds of heaven" (Matt. 26:64).

That same high priest who presided at the trial of Jesus and demanded His crucifixion will be brought out of Hell to face the pierced Jesus. Those in Hell will see Christ's return and later will be dragged out to face Him as He sits on the great white throne, and when God's record books are opened (Rev. 20:11–15).

So will every Christ-rejecting sinner face the Lord Jesus there. "For it is written, As I live, saith the Lord, every knee shall bow to me, and every tongue shall confess to God" (Rom. 14:11).

And Philippians 2:9–11 tells us:

"Wherefore God also hath highly exalted him, and given him a name which is above every name:

"That at the name of Jesus every knee should bow, of things in heaven, and things in earth, and things under the earth;

"And that every tongue should confess that Jesus Christ is Lord, to the glory of God the Father."

Not a sinner can escape facing the pierced Jesus! You may blaspheme His name now, reject the pleading of His Holy Spirit now, refuse to love and serve Him now; but the time is coming when every sinner will kneel before Christ and confess Him as Lord. "They shall look on him whom they pierced" (John 19:37).

3. Through eternity Christians will see the pierced Jesus.

The Jews will face Christ when He returns to reign. Seeing Him, they will be convicted and saved.

All unconverted sinners will face Jesus. They will see His return and later be judged by Him.

Christians too will see the Lord Jesus. Throughout eternity the pierced Jesus will be our delight and joy.

Jesus will be the only One in Heaven with scars. His wounds will be the eternal reminder of salvation by God's wonderful grace through faith in the death of His Son.

We have good reason to believe that when Jesus comes and our vile bodies are changed and glorified, we will have no more scars.

In Isaiah 35:5,6 we are told that at the resurrection

"...the eyes of the blind shall be opened, and the ears of the deaf shall be unstopped.

"Then shall the lame man leap as an hart, and the tongue of the dumb sing."

The weaknesses, the frailties, the scars of our mortal bodies will all be cured in our glorified bodies. In Romans 8:23 Paul reminds us that "ourselves also, which have the firstfruits of the Spirit, even we ourselves groan within ourselves, waiting for the adoption, to wit, the redemption of our body."

Our bodies then will be free from the marks of our sin. Every Christian then will have a body as perfect as that of Adam and Eve in the Garden of Eden before they sinned. This crooked nose I got playing college football will be straight. And many another crooked thing about me will be cured in that good day.

When I was called to the army in 1917, the induction papers carried a record of the scar on my right wrist, cut by an ax; of the slash on the side of the left elbow, cut when a young bull ran into the fence with me. But in Heaven those scars will be gone! The army record will be out-of-date!

I believe the dying thief, who trusted the Lord Jesus and went that day with Him into Paradise in the resurrection, will not have even the mark of the nails that held him to the cross.

But it will be different with Jesus. He will still have the scars. When He arose from the dead, He saw the doubting disciples and "shewed unto them his hands and his side." He encouraged the doubting Thomas to thrust his finger into the prints of the nails in His hands, and to thrust his hand into the wound made by the spear in His side. Jesus still had the scars in His resurrection body.

And He will still have those wounds when He returns to reign, for Zechariah 13:6 records that Jews will ask, "What are these wounds in thine hands?" and He will answer, "Those with which I was wounded in the house of my friends."

If we can imagine that anyone in Heaven could seriously question the right of someone else to be there, I can imagine that I would have to say frankly that Hell ought to have been my portion and destruction, my just due. I know that I do not deserve my salvation. Only the mercy of God keeps me out of Hell.

But if such a question could be raised in Heaven, I would run to the Lord Jesus and beg to see again His wounded hands and ask if I might put my hand into His side and feel the wound made by the spear. And as long as the scars are in the hands and feet and in the side of the Saviour, then that long my soul will still be safe in Heaven. I will have that constant proof that my sins are paid for and that I am bought with a precious price that satisfied all the demands of God.

Though Christ never sinned, He will be the only One who will retain the marks of sin. Since He suffered the punishment of all the sinners in the world, He will always have the eternal reminder of the price He paid to save sinners.

> **When my lifework is ended, and I cross the swelling tide,**
> **When the bright and glorious morning I shall see;**
> **I shall know my Redeemer when I reach the other side,**
> **And His smile will be the first to welcome me.**
>
> **I shall know Him, I shall know Him,**
> **And redeemed by His side I shall stand;**
> **I shall know Him, I shall know Him**
> **By the print of the nails in His hands.**

"They shall look on him whom they pierced"!

JESSE HENDLEY
1907–1995

ABOUT THE MAN:

Jesse Hendley was for fourteen years pastor of a great Southern Baptist church with a membership of over 2,300, in East Point, Georgia, a suburb of Atlanta. For more than fifty years he was the director of the Radio Evangelistic Hour gospel broadcast. In addition, he was one of the most successful evangelists in the country in the 1940s and '50s. His preaching was unique and very effective. This devoted, humble Christian was easy to admire, easy to love, and easy to work with.

In a write-up by a Georgia journalist who "covered" one of his meetings in the earlier years, Hendley is described as one who "reads his Scripture from the Greek New Testament but preaches like Billy Sunday."

He was educated at Georgia Tech, Columbia Seminary and Southern Baptist Theological Seminary, Louisville. He was also a remarkable Greek scholar.

But Dr. Hendley was preeminently a soul winner with a passion that knew no bounds. This passion characterized his preaching, making it at once fiery, fervent and penetrating. Who can ever forget his tremendous and famous message on "Sin—Hell—Salvation"!

Yes, evangelism was his very life.

Once in Atlanta he began a meeting in a large tent. When it turned out to be too small, he moved to the Atlanta baseball stadium. Hendley rigged up a mike over home plate and delivered his sermons from there, speaking to as many as 7,500. Hundreds were saved during that revival in 1945. He held other large campaigns in his heyday and had God's blessings on each, leading thousands to Christ. Dr. Hendley was one of the main speakers at Sword of the Lord Conferences at Winona Lake, Indiana in those early years.

XVII.

Wonderful Jesus!

Wonderful in His Preincarnate Glory and Deity; in His Humiliation; in His Marvelous Birth and Life; in His Marvelous Teaching; in His Healing; in His Atoning Death; in His Glorious Resurrection

JESSE M. HENDLEY

"God, who at sundry times and in divers manners spake in time past unto the fathers by the prophets,

"Hath in these last days spoken unto us by his Son, whom he hath appointed heir of all things, by whom also he made the worlds;

"Who being the brightness of his glory, and the express image of his person, and upholding all things by the word of his power, when he had by himself purged our sins, sat down on the right hand of the Majesty on high."—Heb. 1:1–3.

This first chapter tells us that God spoke all through the Old Testament period "by the prophets." That phrase is used by Zechariah and the rest of the prophets. God spoke to them, and they wrote down what He spoke. But now God is speaking to the whole human race, not by prophets, but by His Son—Jesus. Then He describes seven wonderful things about Jesus.

First of all, God has appointed Jesus heir of all things. Everything in Heaven belongs to Jesus. Everything on earth belongs to Jesus. Everything in Hell belongs to Jesus. Everything in the entire universe belongs to Jesus.

"By whom also he made the *worlds*." The Greek word means "ages." Students study about the ages of the rocks. Well, Jesus made it all—the Stone Age, the Iron Age and the rest of the ages.

"Who being the brightness of his glory...." That word for *brightness* means "effulgence." You do not see the actual sun when you look at it; you see only the effulgence of the sun. You see the rays emanating from the sun.

No man can see God. But when you look at Jesus, He is no less than God Himself; but He came into human flesh in order that we might see God.

Jesus is the brightness of God's glory. Jesus is the express image of God's Person. Translated, *express image* is the word *character*. In using the stamp or a die, you leave the absolute impression of the stamp or die. Christ is the absolute impression of the Father. He is like the Father in every respect.

Then we read that He is "upholding [bearing] all things by the word of his power." It is the present participle. Jesus is carrying the entire universe.

I used to wonder about Atlas, that fictitious personality's, carrying the entire world on his shoulders. But Jesus is in reality the great Atlas who carries the entire universe.

Then we read, "...when he had by himself purged our sins...." There is a precious word. Jesus was all alone at the cross when He took our sins away.

Then we read there in the closing words that He

"...sat down on the right hand of the Majesty on high;
"Being made so much better than the angels, as he hath by inheritance obtained a more excellent name than they."— Vss. 3, 4.

The Lord Jesus Christ is greater than all angels. He is God!

We read on:

"And, Thou, Lord, in the beginning hast laid the foundation of the earth; and the heavens are the works of thine hands:
"They shall perish; but thou remainest; and they all shall wax old as doth a garment;
"And as a vesture shalt thou fold them up, and they shall be changed: but thou art the same, and thy years shall not fail."— Vss. 10–12.

Now with that solemn fact that Jesus Christ is God, we go into the second chapter.

"Therefore we ought to give the more earnest heed to the

things which we have heard [about Jesus and about His great Gospel], *lest at any time we should let them slip."*—Vs. 1.

Slip to what? Slip away from Jesus!

"For if the word spoken by angels was stedfast, and every transgression and disobedience received a just recompense of reward;

"How shall we escape, if we neglect so great salvation?"—Vss. 2, 3.

Why is it called "so great salvation"? Because it has to do with a great Saviour. The theme of the Epistle to the Hebrews is Jesus. All through the entire epistle there are solemn warnings about falling into sin. They are not warnings about backsliding, getting drunk, committing adultery and gambling, but the warnings about slipping away from Jesus!

In the third chapter we read these words:

"Take heed, brethren, lest there be in any of you an evil heart of unbelief, in departing from the living God."—Vs. 12.

When you leave Jesus, you leave the "living God." The danger of these Hebrew Christians was that they would leave the Lord Jesus and plunge back into their old ritualism of the Old Testament times.

I repeat: It is a "so great salvation" because it has a great Saviour.

We read in verse 9 of chapter 2 that "we see Jesus." Brother, whom do you see when you think about salvation? I see no one but Jesus! I do not see the church—it cannot save. I do not see baptism—it cannot save. I do not see the Lord's Supper—that cannot save. I do not see good works—they cannot save. I see Jesus, the only One who can save. He is the Saviour, so it is a great salvation. In neglecting Him, you neglect "so great salvation," the thing most precious to you.

"But we see Jesus." I wonder, friend, have you ever seen Jesus? You are not saved unless you have. Salvation has to do with a Person, the Lord Jesus.

Fanny Crosby was born blind. She wrote six thousand hymns and more. She never saw the face of anyone—not even her mother.

One day a friend who was pitying her, said, "O Miss Crosby, just to think you have never seen the face of anyone!"

Her face lighted up like the sun—radiant Christian that she was—and she said, "Don't pity me! Just think, the first face I shall ever see will be the face of my Lord!" She was looking forward to the time when she would see Jesus.

The minute my heart stops beating, I am going to look into the most beloved face I have ever seen—Jesus! You go on in sin if you want to; you go on and look into the angry, malignant face of the Devil and his demons. Not I! When I die, I shall see Jesus, wonderful Jesus!

Five hundred years before Jesus was born, God gave to the Prophet Isaiah a vision of Jesus. He let him see Jesus and His marvelous work before He was born. Isaiah cried out, 'He is wonderful! His name shall be called Wonderful!'

1. Jesus Was Wonderful in His Preincarnate Glory and Deity

No one is so wonderful as the Lord Jesus Christ. Before Jesus came to this earth, He was with the Father in Heaven.

"In the beginning was the Word, and the Word was with God, and the Word was God."

"All things were made by him [Jesus]; and without him was not any thing made that was made."—John 1:1,3.

"In the beginning God created the heaven and the earth" (Gen. 1:1). Back there the Son and the Father were in fellowship together, but Jesus flung the worlds into space. He created them with the power of His own word.

Jesus Christ is God! He is marvelous in His preincarnate deity and glory and heavenly life.

Now in Colossians 1:16,17 we read:

"For by him were all things created, that are in heaven, and that are in earth, visible and invisible, whether they be thrones, or dominions, or principalities, or powers: all things were created by him, and for him:

"And he is before all things, and by him all things consist."

He is the One who holds things together today. Jesus Christ is still on the throne. If you are a child of God, you need not worry about existing conditions. Things will never get out of His hands as long as He sits at the right hand of the Father. To be sure, He will permit trouble. But as long as He holds the reins in His hand and is the Ruler of the kings of this earth, you and I have nothing to fear!

He is ruling the earth! When the time comes, our Saviour shall have every bit of power and authority and assume the rulership of this world, as it is written in Revelation. Every knee shall bow and every nation shall hand over the reins of government into His hands! He is God.

Christ is wonderful in His preincarnate glory and deity with the Father, with the angels worshiping Him as God's only begotten Son, back in the age of eternity, before the earth was ever made, before the universe or any man was ever created. Jesus is wonderful!

2. Jesus Was Wonderful in His Humiliation

Not only is He wonderful in His preincarnate glory and deity, but He is also wonderful in His humiliation. In Philippians 2:5–11 we have one of those great statements about Jesus and His humiliation:

"Let this mind be in you, which was also in Christ Jesus:

"Who, being in the form of God, thought it not robbery to be equal with God:

"But made himself of no reputation, and took upon him the form of a servant, and was made in the likeness of men:

"And being found in fashion as a man, he humbled himself and became obedient unto death, even the death of the cross.

"Wherefore God also hath highly exalted him, and given him a name which is above every name:

"That at the name of Jesus every knee should bow, of things in heaven, and things in earth, and things under the earth;

"And that every tongue should confess that Jesus Christ is Lord, to the glory of God the Father."

In Colossians we are told that Jesus redeemed all things in Heaven and earth, but there is nothing said about His redeeming things under the earth. There is no redemption in Hell. They bow down there, but it is too late. Someday every unsaved soul shall bow his knee and confess Him Lord in the flame of Hell.

Sinner friend, it is a lot better to walk down this aisle tonight than to do it down there in the fires of Hell; do it willingly now, when it would mean salvation, than do it down in Hell, where it will be too late. There is no redemption in Hell! No Christ is coming to you there. No Saviour can reach you then. His arms are not long enough to save a soul in Hell. Openly confess Him now. Accept Him now.

3. Jesus Was Wonderful in His Marvelous Birth and Life

Jesus is wonderful in His preincarnate deity and glory and heavenly life. Jesus is wonderful in His humiliation. Jesus is wonderful in His marvelous birth.

I am glad that Jesus was not born as I was born. A mother takes her baby in arms and says, "My, he's innocent! My, he's perfect! My, he's a little angel!" But before he is a month old, Mother will find out differently. Babies are not angels, with their selfishness, malice, anger. They are born with a sinful nature. It shows up before they can say a word. Selfishness is at the root of all our hearts, and it is sin.

In a Chicago station, there were two tiny tots who were scarcely able to talk. Each had a little train. There they were, fighting over them. People were laughing at that, but it wasn't a laughing matter. That sin will damn them if they don't get a new nature from Jesus Christ. It is written, "Ye must be born again."

I am so glad a Child was born two thousand years ago who was not born as we were. I cannot die for you, and you cannot die for me. We cannot save each other.

The Angel Gabriel was sent from Heaven to a virgin to tell her, "Thou shalt conceive in thy womb, and bring forth a son, and shalt call his name JESUS."

And Mary said, "How shall this be, seeing I know not a man?"

And he answered, "The Holy Ghost shall come upon thee, and the power of the Highest shall overshadow thee."

He will not have an earthly father. He will not have a sinful nature transmitted to Him. He will not have selfishness and anger. God will be His Father. He will be begotten of the Holy Ghost in the virgin's womb. He will have a divine nature instead of a human nature and sin.

Brother, don't you ever attribute shame to the Lord Jesus Christ. He is absolutely perfect. His birth was a holy birth! He came into this world like no other child. Thereby He was a fitting sacrifice for our sins.

We read further on in Hebrews that He is "holy, harmless, undefiled, separate from sinners, and made higher than the heavens." Nobody was ever able to find any sin in the Lord—not even His enemies. I have never known anybody else I could worship. But I can worship Him, for He is perfect.

He was marvelous in His virgin birth.

Then, Jesus is wonderful in His marvelous life. Did anybody ever live like Jesus? Into three and one-half years there was packed the most wondrous life this world has ever known!

4. Jesus Was Wonderful in His Marvelous Teaching

No one ever talked as the Lord talked. One time they sent the temple priests after Him, to take His life. When they came and stood on the outside of the crowd where Jesus was talking and teaching, they forgot about their errand and went back without Him. When the authorities asked, 'Why didn't you bring Him?' the priests, with a glow on their faces and wonderment in their hearts, answered, "Never man spake like this man."

Nobody ever talked like Jesus.

I have on the shelves of my study some of the best volumes by the most spiritual men and the greatest intellects the world has ever known, but there isn't a line in any book that is comparable to the words of the Lord Jesus! "Never man spake like this man." Oh, listen to what He says!

Daniel Webster, one of the greatest minds America ever had, read the Sermon on the Mount and said, "I know men, and it wasn't a man who spoke those words. He was more than man." I too tell you, He is more than man.

5. Jesus Was Wonderful in His Healing

Oh, His sympathy and love for human sufferers! Have you ever suffered? I have been around tragedy all my life. Whatever I might say tonight that will be a blessing to any heart, I owe to the tragedy and suffering which I contact.

Jesus moved in human suffering and human tragedy, and He always left behind a blessing.

It was Jesus who said to the leper, "Be thou clean." Then we read that He touched him. Why? Nobody wanted to touch a leper, whose body was rotting; filled with filthy, running sores, a contagious disease. He couldn't live with his wife and family; he couldn't even let his loved ones come near him without crying, "Unclean, unclean!" He had to stay away from everybody. It had doubtless been years since anyone had touched this leper. Everybody ran away from him.

Jesus knew the hungry cry of that man's heart, and He not only cleansed him, but reached out and touched him. Oh, there is nobody else like that! I can trust a Man who opened the eyes of the blind, cleansed the lepers and touched the man who was lame and made him whole so that he was able to walk. I can love a Man like that. Jesus was wonderful in His healing!

6. Jesus Was Wonderful in Miracles He Performed

Jesus Christ was wonderful in His marvelous miracles. He raised Jairus' daughter from the dead.

Jesus stopped the funeral train of the widow's son, who was her only support, and said, "Young man...Arise," and he arose. Jesus restored him to his precious mother.

Jesus stood at the tomb of Lazarus, who had been dead four days, and He cried out, "Lazarus, come forth"! Who on earth is He, if He isn't God! What a big lie has been perpetrated on the human race if it were not so!

But it is so! One of these days I too am going to be laid in the tomb, and I want Him as my Friend when that time comes.

7. Jesus Was Wonderful in His Atoning Death

O friends, this is holy ground.

A song I love very much is this one:

> **There is a green hill far away,**
> **   Without a city wall,**
> **Where the dear Lord was crucified,**
> **   Who died to save us all.**
>
> **Oh, dearly, dearly, has He loved,**

**And we must love Him too,
And trust in His redeeming blood,
And try His work to do.**

That tells of our only hope—the cross of Calvary where He gave Himself for our sins.

Do you remember that wonderful song:

**They are nailed to the cross,
They are nailed to the cross;
   Oh, how much He was willing to bear!
With what anguish and loss
Jesus went to the cross!
   But He carried my sins with Him there.**

The blessed atonement of the Lord Jesus Christ! One thing I know: I have confessed my sins and have turned to Calvary's cross.

Another old song asks:

Were you there when they crucified my Lord?

Every time I hear that sung, I say, "Yes, I was there." I have been beneath the cross. I have seen His precious blood dripping over my poor, dirty, soiled soul and washing away every stain, until now I am as white as the Angel Gabriel; yea, whiter than snow. I can walk straight through that gate of Heaven, walk by the angels and archangels and right up to the throne room of the holy of holies and look God in the face without a single tremor of fear, for on Calvary's cross He made me as clean as an angel.

Do you think I would turn down the cross of Jesus? A man is a fool who does that. No way can a man escape a deserved Hell and walk the streets of gold for eternity but for the way of the atoning cross.

Charles Wesley was walking through a forest while a storm was raging. Suddenly he felt something strike his chest. Reaching up, he found a little bird had flown up against him in its fear. He took it, hid it in his bosom, and there it stayed through the driving rain and storm.

He could feel the rapid beating of its little heart as he went to his house. There he kept it in the safety and security of his home until the storm had abated. Then he took it out into the sunshine and let it fly. Then he went back into the house and wrote these precious words:

> **Jesus, Lover of my soul,**
>   **Let me to Thy bosom fly,**
> **While the nearer waters roll,**
>   **While the tempest still is high!**
> **Hide me, O my Saviour, hide,**
>   **Till the storm of life is past;**
> **Safe into the haven guide,**
>   **O receive my soul at last!**

That is the way I feel: "O receive my soul at last!" There is no other way. The only death is that of Christ and the blood.

8. Jesus Was Wonderful in His Glorious Resurrection

His death would never have meant much if He had not been raised from the dead. Jesus is alive tonight! More real to me than any other fact is the resurrection of the Lord Jesus.

Why do I believe He was resurrected?

First, because it is told us in this Book. Because the men who wrote it jeopardized their lives to tell it and to write it; and men do not jeopardize their lives for a lie!

Every New Testament writer paid with his life, except perhaps John the apostle. Paul laid down his life under the headsman's ax for his testimony. And men do not testify a lie nor jeopardize their lives for a lie. I believe the record of these men today, actual historians who wrote what they saw and felt and knew.

When John said, "That which was from the beginning, which we have heard, which we have seen with our eyes, which we have looked upon, and our hands have handled," he meant that they saw and talked with Jesus, ate with Him and handled Him after His resurrection from the dead. Those men were not lying.

I never was in a war, but I am told there was a World War II. If I say I do not know there was a war in Europe, you think I am a fool. Well, I wasn't there. I didn't see a single plane shot from the sky nor a single ship go down at sea. During the entire war I never heard one shot fired.

But I believe there was a war because credible, honest, trustworthy men were there and saw it. They felt it, knew it, wrote about it. And I believe what they wrote.

For the same reason, I believe in Jesus Christ and His atoning blood and His marvelous resurrection.

There are eight thousand different manuscripts in the world that have to do with Jesus' blessed life. If we had no New Testament today, it could be reproduced from what has been discovered and what has already been found back yonder in the beginning.

When you read the Bible, you are not reading cunningly devised fables, but an accurate account of historians who wrote down what they saw and knew.

Do you know why I know Christ lives? He lives within my heart!

One day an atheist said to an old farmer, "You are always talking about Jesus. How do you know He lives?"

With a twinkle in his eye, the farmer said, "I ought to know, for I talked to Him a few minutes ago."

When I go into my prayer room, I meet Somebody there. Something happens to me there. You can call it psychology, psychiatry, or something else that men have figured out; but I know that when I met Jesus, He did something for me no one else has ever done. He is real. I know He lives within my heart. I know Jesus because I have seen Him, have touched Him, have felt Him, have handled Him.

> **And He walks with me, and He talks with me,**
> **And He tells me I am His own;**
> **And the joy we share as we tarry there,**
> **None other has ever known.**

As I go up and down this land preaching, I am not out just to get numbers. Sure, I want numbers, but I want numbers of born-again people. I am not trying simply to "get people forward." I can preach an easier gospel and do that. I am not eager about that easy, light sort of thing. I want no reputation for doing it. What I want is to see people come and meet Jesus Christ.

In eternity, there will be many people who were fooled. Preachers are packing their churches with church members; but God says nothing but the new birth will get one through the gates of Heaven. "Ye must be born again." You must know the Lord. You must be able to say in your heart, "I am trusting Jesus to save my lost soul."

I was preaching in a great Baptist church in St. Louis, Missouri. The first Sunday morning as I preached on sin, I didn't hold back a thing. I waded into it with everything I had. It was the first time I had ever started a revival meeting on the subject of sin. And when I preach on that subject, I don't play around. I take off the cover and reveal it in all its nauseous condition.

The message was broadcast. In an adjoining state a woman was listening over the radio. After the broadcast she wrote me:

> Preacher, back several years ago when my husband became sick, I began to flirt around in sin. Finally I had an affair with another man, and I clothed my children with the fruit of my sin. For awhile my conscience hurt me; then when I looked around and saw other people doing it, it didn't hurt me nearly so much. But this morning when you preached on sin, it nailed me to the wall. Will God forgive me for this horrible thing I have been doing?

I could sense the agony of that poor sinner's heart.

I went on the air the next Sunday and read the letter. I then told her that the precious blood of Jesus could wash her clean, could put away her sin and give her brand-new life, a brand-new start, a brand-new page all over again.

I have at home her response, which I treasure to this hour. She wrote: "Preacher, He saved me! Thank God, I'm saved!"

She gave up her sin and went to the arms of Christ. Who did that? Not Jesse Hendley. Christ reaches down and saves and forgives all who will come to Him.

When I gave the invitation one night in Lake Charles, Louisiana, many came forward to accept Christ. Among them was a man whom I somehow pitied.

At the close of the service I went to shake his hand. He was in tears as he gave his confession of Jesus as his Saviour.

While people were shaking hands with those who had come to the altar, this man's wife took me to one side, and she burst into sobs as she said something like this:

> Preacher, we were just passing through the city and saw the sign here. We came into the tent. Just the other day my husband said, "Honey, I know I'm lost; I know I'm going to Hell! I've got to do something about it!" I am so glad that we hap-

pened to come by the tent and that we happened to drop in. Now he is saved!

I wanted to say, "Woman, it isn't any 'happen-so.' Jesus sent him into this tent, and it was Jesus who brought him to this altar and saved his soul. The resurrected Christ did it all."

Do you want to know why I trust Him?

First let me tell you about my mother. She suffered all her life. She passed on in middle age with a dreadful cancer. For twenty years she fought for life as only a few people have. I watched that cancer choke her life and take her into eternity.

What I would give tonight if she were to walk down that aisle and I could see her again and embrace her! She has been gone now for nineteen years. My heart is hungry to look once again into her face. And I am going to do it before long. And not only hers, but also the face of Jesus. He is my only hope of ever seeing her again.

I have a daddy who sleeps beside my mother out yonder in Greenwood Cemetery in Atlanta. What I would give tonight to see my dad again! For six days I watched him die in Georgia Baptist Hospital. I watched death choke the very life out of him at sixty-two years of age. But his salvation was secure, and he is yonder in Heaven. I want to see him again. My only hope is the Lord Jesus.

I met a girl in Atlanta, the only girl I ever went with. After four years we were married. I love her more than any other person on earth. I do not want to leave her. We are getting on in years. We are over the top of the hill now and are headed downhill. She said the other day, "Wouldn't it be wonderful if we could just go together?" I have seen other couples like that who wanted to go together, but God separated them.

One day I want to be with her again. We have had great times down here, and I do not believe anything will separate us forever. And my only hope of spending eternity with her is the Lord Jesus Christ.

I have a little twelve-year-old girl whom I dearly love. A lady who keeps her and my boy when my wife is with me, said something very precious the other day: "Brother Hendley, your daughter Helen spends a lot of time in your study. One day I said to her, 'Helen, why do you stay back in your daddy's study so much?' She answered me, 'Well, my daddy's been gone in revivals a long time, and when I'm back here in his study, I feel just a little bit nearer to him.'"

My little girl loves me, and I love her, and I want to spend eternity with her.

I have a little ten-year-old boy. I love him with all my soul. I want to spend eternity with him. And my only hope is the Lord Jesus Christ.

But that isn't all. I trust Him chiefly because I need Him. I cannot do without Him. Christ is a necessity. I have to have Him. One day I am going to die and leave my precious wife, my girl and boy. They can't go with me when my times comes. They will have to kiss me good-bye and step back. When the summons comes, all that medical science can do cannot keep me. In that solemn hour, there is only one Person in the universe who can cross the chilly waters of death and bring me home and into Heaven, and His precious name is Jesus.

Do you think I am a fool? I will never turn Him down.

I turn the pages of this Book and read Psalm 23: "The LORD is my shepherd." Immediately I bow my head. Why? Because I need a Shepherd. My daddy used to take care of me when I was a child, but my daddy and mother are gone. I need Somebody stronger than Dad. I need somebody greater than Mother to take care of me when I cannot take care of myself.

And that great psalm closes: "Surely goodness and mercy shall follow me all the days of my life: and I will dwell in the house of the LORD for ever."

When life's little day is over, I am going Home. I am out in revival meetings so much and away from home so much. But one of these days the great summons is coming, and I am going to leave this world. I'm headed Home! Thank God, it is going to be Home. Why should I be afraid of going Home?

SHELTON SMITH
1942–

ABOUT THE MAN:

Born December 4, 1942, in rural Western Kentucky, Shelton L. Smith grew up on his father's farm. When he was almost nine years old, he accepted Jesus Christ as his Saviour at the family home. At fourteen years of age, and when just a freshman in high school, he announced his call to preach. He preached his first sermon the very next week on January 13, 1957.

Having grown up in a Southern Baptist church, he attended SBC schools and was pastor of SBC churches for the early years of his ministry. An anonymous gift subscription to the SWORD OF THE LORD came to his mailbox one day, and it changed his life and ministry forever. He set out on a course of bold preaching, strong leadership and personal soul winning which has resulted in thousands of souls saved.

In late 1978 he accepted the pastorate of a small church, the Church of the Open Door in Westminster, Maryland. For seventeen years he saw his vision fulfilled as "every dream I ever dreamed came true." From a small group of 200, the church grew to average between 1,500 and 1,600 under his ministry. The church became one of the great growing, thriving centers of fundamentalism and soul winning in the Northeast.

In April of 1995, Dr. Smith was elected to succeed Dr. Curtis Hutson as the editor of the SWORD OF THE LORD. Now in his role as editor, he travels as an evangelist to encourage pastors and Christian workers to win souls, and to assist fundamental churches in reaching their areas for Christ.

Dr. Smith preaches as an evangelist with the same candor, compassion, conviction and courage that he had as a pastor. He is a soul winner, a fundamentalist, a separatist and an independent Baptist.

XVIII.

"This Same Jesus"

SHELTON SMITH

"And while they looked stedfastly toward heaven as he went up, behold, two men stood by them in white apparel;

"Which also said, Ye men of Galilee, why stand ye gazing up into heaven? this same Jesus, which is taken up from you into heaven, shall so come in like manner as ye have seen him go into heaven."—Acts 1:10,11.

The first chapter of the Book of Acts is often overshadowed by the second chapter. While I would not attempt to say that the second chapter is not the bigger of the two, at the same time, Acts, chapter 1, has much great preaching in it. Perhaps a month of Sunday mornings, Sunday nights and Wednesday nights could be expended when the preacher would do nothing but preach the great texts of Acts 1.

I'll not attempt to recite those great themes, and I'll not in this message exhaust the entirety of the two verses I've read, but there is one segment, one little piece in verse 11, that is the thrust and the thesis for what I want to give you. There is a phrase in verse 11 that says, "…this same Jesus…."

Christianity is a faith laden with principles, concepts for living and dying, perspectives for time and eternity. Such valued treasures are important to us.

Christianity is a faith that has abundant and eternal provisions for those who adopt it as their faith—many provisions, great provisions—and they too are so important to us.

Christianity is a faith loaded with promises—the pledges of Heaven, the divine commitment to us—and all those promises are important.

However, Christianity is first and foremost not really about principles and provisions and promises. Rather, everything that is, in fact, the essence of Christianity is focused on a Person. And that

Person is the Lord Jesus Christ. Without the Person, every promise is vain, every principle is faulty, and every provision is empty.

Everything has to be hinged on a Person, the Lord Jesus.

"This same Jesus" who came the first time is promised here to return a second time. In history "this same Jesus" was born in Bethlehem, reared in Nazareth, crucified and resurrected at Jerusalem. Now we are reminded that it is "this same Jesus" who will one day burst forth through the azure blue of the spacious sky, and "this same Jesus" will descend from Heaven with a shout, with the voice of the archangel and with the trump of God. The dead in Christ shall rise first; then we who are alive and remain on the earth shall be caught up together to "this same Jesus" in the air.

It's "this same Jesus" who, though born a baby in Bethlehem, will one day after the Tribulation come riding on a white horse triumphantly and set up His millennial kingdom.

If you go to a church that is the right kind of a church, you may anticipate hearing a lot about "this same Jesus." You can just expect it. There will be songs about Him. You'll hear people referring to Jesus when they pray. The people in their average, everyday conversation will make reference to Jesus.

Certainly whenever the preacher rises to the platform to preach the message, even if it's a message about some other great Bible subject, nonetheless the Person of Jesus will not be forgotten. In any gospel message or Bible sermon there will be many references to Jesus.

The name Jesus, somewhat common in Bible times, is now etched in history as the name above all names, precious to His intimates in faith; and whether whispered or shouted, it is powerful beyond all others.

I. "THIS SAME JESUS" IS THE PREEXISTENT JESUS

This passage says that the One for whom our eyes are lifted skyward is "this same Jesus" who came at Bethlehem. The critics say, "Well, there's a Jesus here, and there's a Jesus there; which Jesus is it that you're looking for?" The answer is, "this same Jesus" to whom this verse refers is the One who is also the preexistent Jesus; that is, He was very much alive before He was born. I mean by that, He had an existence prior to Bethlehem. In every generation of the eternities past, He was a real, living Being.

John the Baptist said, "This is he of whom I said, After me cometh a man which is preferred before me: for he was before me" (John 1:30). Though six months older than Jesus, John the Baptist said, "He was before me." It is for this very reason that the Bible says, "In the beginning was the Word, and the Word was with God, and the Word was God" (John 1:1); that is, at the time of creation, the Lord Jesus who is the *logos* (the Word) was alive. He, even as were God the Father and God the Holy Spirit, was the Source and the Maker of the creation! Preexistent was He!

So in the First Epistle of Peter, it says, "Who verily was foreordained before the foundation of the world, but was manifest in these last times for you" (1:20). Before the foundation of the world was ever laid, Jesus was! Before Bethlehem was a place, Jesus was! Before the earth, Jesus was!

Jesus testified, "Verily, verily, I say unto you, Before Abraham was, I am" (John 8:58). Abraham lived hundreds of years before these events in Bethlehem, and yet Jesus said, 'Before Abraham was born, I was; indeed, I AM.' The Lord Jesus whom we honor and exalt, the Lord Jesus who was, is and forevermore shall be, is the One of whom this passage says, "This same Jesus…shall so come in like manner as ye have seen him go."

"This same Jesus" is the preexistent Jesus!

II. "THIS SAME JESUS" IS THE PROPHESIED JESUS

He is not only the preexistent Jesus, but He is also the prophesied Jesus. Who is this Jesus? Which one is He? How do we know when we see Him? How can we identify Him distinctively and surely? He is the prophesied Jesus.

Isaiah said, "Behold, a virgin shall conceive, and bear a son, and shall call his name Immanuel" (7:14). "His name shall be called Wonderful, Counsellor, The mighty God, The everlasting Father, The Prince of Peace" (9:6).

"This same Jesus" is the One of whom Micah the prophet wrote, "But thou, Beth-lehem Ephratah, though thou be little among the thousands of Judah, yet out of thee shall he come forth unto me that is to be ruler in Israel; whose goings forth have been from of old, from everlasting" (5:2).

The Bible says about Him, "She shall bring forth a son, and thou shalt call his name JESUS: for he shall save his people from their sins" (Matt. 1:21).

It is because of "this same Jesus" that the angel said:

"I bring you good tidings of great joy, which shall be to all people.

"For unto you is born this day in the city of David a Saviour, which is Christ the Lord."—Luke 2:10,11.

Isaiah the prophet, Micah the prophet and others of Old Testament fame and certification testify of the coming of the Lord Jesus, every one of them saying, "Jesus, the Saviour, is coming! He is to be born!" Even the time, the place, such intricate details are prearranged and preannounced unmistakably to set the stage for His coming. "To him give all the prophets witness, that through his name whosoever believeth in him shall receive remission of sins" (Acts 10:43).

When I talk about "this same Jesus," I'm talking about the One who had an existence before Bethlehem. The preexistent Jesus is amazingly, uniquely, clearly the Jesus prophesied of the prophets.

III. "THIS SAME JESUS" IS THE PERSONAL JESUS

I'm also talking to you about the One that I simply refer to as the personal Jesus. Jesus said, "Wist ye not that I must be about my Father's business?" (Luke 2:49).

When you read the record of the life of "this same Jesus" in the four Gospels, you'll find that He was very personally attentive to His own family. He was compassionate with them in the times of sorrow. When friends, and even people that He did not know, had a death in their family, Jesus exercised the greatest care, a compassion bringing comfort even to the point of raising the dead. Look at His tender dealings with Mary and Martha, the sympathetic ministering of His grace at the time of His friend Lazarus's death (John 11).

See Him with warmth mercifully deal with the ruler Jairus when his young daughter had died (Matt. 9:18–26).

Note His pastoral attendance to the grieving widow of Nain whose boy had died prematurely and unexplainably (Luke 7:11–18).

Jesus gave Himself in caring for the hurting, the needy, the broken and people with all kinds of difficulties. He showed Himself, demonstrated Himself, strong in being personally conscious of the needs of every person with whom He came in contact. It's a good example for you and me to follow.

Every one of us would do well to see in the eyes and in the face of every person that we meet somebody for whom Jesus died. And remember that Jesus Himself gave a personal touch to every little boy and girl, every old drunk, every broken person, every crook and every thief, everybody that He saw. There was nobody who was outside the scope of the personal love and compassion of the Lord Jesus Christ.

IV. "THIS SAME JESUS" IS THE PRIZED JESUS

When we talk about "this same Jesus," it is the preexistent Jesus, it is the prophesied Jesus, it is the personal Jesus of whom we speak. I hope it also will be for you, as it is for many of us, that He is the prized Jesus.

You know He was highly prized of God the Father. The Father said, "This is my beloved Son, in whom I am well pleased" (Matt. 3:17).

He was noted and lauded, often commended by men. They said, "Never man spake like this man" (John 7:46). They said, "...even the winds and the sea obey him" (Matt. 8:27). There is a value about Him that every one of us ought to deposit in the bank of our souls! Every single one of us ought to say, "It is with the utmost devotion of my heart and soul that I estimate and esteem the value of Jesus! I highly prize the blessed Lord Jesus Christ." What a treasure He is! Greater than riches! Greater than fame! Greater than life itself! Greater than anything and everything that compete with Him!

No trophy compares! No award so special! No applause so expressive! Jesus is our eternal treasure! He is in every way precious and prized!

We, with sober thoughts, allow nothing and no one to preempt Him or to cause us to give Him anything but first place.

Survey your house and lands, assess your silver and gold, be wise, be faithful, remember it is Jesus who is to be most greatly prized! Amen!

V. "THIS SAME JESUS" IS THE PERFECT JESUS

"This same Jesus," the preexistent Jesus, the prophesied Jesus, the personal Jesus, the prized Jesus, is also the perfect Jesus.

Jesus "was in all points tempted like as we are, yet without sin" (Heb. 4:15). Jesus, "this same Jesus," had no sin; He had no stain upon His life; He had no scars because of His yielding to something that was outside the scope of God's will and God's commandments. He was, in fact, the Just One who came to die for all of us who were unjust—perfect in His character, perfect in His acts, perfect in His attitude, perfect in that all He did was flawless, perfect in that He left nothing undone that should have been done!

Perfect in plan, perfect in precept, perfect in presentation, perfect in plentitude, perfect not just in part, but the whole!

Perfect as God and perfect as Man! Morally perfect! Philosophically perfect! Not one day of regret, not ever! Always in all ways with everything in place; order was the norm! Perfect, indeed!

No degradation! No dysfunction! No dereliction! No dementia! No demerit! No delusion! No debauchery! No debility! No debris! No deception! No decay! No declivity! No default! No defeat! No debit! And glory to God, no debate!

Philip Bliss wrote, "Guilty, vile and helpless, we; Spotless Lamb of God was He...." Amen!

I look at "this same Jesus" and I remind you today—preexistent? Yes. Prophesied? Yes. Personal? Yes. Prized? Yes. And perfect? Absolutely!

VI. "THIS SAME JESUS" IS THE POWERFUL JESUS

The Bible says He is also the powerful Jesus—mighty, yea, almighty—the omnipotent One! Not a superman, not a superstar, no; but He is God with absolute power in His grasp. "All power is given unto me in heaven and in earth" (Matt. 28:18).

He had power over devils. No demon could bring embarrassment to Jesus. No devil could rise up or rise higher to do something greater than what the Lord Jesus did. No disease was able to run rampant in the neighborhood where Jesus was. With power over devils, over disease and even over death, He never walked into a circumstance He could not conquer and control! When death was present, He effected resurrection! Where disease was working, He imposed a cure! The Devil himself was harmless in His presence!

Even when they took His life, He laid it down voluntarily on the cross, just long enough—three days and three nights—to demonstrate the divine plan and power. He took up His life again with resurrection power, illustrating once again His power over the reach and the grasp of death.

It is for this reason that whenever we put our faith in Christ Jesus, we claim for ourselves power and victory over death, over Hell, over the grave. No grave has its victory over us because of the wonderful, almighty, undiminishing, inexhaustible power of the Lord Jesus Christ.

He has power greater than men, power that rises with a dominion as exalted as the majesty of God. He has power greater than cyclones, greater than earthquakes, greater than any of the natural catastrophic events. He has power over sin. There is no sin any person has committed which is beyond the scope of the forgiveness of "this same Jesus."

You might have something in your life of such monumental magnitude that you don't know what to do or where to turn. I have a word for you: Turn to the Lord Jesus Christ with it.

You say, "I don't know how to solve the difficulty that I have." Come to Christ! The Lord Jesus has the power to deal with the difficulty that you have, no matter the difficulty. No problem is too big, no sin too great. You may be a moral leper with a shameful track record of much length. You may have played in the Devil's playland with utter abandon. You may be enamored with the trash, the garbage of life. You may have ignored God. You may have done all there is to do—every wrong thing! Listen to me: There is nothing outside the bounds of His ability to solve. I say to you sincerely, and I believe that whatever the difficulty is, you can know that "this same Jesus," the powerful Jesus, is able to help you with the need that you have.

"Wherefore he is able also to save them to the uttermost that come unto God by him, seeing he ever liveth to make intercession for them."—Heb. 7:25.

VII. "THIS SAME JESUS" IS THE PRAYING JESUS

Now I remind you: Jesus preexistent, Jesus prophesied, Jesus personal, Jesus prized, Jesus perfect, Jesus powerful; but I also want you to see "this same Jesus" as the praying Jesus.

The Lord Jesus, while He was here, found every crisis to be a time for prayer. When there were burdens, He brought comfort by praying. He prayed in agony before the cross and said, "If it be possible, let this cup pass from me." But when it became obvious that the cup was His to drink, He endured the cross, despising the shame. And from the cross, even upon the cross, He prayed with great authority and looked to God the Father in prayer.

Even now, sitting on the right hand of the Father, He still, with great authority and with full advocacy for every one of us, after the cross, after His ascension, is praying like a great mediator, like an attorney, representing you and me every time that we have any need at all.

"If we say that we have no sin, we deceive ourselves, and the truth is not in us.

"If we confess our sins, he is faithful and just to forgive us our sins, and to cleanse us from all unrighteousness."

"My little children, these things write I unto you, that ye sin not. And if any man sin, we have an advocate with the Father, Jesus Christ the righteous."—I John 1:8,9; 2:1.

We don't have the ability to play priest without a High Priest, and Jesus is our High Priest-Mediator who gets us through to God. "Let us therefore come boldly unto the throne of grace, that we may obtain mercy, and find grace to help in time of need" (Heb. 4:16).

Sometimes when I want to call someone I'll call the long-distance operator or check the CD-rom phone directory, but I can't come up with a phone number, and I can't call the person if I don't have the number. As a born-again child of God, Jesus is your Mediator, Jesus is your Advocate, He is your Attorney; and you have no trouble—night or day, at any hour of crisis—getting through to God the Father because you have the number you need to call when you call through Jesus.

VIII. "THIS SAME JESUS" IS THE PREACHING JESUS

"This same Jesus" is the preexistent, prophesied, personal, prized, perfect, powerful and praying Jesus. And "this same Jesus" is also the preaching Jesus.

Sometimes people say, "Well, I never thought about Jesus' being a preacher." They said, "Never man spake like this man." Have you not read the Sermon on the Mount lately? What about the sermon on the plain?

You read the preaching of Jesus, and you'll find that He moved and stirred crowds. Great conviction fell upon the hearts of the people, and they became convinced of eternal truths because of the preaching of the Son of God.

"And again he entered into Capernaum after some days; and it was noised that he was in the house.

"And straightway many were gathered together, insomuch that there was no room to receive them, no, not so much as about the door: and he preached the word unto them."—Mark 2:1, 2.

Imagine the living Word, the Lord Jesus, preaching the written Word!

Sometimes His preaching agitated them, as all good preaching sometimes does. On occasion it ought to agitate. Once in a while it ought to anger, and at times Jesus' preaching did, but He motivated the people and pointed their hearts Heavenward!

There have been many men stand in this pulpit, and I could name a lot of them. There are many of them for whom I have great and high regard. In fact, I don't know of anybody who has stood here but that he was one for whom I have respect and regard. But I say to you, none who have stood in this place, none who have stood here to open the Bible and preach the Word of God, not one of them compares to the Preacher who is the Master of preachers—that is, "this same Jesus," the Lord Jesus Himself!

IX. "THIS SAME JESUS" IS THE PROVIDING JESUS

"This same Jesus" is the preexistent, prophesied, personal, prized, perfect, powerful, praying and preaching Jesus. "This same Jesus" is also the providing Jesus.

Can you see what He gave up so that you and I might get up? He came out of the grave so we might come out of the wallow! He gave up Heaven so that we might get up and grow up in Him and so that one day we might go up to be with Him.

Look at His life and His death, His resurrection and all that He provides, the salvation that is there for sinners like you and me. Look at it all. The providing Jesus descended out of Heaven that one day we might ascend up to Heaven.

He became poor, having all of the riches of Heaven, in order that we, poor as we are, might ourselves indulge in the riches of Heaven. He was born in Bethlehem so that we might be born again. He became a servant to all of us so that we might become the sons and daughters of the living God. He who had the greatest of all residences in Heaven came to this earth and had no home in order that you and I might have a home in Heaven.

The Lord Jesus was often hungry that we might be fed. He Himself endured thirst that we might drink at the wells of salvation and have our thirst quenched.

The Lord Jesus was often wearied in order that we might rest. He was stripped in order that we might be clothed. He was forsaken in order that we might never be forsaken. He often became sad in order that we might be glad forever. He was bound that we might go free. He was made sin that we might be made righteous.

The Lord Jesus died on the cross in order that we might not have to die but instead have life eternal, everlasting. He came down from above in order that one day we might be caught up when He returns. What a provider He is, "this same Jesus"!

X. "THIS SAME JESUS" IS THE PREEMINENT JESUS

One final thing! Just as He is the preexistent Jesus, the prophesied Jesus, the personal Jesus, the prized Jesus, the perfect Jesus, the powerful Jesus, the praying Jesus, the preaching Jesus and the providing Jesus, He is also the preeminent Jesus.

There is not a name higher than the name given to Him. Above all other names there is one that stands at the top of the heap—Jesus, Jesus, Jesus! What a name!

He is preeminent in His name. He is preeminent in the position that He has, because as the Lord of the universe He has a position higher than all other positions.

He is greater than the potentates. He is greater than the prime ministers. He is greater than the presidents. He is greater than them all because "Lord" is the greatest position of all.

He has a place that is greater than all other places—sitting at the right hand of the Father. The preeminent Jesus has three special offices: Prophet, Priest and King.

The prophet is one who represents God before man. Certainly the Lord Jesus has come with the message to tell us the sweet story of salvation and to give what God wanted to be given to men.

The priest is the individual who represents man before God. Jesus, now our great High Priest, sits on the right hand of the Father, making intercession on our behalf, being our Advocate. What a High Priest He is!

Not only is He preeminent as Prophet and preeminent as Priest, but He is also preeminent as King—not just *a* King, but *the* King of Kings.

The king is someone who rules on behalf of God, and the Lord Jesus issues edict and mandate to those who call themselves kings. The Lord Jesus becomes the King who dominates even the rulers of the world.

I look at His threefold office—Prophet, Priest and King—and I am reminded that the Lord Jesus—more than any other man who ever lived, greater than anyone else who was ever born, greater than anybody else who ever donned human flesh—is the preeminent Jesus.

I'm talking about the Lamb who was born, the Lord Himself, the Lion who is coming.

"We see Jesus, who was made a little lower than the angels for the suffering of death, crowned with glory and honour; that he by the grace of God should taste death for every man."—Heb. 2:9.

"This same Jesus." He has come already so that you and I who did not have eyes to see God could see Him; so that every prophecy that had ever been made about a Messiah would be fully and entirely fulfilled; so that every promise of God would come to reality and fruition on behalf of every person—no matter who we are, where we come from, no matter the culture where we're born, no matter what color our skin, no matter what our character is or is not. The fact is, whoever we are, from wherever we come, we have the privilege to know that God prophesied long ago and fulfilled every word of His promise in the preeminent Jesus.

"This same Jesus" came to make sacrifice for sins, to reconcile you and me to God, to provide for us what we could not provide for ourselves, to destroy the Devil's works and to keep him from becoming the victor in our lives, to erase that old curse that had been placed upon us because we were sinners, the sons of Adam, to allow us to escape from that curse where death passed upon all men and to give us life that is sure and abundant and everlasting.

The Bible says that the old Devil, like a thief, comes not but for to kill and to destroy (John 10:10). In fact, if you do not have the Lord Jesus in your life, the Devil no doubt is sitting somewhere with a little smile and smirk on his face thinking he's got you wrapped around his finger. And one day he will jerk you off your feet and suck you down into the pits of Hell simply because you have not embraced the Lord Jesus as Saviour.

I want you to know that even if that old Devil, the thief, comes to steal and to kill and to destroy—and he has such horrific designs on your life—the rest of that verse says, "I am come that they might have life." "This same Jesus" is the antidote for the Devil's poison! They whom the Devil intended to steal, they whom the Devil intended to kill, they whom the Devil intended to destroy—Jesus said, "I am come that they might have life"; and not just a little, measly existence, but that they might have a life more abundant than anything that they could know otherwise.

Life everlasting and abundant—what a privilege it is to know a Saviour like that! And the Lord Jesus, "this same Jesus" who is the mighty God, the Master, is my Redeemer.

Years ago as a lad, I heard the name and the plan and trusted the Saviour! On my knees in a little out-of-the-way spot in the river bottoms in Western Kentucky, I invited the Lord Jesus to come into my life and be my Saviour.

He who is the Mighty God, the Master, became my Mediator on

that day. He who is the Rock, the Rock of Ages, the Rose of Sharon, became my Redeemer. The Son of God, the Great Shiloh and the Great Shepherd, became my Saviour. And He, "this same Jesus," can become your Saviour too!

According to Acts, chapter one, He went back to Heaven literally. He went up visibly. He went up bodily. And "this same Jesus" will come back down literally. He'll come back down bodily. He'll come back down visibly.

I ask you now, What do you think about Him? I'm talking about Him who is the altogether lovely One, the Chief Cornerstone, the Bright and Morning Star, the One who is called the Door, the Way, the Truth and the Life, and the Light of the World!

He is the One who is absolutely unsearchable riches, the Comforter, the Anchor on troubled seas, the Great Physician, the Master Teacher, the Lord of the harvest, the One who is a Friend who sticks closer than a brother, the Rose of Sharon, the Lily of the Valley and the Rock of the Ages.

He is the One who is the propitiation, the vine, the hidden Treasure, the Rest-giver, the righteous Judge, the true and faithful Witness, the Pearl of great price.

He is the Advocate, the Son of God, and God the Son. His birth is announced as tidings of great joy for folks such as you and I.

I am talking about Him who is the Friend of sinners, the unspeakable gift, the veritable Word of God, the Water of Life, the Bread from Heaven.

He is the Living Stone, the Lamb who takes away the sin of the world.

He is the Sun of Righteousness that arises with healing in His wings. He is the Author and the Finisher of our faith, rest to the weary and cause for living, giving us hope when we are dying.

Oh, the great, great "I AM"; our all in all; the great, eternal Amen!

That's the Jesus I'm talking about.

"This same Jesus," born in Bethlehem, is one day coming down from Heaven again to gather up His own. And we become a part of that great family of believers whenever we put our faith and trust in

Him and say, "I, a sinner, need a Saviour."

And it is "this same Jesus" who is preexistent; "this same Jesus" who was prophesied; "this same Jesus" who is the personal, prized, perfect, powerful, praying, preaching, providing and preeminent Lord. I believe it is He, and because of that, I simply submit to you "this same Jesus, which is taken up from you into heaven, shall so come in like manner as ye have seen him go into heaven."

For a complete list of books available from the Sword of the Lord, write to Sword of the Lord Publishers, P. O. Box 1099, Murfreesboro, Tennessee 37133.

(800) 251-4100
(615) 893-6700
FAX (615) 848-6943
www.swordofthelord.com